ROUTE...

A POEMEMOIR

DORIAN HAARHOFF

Published in Australia (2023) by

Heart Space Publications
PO Box 1190
Bakery Hill, Victoria, 3350, Australia
Tel +61 450260348
www.heartspacebooks.com
pat@heartspacebooks.com

All rights reserved under international copyright conventions. No part of this book may be reproduced, stored in a retrieval system, or transmitted in any form or by any means electronic, mechanical, photocopying, recorded or otherwise without written permission from Heartspace Publications.

Whilst every care has been taken to check the accuracy of the information in this book, the publisher cannot be held responsible for any errors, omissions or originality.

Copyright: Dorian Haarhoff 2023
ISBN 978-0-6486524-5-8 Route 77

Foreword

Many of Dorian's followers, friends and the hundreds of people that have attended his workshops will be delighted with this publication. In it, Dorian shares a lifetime of reflection on the insights his work and reading have given him, the skills that he has acquired, and above all the many stories of Dorian, the consummate storyteller. You will meet again Oom Schalk Lourens who knows how to weave a yarn beside the fireplace, and you will meet too Dorian the Methodist, Dorian the Jew, Dorian the Hindu and Dorian the Buddhist and each one will give you a surprising and new perspective on life.

Over the years Dorian has invited many people to the pen and the empty page to begin the magic and mystery of writing their own story and through that process to heal and re-imagine and re-story their lives. In that sense his work has been transforming in the lives of many, who have found their voice and have gone on to produce their own memoirs, write stories and publish their works. Add to that his work amongst children and young people in Namibia. In schools, colleges and university his work has helped to uplift struggling communities of children, and searching students.

Then there is the poetry, and know that Dorian has written over one and a half thousand poems, a small portion of which are in this publication. New readers to the poetry may find that while the prose passages move smoothly with Dorian's lightness of touch, the poems slow things down and call for a different way of reading. Poems often require that you read them aloud over and over so that you pick up their rhythms, their music, their subtle levels of meaning. However, you may not want them to slow you down so I suggest you read them once, and come back to them later, when you can give more time to them. You may want to use them in your own quiet times, reflections and meditations.

Thank you Dorian for sharing so much of your journey with us in Route 77.

Bob Commin (February 2023)
Poet, priest, storyteller and life-coach. His publications include: From a Still Point, Someone Dreaming Us, Becoming Human, Meditations on the way of the Cross, and Under the Ilex Tree.

Whether sharing a glass of wine at sunset under the Helderberg and ruminating together over books, life and poetry, or sharing teaching input sessions on a retreat, or walking and swimming on a beach or in a lagoon, Dorian's confident, buoyant humanness is always consciously present.

Linked in loyal friendship through the years, through a love of words, friends in common, similar fields of study and research and his psychotherapist sister (Joy), Dorian brings gifts of poetic artistry and eloquence, mythological reflection, magical storytelling, and quirky, witty commentary in all his engagement with Life.

This remarkable anthology revealing the loves and encounters and questing through seventy-seven years is spun on the axis of earning a living and earning a life as DH Lawrence indicates. The body of writing; a collection of essays, an engrossing autobiography or a richly textured fabric of poems asking to be read out aloud. Route 77 is a unique gift to his immediate family and to the descendants who will follow. In terms of it being a study in creative writing and storytelling it also holds interest and value to the non-family reader.

Written at a time when after our three score and ten years, thoughts and realities of mortality are more present and real, Dorian is not without some close encounters with death in his living years and his partnering takes him right into that edge place of leaving and transition. In a story I once read, the Rabbi is questioned by a child about why we have to die, and the Rabbi answers, "Because that is what makes life precious".

The Greek derivation of the name *Doron* means *gift*. Dorian has brought his gifts in this anthology in wordcraft and meaning through his detailed recall of events, of places and of people in his life from an early age. Several of the persons he describes and remembers I knew in common with him as a Rhodian. He honours Prof Winifred Maxwell of the History Department who affirmed his talents and skills. She wasn't one easily given to praise or flattery. These talents and gifts are then translated into his later working life as educator and teacher, as an academic, as a story teller and poet, as a creative writer and retreat leader, as a mentor and editor, and father. His skills as an editor assisted me when in 2003 I co-authored a book on Dying.

There is an eclecticism in the sources that he draws from that influence him in inspiration and imagination from Dante to Jung, Francis Weller to Jacob Needleman, Kabbalah and Buddhism, Christian mysticism and Sufism, James Hillman, Gerard Manley Hopkins and Joseph Campbell. These sources get included in his expression in a way that ambiguity and paradox are respected and the spiritual quest for transcendence and timelessness are explored and held in delicate balance.

Unconventional and non-traditional as a husband or partner and generously mindful and supportively present to his children throughout their growing years and also later in their lives, Dorian has these themes criss-cross the chapters and seasons of his Life. There is through all the decades that capacity to reinvent himself in the face of Life's threats and challenges and to land on his feet. Life is no small brief sputtering candle to be snuffed out by the breeze. It is to be embraced, fully taken in both hands and shaken until the hidden connections and synchronistic coincidences get woven into the fabric of the Life he is living.

In Jungian typology the Journey through Persona, Shadow, Anima to Authentic Self is never a smooth straight line. This journey is honestly traced and told in these writings. Likewise, in the masculine aspects of Lover, Warrior, King and Magician that as men we get lost in the labyrinth of at times, Dorian bravely and thoroughly traverses this territory and I leave you to decide where the emphasis is prioritised.

Peter Fox (February 2023)

Peter Fox is a minister and a counselling therapist involved in Hospice work. He co-authored *Dying: the Practical Guide for the Journey* (2009) and has lectured at the South African College of Applied Psychology.

Seven Circlings – travelling on the back of a Tortoise

For helping angels, for all those in these pages, for great-grands yet unborn and for those ancients in this poem:

<blockquote>

If Ancestors were Apples

when one apple ripens
in the bowl
on the kitchen table,
apple ancestors,
granny, starking,
ripen in reverse.

they lose their bruising.
reseed their rotten core
from bitter black.
the pink lady
unwrinkles her skin.

they sweeten again
crisp, fiber-white,
golden delicious,
to juice the Eden tree.

</blockquote>

Whether I shall turn out to be the hero of my own life,
or whether that station will be held by anybody else, these pages must show.
(Dickens)

My father Reggie and Uncle Allan Haarhoff (1890)

Contents

FOREWORD i

    Seven Circlings – travelling on the back of a Tortoise v

PREAMBLING THROUGH THE YEARS xiii

ONCE THERE WAS A DORIAN 1

    A Story about a Storyteller 1944 – 1956 (0-12) 1

    Bill Haley, Pat Boone, Elvis and teenage me jiving in luminous green socks 1957 – 1961 (13-17) 27

    Encountering the Poets 1962 – 1965 (17-21) 33

    Teacher Man 1966 – 1968 (21-24) (title courtesy of Frank McCourt) 41

    The Fairest Cape 1969 – 1978 (24-29) 46

    Wrist and Rib 1973 – 1978 (29-34) 52

    Wild West Land Namibia: Teacher Trainer (1979–1983) 60

    University Days 1984 – 1997 (40-53) 67

    Leaving Prof Behind 1998 – 2003 (53-58) 90

    Under the Helderberg 2003 – 15 (59-72) 102

    Pringle Mingle Bay 2016 – 2022 (72-77) 107

EDGE MOMENTS **123**

    Across a Crowded Room 123

    Eating with the Troll 125

    Images, Triangles, You and Me 130

    Leo 140

    Ho Spice 146

    The Same Rainbow's End 150

    Galway Bay and Billy Collins 151

    Walking on Water – North America 154

    Living the Stories I tell: The Faces of Bulawayo 156

    Petty Thieves and Angels 161

    Hiking Haiku 163

FAITH **169**

    The Pliable Eclectic Bubble 169

    A Myth? What is a myth, Grandpa? 173

    Listen with the Deep Ear in your Chest 177

    Inhabiting the City of Synchronicity 181

    Give us this Day our Daily Quote 184

    The Feminine Face of God 189

    Rabbinical Mysteries 192

    Creativity, Imagination and Midrash 197

    A Buddhist Flower 203

    Indian Mythology 207

    Mystics and Gnostics 209

VOCARE 213
   Tortoises all the way down – why I do what I do 213
   Cosmic Land and Ocean: Logo 220
   A World of Stories 224
   Two Sisters: UNICEF and SLED 229
   Please Sir, may I have some more? Namibia 231
   Mentoring: You one foot, me the other 233
   Can you Speak Cow Talk? 234
   Reflickology, Your Life, Your Movie 239
   Living the Myth 241
   Words on a Mirror: Remembering our Stories 244

WRITING LETTERS 249
   No, no it happened like this 249
   Taking Words for a Walk: November 2016 252
   Maps and Scape in Storyland: April 2017 255
   Postcards from the Edge, August 2017 260
   GAGA, January 2018 262
   The End of Story? June 2018 265
   The Phantom in the Word: Writer's Block, April 2019 270
   Anansi the Spider, August 2019 273
   World Concern, Social Distancing and Space, April 2020 276
   We are Here, June 2020 279
   Losing and Finding Words, January 2021 281

ACHILLES HEAL – IN POETIC PRAISE OF HEALING... 289

- The Myth of Achilles 289
- Alpha to Omega: Letters, Breath, Music, Words and Meaning . 290
- Our Beginnings – Growing Soul through Poetry 297
- Ecology: Trees, Poetry and Belonging....................................... 303
- Acorn to Oak Leaves 311
- Observing Worlds: Retraining the Eye 314
- Ritual, Mantra and Meditation 319
- Ways with Words – Ambiguity, Paradox, Irony and Word Play . 322
- Saved by a Poem 326
- Temenos Garden of the Beloved.. 328
- Praise Poems 331

LOVES WITHIN, LOVES WITHOUT 337

- The Night Novel – Dreams.. 338
- Dream Chef.. 340
- Crossing Orange – River Sea Mountain Forest 345
- Eleven Just Men... 349
- Eleven Just Women.. 357
- Child Tribe 369
- Stories within Stories 382
- Music of the Spheres.. 391
- Otherworlds... 393
- The Emmaus Road, the Inn, the Traveller and a Journal............ 395
- 27 July 400

ENDWORDS **407**
    Wealth Cycles 407
    Fare Forward Traveller 409
    Some of Dorian's publications 415

PREAMBLING THROUGH THE YEARS

A man should never earn his living.
If he earns his life he'll be lovely.
(D H Lawrence dubbed Priest of Love)

In Herman Charles Bosman's *The Love Potion*, one of the Oom Schalk Lourens stories I tell by heart, the farmer Krisjan, in minute detail recounts his life to shy Gideon, the policeman, who has come to court his daughter Lettie. And in *Mafeking Road*, the wise veld philosopher reminds us that *it is not the story that counts. What matters is the way you tell it. The important thing is to know just at what moment you must knock out your pipe on your veldskoen… Another necessary thing is to know what part of the story to leave out.*

I trust that my story follows this advice, and that I will not overtell, nor forget what to leave out. Some intentional leaving out also ghosts between the lines. Shared stories not mine to tell. Secrets not mine to share. Friends who read *Route 77* will recall shared memories. Were I to include them, this tome would double in length. So cricket-wise, it's an ODI, a one-day game, not a five-day test.

I gather up the story hidden in laptop mazes. Hunting through fifty journals, stories, poems, articles, newsletters, and memories, dreams, reflections (Thank you, Carl Jung). Then writing the gaps.

How to structure and shape this under-telling? Here is a kind of Babushka with seven dolls – not sure which is inner and which outer. Imagine each doll decorated with eleven symbols, images and squiggles. Holograms.

Why seven? It's prime. A story number. A mythic one. The wonders of the Ancient World. The Old Testament, God's span of days; the New

Testament's four corners of the Earth plus the Trinity. We are called to forgive seventy times seven. The Book of Revelation's angels, seals, trumpets and stars. The Koran's heavens and number of circles Muslim pilgrims walk around the Kaaba in Mecca. In Hinduism seven higher and seven underworlds, while newborn Buddha takes seven steps. And don't forget the dwarfs.

Among many blessed influences, Carl Jung's, *Memories, Dreams, Reflections* and Dante's *Divine Comedy* serve as guides. Here are tributes, myths, stories, poems to the rich pantheon of characters who have consented (or not) to be in this play. Many teachers at the way stations along the Emmaus Road.

Revisiting in memory the people, spaces and places, along this *Route 77* involves acts of forgiveness. Learning to love the sometimes arrogant, chaos-causing, unaware, asleep young and middle-aged man. "One who has ever slenderly known himself" (Lear).

Here's poet Paul Mathews:

> Go my Songs and beg
> forgiveness from the ones
> you brought into confusion.
>
> If any girl admired
> your glittering syllables
> confess that they deceived her…
> go my songs. the air
> upon the open field
> is reft of melody.

(Publishers note; Dorian's poems are in blue. Poems from others are black.)

In Thomas Moore's books on influences, (*The Education of the Heart*) he celebrates his reading lineage. I do too. Tussentak. A thousand thanks to those who have educated (or tried to) my heart. Those helping angels in books and in person. When Francis Weller (*The Wild Edge of Sorrow: Rituals of Renewal and the Sacred Work of Grief*) was consulting maverick Jungian psychologist James Hillman, he dreamt of a drawer with reams of influences. In *Route 77* I slide open a few of these drawers too.

Tagore's *My Reminiscences* too is my guide:

> I know not who paints the pictures on memory's canvas...
> Life's memories are not Life's history, but the original work of
> an unseen Artist. The variegated colours scattered about are not
> reflections of outside lights, but belong to the painter himself,
> and come passion-tinged from his heart...

I trust too that in creation, memory and art I adhere to this Osiris myth, a touchstone poem, written decades ago:

Feather Prayer

in Egypt, Osiris,
Lord of the underworld,
weighed the hearts
of those who crossed over
against the plume of truth.

those light of heart,
lived in his chambers
endlessly. while the crocodile,
monster of the Nile,

devoured souls
heavy with matter.

weigh my quill of words
on the scales of space
so they measure against
what the guinea fowl
has left on the grass –
the lightness of a feather.

Begin anywhere. Read at random. Dip in here or there. So hop on the *Route 77* Greyhound.

1

ONCE THERE WAS A DORIAN

*Tell me what created timelessness for you as a child for
therein lies your myth to live by*
(Joseph Campbell)

A STORY ABOUT A STORYTELLER 1944 – 1956 (0-12)

Here's John Irving:

A fiction writer's memory is an especially imperfect provider of detail; we can always imagine a better detail. Being a writer is a strenuous marriage between careful observation and just as carefully imagining the truths you haven't had the opportunity to see.
(Trying to Save Piggy Sneed)

As Dylan Thomas intones 'to begin at the beginning.' So here's to my parents, Reggie Haarhoff and Patricia Purchase who married in 1941 in Kuruman.

Route 77

Tender Love Story

the widower of 56, with a retarded son,
chugs down Jones Street in his V8 Ford.
sees a nurse of 26 window-shopping
outside John Orr's with his cousin's daughter
(who will become my godmother) courts her.
the war rumbles far away in Europe,
near in news, shortages, coupons
and a desert death toll.

and she escapes from this diamond city
to a military hospital in Middelberg,
somewhere in the Transvaal nowhere
to put miles between this age gap
and bringing up a backward son.
the man writes letters in his lovely hand
blue-black Quinck on blue bond
from a ticket booth at a rugby match
where he earns Saturday cash.

and one day off duty, she enters her room
in the nurse's quarters. the winter smell
of freesias in full bloom announces
he has come for her. they marry with
a promise of release within six months
if she, number fourteen of fifteen children, is not happy.
(they share fifteen years before his heart stops.)

and as they sit down to their
first wife-cooked meal –

meat, potatoes, peas and rice,
he scrapes blade against sharpener

Once there was a Dorian

<blockquote>
as if washing hands. yet still
the roast resists the knife.
he speak his fatherly words
never mind, my dear.
at least the gravy's tender.
</blockquote>

My parents' wedding: Reggie Haarhoff and Patricia Purchase

I was born in a flat above a cinema and a bank, across the road from the market place. A fine balance between left and right brain. 27 July 1944. A Leo. My late uncle Alan Christie's birthday. The doctor, nowhere to be found, so Great Aunt Gerty, midwife extraordinaire, brought me into the world. "Looks like a drowned rat," mused my father. Perhaps this is where the story begins.

I was a mistake. After my sister's protracted birth, the doctor told my mother, "No more children." But somehow I wriggled into life.

Route 77

gatherer of family) when I tumbled head-first, nose grazed, from a teak feeding chair, which converted to a rocker. Coming ninth in a class of thirty-two, I'd offer solace, "Don't worry, Mom, there are twenty-three others behind me." At eight, the school doctor declaring, "Your right eye is weaker than your left." Me to Ma, "He says my one eye is stronger than the other." Enter spectacles.

Down the road, the cafe, Mookery's, divided our white 1940s suburb from Kimberley's Malay quarter. Here we met the other South Africans. Buying sherbet. In 1948 I heard my mother, hunched over the old valve radio, crying as she listened to the insistent beep-beep announcing that Jan Smuts had lost his seat in parliament. Later I wrote a story, *The Silver Tickey*, about that day. Not even my silver tickey could console her.

Memories unfold in a love for water. I learnt to swim in the Vaal and Modder Rivers on the Smith's farm. Drinking milk from the cascading corrugated sheet, the white waterfall. Another memory of a four-year-old, from a beloved six-years-older cousin, Joan Peirson, now in Wales. Joan's pilot father Donald was killed in World War II. So Joan, Chris, her brother, and Aunt Erica often holidayed with us. Four children elbowing for space, making imaginary 'my side' borders, asleep in the backseat of the Ford V8, three adults up front. Driving 1000 km through the night to Herold's Bay or Ganzekraal, Lillian and Percy's farm near Darling. Here's Joan's gift:

> Long before you wielded words
> We dug runnels in the sand
> At Herold's Bay. In play mode
> I taught you to curl your tongue
> Like the crisp wave breaking;
> When the consonant crested
> Your lips, we shouted

Once there was a Dorian

    The twisting words in rhythm
    To our stamping, splashing feet,
    Laughing.
    Your father alone, was saddened.
    He loved your
    Lound the lugged locks
    The lagged lascal lan.

Until then I had thought that my father, old as a grandfather, had scant connection to me. This gift gave me another perspective. I need to reinvent myself and change my story. The past is not fixed – it's a moveable feast.

Enter the imagination. Another 'memory' from the annals of Dorian @ four:

A Motorbiker and A Boy

I imagine you on your bike,
goggle cap, ear flaps,
jacket, leggings, gloves.
on a Saturday spin, 1948,
purring past the park in leather trim.
350 CCs bloodred, silver streaks.

then a boy roars suddenly
out of the fete gates,
under your wheels.
no time to swerve,
to lock brakes.

Route 77

> you skid leather along
> the tar in a screech-scream,
> the bike stripping paint
> in a wheel buckle blowout.
> you metal-slide for
> a jangle-tangle moment.
>
> when stillness descends,
> a boy, aged four,
> with a leg as bent
> as your front wheel fork,
> lies, out cold, in the road.
> when the ambulance
> has sirened him off,
> you answer the cop's questions,
> shaking like a rattle nut.
>
> you drag bike and you home,
> tend to the exhaust burn
> mercurochrome knuckles,
> knees, elbows, kick start ankle.
> sixty years on in an age of helmets
> and padded jackets, finger-flick starters,
> the boy thinks of you and says
> I'm sorry I wrecked your bike.

And a beloved half-brother, Allan, older, much older, from my widowed father's first wife. Strange stories about her – passing herself off as an Egyptian princess in Cape Town. My father struggling to support her. Hysterical when she discovered she was pregnant. Did she harm her baby son? Let him fall? Who knows. In his forties his heart stopped beating.

Once there was a Dorian

Bronzed Shoe
for Allan (1921–1968)

your shoe stood on
the mantelpiece
above the fireplace
where your father lived
with his second wife
and us, your siblings.
it rested alone,
its left-foot friend, long lost.

I often balanced it,
cool in my palm.
studied its leather tread
glazed in a bronze age.
hand stitched, double thread.
the shoemaker's elves
could have shaped it.
tongue, eye, sole and instep
sang in unison.
the nails tacked
a horseshoe heel
for the luck of the road.

your body trod to
a kind of manhood.
you wrote gentle letters
each birthday, in pencil,
from the Home, with poems
copied letter by letter.
for you never stepped
to cursive script

Route 77

> with run-on lines racing
> to the edge of the page.
> your mind had long gone wandering
> still shod in its childhood shoe.

Of four grandparents I saw only one in the flesh – Granny Harriet. And one anecdote only of my father's mother, Susannah (Olivier) to Japie, father Reggie's dad. "Japie, do you think you are a boarder in this house?" she asked. I have been wife-told that I carry such genes. In her eighties, Granny Harriet walked around our midnight kitchen, singing, 'Tell Me The Old Old Story', the motion of her wrists and hands kneading endless bread:

> ## Keeping Track
>
> the old coke cooler
> with its flatpan tray,
> stood outside the window
> where Granny Harriet,
> with thirty-three grandchildren,
> slept her senile sleep.
> raised on bricks like a tokoloshe bed,
> it sagged, rusted in chicken wire
> and trusses with trickle holes.
> woodrot spat out screws and splinters.
>
> this ruin, taller than a ten year old,
> was my robber bank, bars for badman,
> shoot-out rock, crow's nest
> for island sighting,
> but most of all

Once there was a Dorian

my pitstop and grandstand finish
for the tricycle track.

legs over handle bars
I pumped round trees
citrus, fig and vine
circled in a brick blur
past the corrugated fence
with a green-flake paint ad,
sandpit S-bend,
grape-shaped bridge
and down the straight
ringing the finger bell,
frantic at last lap,
flashing by the check flag
and crowd roar from the cooler,
spinning a Trinity of wheels.

then, laurelled and champagne-sprayed
I fizzed into the breakfast room
where Granny, woken from slumber,
looked up at me and quizzed
ferreting the fridge of her memory,
'Now who are you again?'

And watching my father at his shaving ritual:

Magnified Moment

one morning I saw it,
watching my father shave
in his swivel mirror.

Route 77

> one circle showed his human face,
> aged, grey, wrinkled, nicked skin.
> then he swung it on its axis.
>
> in the reverse moon
> his face magnified,
> bristles thrice their size,
>
> pores a diamond design.
> a blood river cut
> through a wild sea.
>
> over his shoulder
> in a ring of silver,
> I saw a thousand fathers rise,
> large as gods.

Then one day King George VI came down our road:

King Dreams

> my boyhood filled
> with the Idylls of Kings.
> their fine robes and gold,
> their off with your head
> ascendancy.
> from old King Cole,
> to sovereigns, monarchs,
> to Fairy Tale Tsars and
> High King Sundays,
> we read, played and sang
> their sceptres into being.

Once there was a Dorian

and then, in '47,
an earthly King came
down Dalham Road
from the war memorial,
with the Long Tom
Boer War gun,
to the Malay Quarter.
coming to the city
which bestowed
the Big Hole diamond,
embedded in his crown.

I took my riempie chair
to the pavement's edge.
fingered for luck
the George Rex tickey,
scrubbed, in my pocket.
Union Jack, homemade,
at the ready, unfurled.
crowds jostled under pepper trees
waiting in the sun.

and he came down that road
made royal for a day,
the engine purring past.
perhaps he gave the backseat wave.

as the cavalcade
drove from sight
and the crowd changed
back to neighbours,
like a mustard seed,
a pepper berry,
the deep King stirred,

Route 77

> regal, royal,
> constellating kingdoms,
> palaces and succession,
> made conscious in me.

Off to school at six. Behold the report. Like doctors and dentists who display qualifications on their consulting wall, as a Prof of English forty plus years later, up this went, enlarged, behind my Windhoek desk.

Sub A (Grade 1) School report

From red trike to bike. Hercules. Black like Henry Ford's Fords. Bell and dynamo. Sweet mobility. I peddled bicycle (it steered itself) to the Victorian library near the Kimberley Club where Rhodes plotted and dreamed. I'd climb the patterned spiral staircase in search of adventure. Secret Seven, Hardy Boys. Back home I played imaginary games, sometimes alone in the backyard, marked by the citrus, and fig trees, a grapevine. Constructing narratives in which I was hero. Later to encounter the myth of the archetypal hero's journey.

Dynamo and GPS Dream

I cycle in the dark,
along a country road,
a breeze blowing
through my shirt.

I find clamped
to the front fork
that simple bit
of bottled physics.

it decked a boy's bike
with rotating coils,
magnetic fields
and pulsing current.

I flip the dynamo spring.
the head settles, nests
once more on the front tyre.
whirs to pedal rhythm.

pump legs to meet this
necessary resistance
and speed to steady this
broad-as-a hand beam.

for I need this bright genie
of the silver lamp,
balanced like a nose
on a handlebar moustache.

yet how to follow the road
through moonless twists
shortcuts left-rights, straight-ons
in this all night saddle ride?

a GPS lights sudden
on the crossbar
like a bird and perches
on the bit that turns the wheel.

this global voice and leglight
in tandem, sing, shine, hum
direct me through motion
to a dawn destination.

As soon as I could escape I was swapping comics in a Saturday morning bioscope queue. And stamping my feet as the stagecoach, with the runaway horses, raced towards the precipice, following the fortunes of *Francis, the Talking Mule.* Then anguishing over the doctor who had taken his suffering wife's life, a mercy killing, and disguised himself as Buttons, a circus clown, to escape detection. Who never removed his painted face. Cecil B DeMille's *The Greatest Show on Earth* with James Stewart as Buttons. 1952, an impressionable eight-year-old, the story moved in me. When the circus train crashes, Buttons is about to leave and shake off the FBI agent shadowing him, but he returns to save a life, administering a blood transfusion. The agent assists Buttons. Then the reluctant arrest. My early introduction to irony, understatement and letting the audience/reader add the two and two. Buttons off to 'meet his girl.'. The death penalty implied.

A first. "I'll show you mine if you'll show me yours." Madelaine, she's eight, me six. She, the initiator into these mysteries. At their Modder River home in a dark secluded shed. Madelaine. A name that still holds electricity, like Guinevere (a triangle with Arthur and Lancelot), another myth that inspired and set me yearning for I knew not what.

First music. The love songs that my parents courted to in the late thirties. Nelson Eddy and Jeanette Macdonald in brittle 78rpm on the gramophone. *Wanting You, Indian Love Call* and Richard Tauber's tenor voice crooning *One Day When We Were Young*. And the Sunday school Elim choruses and jubilant Wesley hymns in the hymn book. Seventy years on I can sing many by heart. And organist Tommy Marnitz in our Gothic Trinity Methodist Church. Long before stories took me up and away beyond conventional religion.

Music Man

so there he was on Saturdays
honkey-tonking a piano
hauled up the grandstand steps
ungrand lid flung open
to the corrugated roof
draped in black and white
at the school derby versus
the local college green and gold.

he twisted and thumped
underneath the arches

Route 77

old tunes into ra ra ra
Lili Marlene
we're proud of our school yes
we're proud of old boys' high
Pistol Packing Mama
rugby playing KHS
put the college down.

on schooldays he turned
choir master for a period
trying to harmonise
testosterone groans
with broken voices
teach them the base for
Carol of the Drum
ram pap pa rum rum pap pa rum
his discipline thin
as his waving pencil.

on Sundays he left
the raucous boys
and lethargic masters behind
fingers and feet pressed
in service to his great love.
shed of other roles he sat
before ivory stops pedals
in the Gothic church.

before organ pipes
thick as rugby posts
thin as his pencil
he played a Bach fugue
kept choir anthem company
piped Wesley hymns

Once there was a Dorian

>oh for thousand tongues to sing
>to Lazarus the dead
>transformed aglow, this maestro
>now at home, no longer alone.

Given my father's heart-struggle for breath, my matron mother donned her starched uniform with epaulets and went back to nurse. She, during her training, a gold medal winner at Kimberley Hospital. Our V8 downsized to a blue Ford Poplar.

A Snap in Time

the three of us stand, Kodaked
beside the house with corrugated roof
half squinting into the sun,
Sunday dressed for church.

my mother in a navy frock
with white trim around her neck
my sister in a flared mid-fifties dress
both with bags and matching hats.

me in a black and white blazer
a size too big, grey shorts,
school shoes, grey socks
Brylcreamed hair, arms hanging.

behind us rests the A-frame swing
with flaked paint and two slatted seats
facing each other like a couple
hooked to a shared footrest.

Route 77

> weeks before his finger click stills
> and the coffin lid snaps shut
> my father's morning shadow unsuited,
> falls onto the edge of the photograph.

We took in boarders. One, John Taylor from Swaziland, at school with me, us sharing a room. A multitude of imaginary adventures. After the death he left our house and school. Where is he now?

A cautionary tale. Once cycling with a friend in the veld after rain. In the cub's green cap with yellow piping. Two 'coloured' youths cycling nearby. I made some sotto voce side-mouth remark to my companion. One of the guys cycled slowly towards me, lifted my cap off my head and dumped it in a muddy puddle. It shrank. Each time I wore it, I was reminded of my too-large-a-head folly.

And outside my bedroom sash window, this:

> The Orange Cosmos
>
> each season the tree grew
> its solar system
> with a hundred suns.
> we stretched on bare toes
> into evergreen heaven
> and when we landed back,
> feet flat on earth,
> we clutched an orange orb
> in our fingers.
>
> the rolling and squashing began.
> we thumped with the base of a thumb,

Once there was a Dorian

roller-skated it under foot,
and worked its leather.
roughed it up and down
the brick wall until it was putty.

we punctured it
with a needle.
a windmill shaft
tapped a citrus aquifer.
as the crochet point withdrew,
a drop of juice surfaced
on the pock-marked lip.

we sucked this ball
of sweet and sour fire,
until the well was dry.
turned it inside out
and tore the pulp with milk teeth,
spitting pips and inner skin
till bitter rind remained.

then we stretched our length
travelling through space
to land astronaut fingers
on another aromatic planet.
our lips glistened in a kiss.

Route 77

Fifteen years passed in Dalham Road. On a visit around 2000, our shrunken home, now transfigured:

A Bedroom and a Chapel

fifty years on in Kimberley
I visit my childhood home,
a small Victorian with stoep,
corrugated roof,
three tiled fireplaces
and a front door with a bird
set in stained glass.

the Catholic Bishopric,
a grand Victorian brother,
stood solid as faith next door.
the fence came down
when the Church bought
and blessed the house
after our departure.

in a timeplay overlay
I walk room to room
to the murmur
of a confirmation class.
in the kitchen that held
the Aga icon and an eight seat table,
nuns ladle Friday soup
to vagrants who queue
under the old lemon tree
bitter-sweet on the tongue.

Once there was a Dorian

I enter my parents' room
stand next to the hearth
with its marble mantle.
green lilies bloom on the tiles
under a pressed ceiling

where my father in pyjamas,
the crotch gaping a little,
home between heart attacks,
writes me a note for school
in a pencil scribble scrawl.

where my mother, days later –
her eyes have not slept all night –
summons me on Ascension Day '56
your father slipped away to Jesus.

in their bedroom
a statue of Mary now
altars the bay window
in this Our Lady's chapel.

her sceptre holds sway
over these instants,
mottled lemon yellow.
this house, this home,
absorbed into her Queendom.

    At age eleven, my first poem landed to hold the grief surrounding my father's death. Spinster, Aunt Edith, my mother's older sister, stayed with us. She helped me. Writing and healing were to become twins. Edith had returned from the Transkei in her brown Citröen, that classic with the

Route 77

running board, lamps and mysterious hydraulic elevation. The only one of fifteen siblings to attend university. Edith headed a mission school. Rumour has it, she never married, saying no to an alcoholic's proposal. Why? Grandfather Henry James Purchase, their father, a charismatic Native Commissioner, horseman, anti-Boer jingoist, womaniser, and alcoholic.

Later I revisited this first death:

My Father's Face

sedan doors shut sharp as gunshot.
we walk a mourning step
to the parlour corner
near the mine museum
and man-made hole
flooded in days when he hung
a young man's moustache.
the street, paved with the living,
sparkles like the gem
that polishes the city.

frosted panes in coffin scroll
announce the partnership.
Human and Pitt. Kimberley.
he always quipped at names
undertaking the grim humour of death.

he lies in a room
shaved of smell,
upper lip scraped
in the blue of morning,
clean as my chin

Once there was a Dorian

its stubble still inside its skin.
and that mouth so dry.
no jest can bud around his tongue.

the pocket, bereft
of his flourishing pen,
surrenders a white handkerchief.
beneath the pin stripe and tie,
his heart, that offending organ,
which plucked his fine-hair breath,
lies deep in its earth,
mined of its diamond.
I see my first death mask
shrunken in the retreat of cells.

and after the black car
had purred us home,
I took to pencil and pulsing type
and, in the erratic clatter of passion,
rhymed to my father's face
my first boy's ballad.
I kissed my words as full stop
on his sweet-fleshed fontanel.

Yes, there are dogs in this story:

The Ride Home

after my father's death
our dog Duke went
on daily walkabout.
trotting to town, calling at

Route 77

> the baker, for breadcrust
> the butcher for bone
> the barber for a pat.
> and at office for a meeting.
>
> he'd arrive after five
> sitting on the back seat
> Of a thumping V8
> Buick, de Soto, Hudson
> I half waited for a royal paw.
>
> doctor, magistrate, magnate
> in chauffer mode, opened the door
> and out stepped Duke
> with a tail wag.
> back at the pillar and bronze plate
> Hilton 18 Dalham Road
>
> so Duke showed a boy
> the pattern of a working life.
> I venture forth into the world,
> ply the writing route
> faithful to images and rhythms
> after twists, turns, surprises
> I arrive sure as story
> dropped off at the front gate.

Exit childhood. In hindsight I carried these two thoughts with me. 'The inner child is the carrier of our personal stories,' says therapist Jeremiah Abrams, and Alice Millar writes 'Only when I make room for the voice of the child within me do I feel myself to be genuine and creative.'

Once there was a Dorian

BILL HALEY, PAT BOONE, ELVIS AND TEENAGE ME JIVING IN LUMINOUS GREEN SOCKS 1957 – 1961 (13-17)

The son of a widow, told to emulate a dead perfect father, to be man of the house. No place to rebel. The result? A protracted adolescence and a subversive, continuing rebellion. A late developer. A mediocre school C 60% performer.

Yet learning poetry by heart. Quotes cling like the burs in my socks walking through the veld. As a teenager, when dealing with the 'thousand natural shocks that flesh is heir to' (Hamlet) I recited quotations written in my left-hand scrawl, recited until a sense of euphoria, courage and possibility rang through my cells. 'Diamonds are made under pressure' (appropriate for a Kimberley boy), and 'oaks grow strong in contrary winds'. I took to lifelong foam, brush and razor, a ritual link to a lost father.

Skin Deep

in the mornings
I lather my father alive
in shaving foam.
the tube breathes him
as I unscrew and snake
lime, camphor, menthol
onto soft bristles.

And in the church choir I sang, *How Sweet the Name of Jesus Sounds*. Dorian to solo-sing the third verse. Organ plays opening bars. This is how it goes on the day:

Route 77

Dear Name the Rock on which I build.
(no words come out of my mouth)
My Shield and Hiding Place, (Choir mistress sings solo, looking at me)
My never-failing treasury filled (Dorian joins choir mistress in duet)
With boundless stores of grace! (Dorian sings last line alone)

And of this choir mistress:

The Singing Teacher

twice a week
one hour alone with her.
all body and auburn hair,
she teaches an adolescent
through images and fingers.

the singing is already there
in the instrument, in the body,
plexus, chest, throat, head and mouth.
she touches each with her palm.
let it unfold its smoke.
my eyes follow her flowing dress.

now her hands lie flat
on her diaphragm.
light the breath on the banks of –
she gestures – subterranean rivers,
so it rises from the hot core.
deeper, draw it from
deep inside you.

Once there was a Dorian

she strokes her throat with her nails.
the polish matches that hair.
clear the chimney of debris and dry rot
so the timbre can climb on tendrils.
she waves her wrists
and leaves a scented breeze.
let sound ascend on an updraft.
yes, like that. beautiful
through the roof of the cave.
your head is a cavern, you know.

the river narrows between us.
she reaches forward
and places her thumbs and fore
on my cheek bones.
she taps the spot exactly
where my eyes and nose meet.

these holes here
ring and resonate.
let the voice currents
echo in these chambers.
tap... tap... tap.
she is a bright woodpecker.
here... here... here.
you are a maze of passages.

she touches my ears with
her thumbs. they pulse.
hear the humming of the bees
from deep inside the hive.
her fingertips on my lips
now open, open the cave. like this.
I see her tongue stir

Route 77

> below a front-row
> audience of teeth.
> beneath a palate dome
> built for arias.
>
> your notes will rise
> sure and sung through,
> exalting the valleys and mountains
> with songs for all seasons.
> just sing, sing, sing.
>
> her mouth closes. red lips rest.
> the river widens between us.
> she drops her arms. The hour's up.
> I swoon from the hive of her.
> All those caves, those passages.

Kimberley. Hot, dry thorn-tree country. Geographic heaviness. A longing for the road south, those 1000 km to the Fairest Cape. Driving with Aunt Edith in her Hillman (which replaced her Citröen), and my friend Rob Dowie (Daffy). Off to cousin Lil's Ganzekraal farm. Or with Dr Portnoi in his 90mph Zephyr to stay in Mowbray in Standard Nine – that's when I got converted by an older girl missionary Bee, who let slip that if I were older there would be a love interest.

At school, taking Latin. It was either that or Commerce. Our teacher a defrocked Irish Presbyterian minister with a Belfast accent who frothed when he spoke. Somehow in Latin matric fourteen in the class. Eight managed G symbols – me included. Poetry escaped me. TS Eliot beyond comprehension. I wrote a parody, one line, being 'the bell rang ding dong dung'. I too could choose not to make sense.

Once there was a Dorian

Vice-captain of the under 15A rugby team, me playing on the left wing, my mediocre right eye not always connecting the pass. I could sprint, one of the fastest in the school but when we played CBC, the opposing wing bulleted past me. We lost 36-0, and as the saying goes, lucky to get zero. Once as he dived for the corner, I could have pushed him airborne out of touch but a fear of hurting him held me back and so he scored yet another spectacular try.

On one momentous school Sports Day, I ran the 100 yards heats, semifinal and final, the same three races for the 220 yards, then the 440, and the house relay. No wonder I gave up sport in my final two school years.

Friday nights. Boy scouts clashed with the youth guild. The latter had girls.

The ugly duckling never finding a girlfriend for long. In excitement, writing Roma's name on my ruler, scratching it out when on our first movie date she brought along a friend. And those Methodist youth camps escaping into the dark. Cuddling. And Daffy who ran his gran's Morris Minor, silent out of the garage for our joy rides.

At fifteen acquiring a non-stepfather, HJ. Afrikaner and racist. How he liked it when I fell from grace. Never missing a day of school, Daffy and I did a bunk in our matric year. My mother, friendly with the headmaster, phones the next day to wish him happy birthday. He asks, "How's Dorian?" Six of the best. My mother with a migraine for days. Says headmaster's wife, "Dorian is tired of being good."

Years later, I compiled a list of people who had seen my potential. I could not include one teacher. A motley crew. One, an Anglican priest who quoted George Bernard Shaw, "You speak the language of Shakespeare and Milton and stand there muttering like a bilious pigeon," and who fiddled girls; another an alcoholic; a third who reset exercises and read his newspaper.

Three influences, close in time, shaped my imagination and spin. My father's death, and a school inspector who pranced around the classroom reciting the Battle of Lepanto. The Sultan receives news that "stirred the forest darkness, the darkness of his beard", and seduces me into metaphor. Then a visiting missionary infused me with the desire to be one too – but was too rebellious and randy. No one told me that sexuality and spirituality are kissing cousins.

My first exposure to teenage lust was via Solly's magazines. He lived down the road with a glandular defect. Obese. Two years older. A distorted sex education. I wrestled with hormone guilt.

Years later I read of a study about men in their thirties. The study could easily separate the men into two categories. Boys who had been more mature than their peers because they were a year older in the same class. If only I had started school a year later.

Down the line I wrote this article, 'Goldilocks and the Three Bare Boys: Myths of Male Potency'. Tried a few psychology magazines. Unpublished. Here's the gist of it. Imagine Goldilocks, as a woman, returning to the woods to find a boys' school swimming pool built on the site of the three bears' cottage. She peers through the change room window to see three sixteen-year-old boys showering. Rod Hardy, Lazarus Limpman and Justin Goodenough. She eavesdrops on their conversation about penis strength, breadth, and length. Goldilocks sighs and whispers. And what secret did she whisper? "This penis is too hard, this one is too soft, this one is just right."

And rock. For the first time hearing *Rock Around The Clock* in the school's quadrangle. Around me, in short back and sides, Brylcreamed, the bolder ducktails. And the jiving. Learning to dance for the matric farewell. Quick quick slow. Pat Boone was 'safer' than Elvis though I collected his 45rpms and jived in my luminous lime green socks.

ENCOUNTERING THE POETS 1962 – 1965 (17-21)

My mother thinks Building Society work first as a prelude to study. Headmaster Herbie says, "He probably won't ever go to university then." The only way to get to university was via a teaching Bursary, with R5 pocket money a month. So off to Rhodes with the headmaster's son, Chris. We take the Kimberley train to Bloemfontein, linking up with the student train from Johannesburg. Six to a compartment. We change trains at 4:00 in the morning. Grahamstown through the early dawn. I think it is an immense city until I realise I'm seeing the cathedral from different angles as the train chugs a wide circle.

All first years in Jan Smuts residence. Me top floor cell. Basic monk's cell. Minimal. Supper in academic gowns. Long tables. At the dais, up front the Professors. The Latin grace; *Benedictus benedicat. Per Christum dominum nostrum.*

Subjects. To keep the minister in me alive, Biblical Studies, and Introductory Greek. To serve the teacher, English and History by default – a timetable clash.

So arrives the first history class, Professor Winnie Maxwell, formidable dame. In the first lecture she quizzed, "Who of you took history at school?" We raise our hands. "Who of you have not done history at school?" Newcomers raise their hands. To these who answer in the affirmative, she says, "You, my pets, are at a distinct advantage." Another favourite phrase, "This is what I think but there are no prizes for agreeing with me."

Somehow in my third year I emerge with a history distinction, one of two in the class. Me? The one with a mediocre matric? Then a personal letter from Winnie saying that by the end of the year the jaded lecturers were impressed by my handling of the questions. She offered me Honours but the Department of Education said, no. So the path via Hons to an MA at an American University was blocked.

The Graduate

Once there was a Dorian

Here is my tribute to my academic mother and mentor. The first person to see my potential. To hold up the mirror. Winnie Maxwell (1907-1984):

> Terminus Steam
>
> 'Flying Scotsman,' iron maiden,
> puffing away across campus
> through the lecturing landscape of history
> with its frontier settlements
> from Versailles to Transkei,
> Charlemagne to Chaka,
> its monasteries and laagers,
> sun kings and cattle killings,
> you have arrived at this station
> and let off terminus steam.
> your brilliant-furnaced mind
> ahead of time, raced on its own track
> pistoning past booms of prejudice,
> rocketing thought small-law points
> and signals that flashed warning,
> steaming through school-text sidings
> with water tight towers of thought
> spitting sparks at us
> clattering and shaking
> in your whistling wake.

As for English, twice I failed the June examinations then emerged with a second-class pass. Guy Butler, huge in reputation, was like the story of the girl with a curl in the middle of her forehead. 'When she was good she was very good and when she was bad she was horrid'. Luckily

Hopkins was on his on day, "Place him next to your Bible on your bedside table."

Entranced, I was swept to the heavens via sprung rhythm. From him I learnt the play and pull of sound:

> I caught this morning morning's minion,
> kingdom of daylight's dauphin,
> dapple-dawn-drawn Falcon, in his riding…
> My heart in hiding
> Stirred for a bird, – the achieve of, the mastery of the thing!

And oh yes, meeting John Donne the playful priest and lover:

> Batter my heart, three-personed God, for you
> As yet but knock, breathe, shine, and seek to mend;
> That I may rise and stand, o'erthrow me, and bend
> Your force to break, blow, burn, and make me new.

Biblical studies. A prelude to the stories and myths I'll draw on in my poetry. Rev Prof Leslie Hewson, our lecturer. Later, I'll teach history with his son Glyn who will calligraphy my first poetry volume, Wrist and Rib, 1979.

I work hard. See myself on the 'dof' end of the scale. Medium-bright, don't understand yet that there are many intelligences and I hold a poker few in my palm. I inherited from a past student an armchair with flat wooden arms. Across this I place an elongated plank where I arrange reading and writing books. On the plank I'm lost in maps of historical Europe as boundaries shift before my eyes. And in my teaching diploma, a biology course. Overlay maps and charts of the intricacies, miracle mystery of the body magnificent. I carry the chair on my head and upstairs when I change residences. My study chair sees me through four years beyond tick-tock time.

Social life. A teetotaler through all four university years, emulating my father. First alcohol a beer shandy when twenty-one. I hang out with the Christians, loving the hymns. Commemoration Methodist Church with Welshman Emyln Jones, brilliant preacher. One sermon on how Christianity is woven web and weave into Western art, culture, music. Lyrical preaching.

1964. I'm working a holiday job in John Orr's toy department. Where you insert cash and slip into a capsule and slide it closed. With a whoosh the tube siphons and suctions it to upstairs accounts. Then it zings back to you. One day the phone goes. My mother. She could not resist opening the Rhodes results telegram. History First, English Second class obtained degree. Not possible. She must have misread it.

While selling toys there I meet Sipho who is sweeping the floor. He has a B matric. Better than mine. We begin sharing our lunch time, sitting on sacks in the backyard. He is also a Methodist, so we know the same hymn tunes. Different words in English and Xhosa:

> Love divine all loves excelling
> Joy of heaven to earth come down
> Fix in us Thy humble dwelling
> All Thy faithful mercies crown.

> Loo nto ayithiyileyo,
> Lowo unguThixo wam,
> Ma ndingabi ndiyafuna
> Ngayo intliziyo yam.

Route 77

In 1964 there is nowhere for us to meet so we cycle around the city to the Free State border five miles away. My stepfather would not allow me to bring Sipho home. My mother did not challenge this. I say the harsh words, "I never thought the day would come when I would be ashamed of my mother." Later in her senility in the late 80s, the nurses in a home who had been under her Matron's supervision and were now looking after her in the same frail care, told me "Ask your mother to sing to you." This is what she sang:

Nkosi, sikelel' iAfrika
Malupakam' upondo lwayo
Yiva imitandazo yetu
Yihla Moya, Yihla Moya
Yihla Moya Oyingcwele

'Nkosi sikelel iAfrika,' to become part of the national anthem after 1994. Mom must have learnt this by heart in Kuruman as a teenager in the 1920s. I revise my judgement.

Back to Rhodes. UED. Teaching diploma. Fourth year. I can relax a little. I miss the odd class. In a subsequent one, I ask a question. The lecturer responds, "Mr Haarhoff, I dealt with that question in the class you chose not to attend." The Afrikaans lecturer tells me TJ Haarhoff (classics Professor at Wits University) was a personal friend so he gives me a bilingual Big A – I who splutter in Afrikaans. I encountered the language in the mouth of racist politicians and officialdom and so I missed out on the Afrikaans poets of the sixties.

The annual Grahamstown to Bathurst fifty-mile walk. I soak my feet in paraffin to toughen them, don well-soaped double socks, and wear slip on leather shoes. No hat. Off I stride. Passing the five mile marker every

Once there was a Dorian

hour. At twenty-five miles turnaround in Bathurst, salt pills offered to us, still going strong, then take a rest under a thorn tree. As I rise, rested, lactic acid has locked my leg muscles.

I stagger on up a pass backwards. By now I am seeing three roads and so some five miles short of my blue tie with the fifty circle on it as reward… I hitch a ride. That night I send a message to girlfriend Irene, "I think I'm dying." Yet this becomes the start to a hiking life.

The age of first girlfriends. Aileen, at the Training College – a walk through the Botanical Gardens. Met at the church Guild – had to be a Christian. No sex before marriage. After I broke off some six months later, I insisted on a weekly friendship to the chagrin of the next girl. Irene. Ex Head girl at Kimberley Girls'. Impressed by this. We took the holiday trains together. Then on a walk I broke up with her. Her response, "The next time you want to break up with someone, don't take them take them on a long walk and announce this far from home." I'm the guy in the song who gets D in love.

There was the possibility of Cynthia. Looked like it was going somewhere. Until the embarrassing moment. We walk downtown to a function below the cathedral. Back uphill to the Drostdy Arch. Then diarrhoea hits, the foul sludge drains down my inside thighs. The 'train smash' residence supper. We were both too embarrassed to mention what was happening. So I wrecked my only second pair of trousers and any next date.

Then from Kimberley, Margaret, nursing in PE. Chubby letters of a dozen pages in pastel scented envelopes sought for on the letter board. A romance in between romances. In my fourth year, when friends host me in East London, I meet around the corner, playing the piano. D-J, Apostolic faith, works in a building society. Those romantic songs seduce this junkie. I sing along as she plays Cliff Richard crooning, "When the girl in your arms…"

Once, going from Grahamstown to East London to see D-J, I borrowed a purple and white striped Rhodes blazer to hitch in. Italian driver in a Volksie picks me up. He waves both hands while driving. Enters a bend at 80 mph. Touches his brake. The rear engine car flips twice onto its roof. He lies under the car with a broken femur. Pineapples scatter across the road.

I find myself standing next to the open passenger door. Gathering motorists ask, "Was he alone?" "No, I was with him." They look at me as if I am a ghost. I wear a scratch on my nose where spectacles, unbroken, pressed against the bridge. I sit up front in the ambulance taking him to a hospital in King William's Town then hitch the rest of the way to East London. Harry Casual. That night at a movie, I begin to shake like a rattle-nut. Years later my psychologist friend, Aneta will introduce me to tremoring to unlock trauma in the body. Yet again Dr Death had nudged my shoulder.

What affected girlfriend choices? Watching my mother, the widow at forty, grieving for her lost love, plus early girl rejection. Contracting with myself in the hidden part of the iceberg. I would never love somebody so much that I would be devastated if they left. And so choosing girls who were more in love with me than I with them. As in the musical Oklahoma I was the boy who could not say no. If someone said she loved me, I returned the sentiment. Hurting in not wanting to hurt. Years to break this pattern. As 1965 ends, Billy Rowles, head of Dale College, recruits me. King William's Town, not too far from D-J in East London, which would have been my chosen posting.

And so to teaching.

TEACHER MAN 1966 – 1968 (21-24)
(title courtesy of Frank McCourt)

January 1966. Lotto recruiting army call up papers plus a train ticket arrive. "Report to Voortrekkerhoogte." After several deferments the lotto draws Private Haarhoff. I phone headmaster Billy. "Leave it to me." Soon a telegram "Exempted from all military training. Return all papers." Close call. Last I ever heard from the Army. Another turning point. What would the me have been like had he'd been down that make-a-man-of-you funnel? Owe you Billy – with some high up army rank. Luck of the draw.

Off on another east Cape train ride. Crack of dawn change of trains. At 22.5 years I arrive as hostel master. The seniors are 18.5, not much leeway. So it's me or them. And it ain't gonna be me. So in comes, to my shame, the cane. Harder rather than softer. For Pineapple brewers in the loft, six of the best. Passing on the six I got for bunking?

First salary R180. Saving half each month, despite paying back the University loan.

In the classroom having to wear suits with buttoned jackets. In the heat. Me once at the notice board with an unbuttoned jacket. Old Mr B approaches. "We don't wear our jackets like that here." I wish I'd had the courage to say, "We do now." Only encountering much later this Robert Fulghum story:

Norman, the Barking Pig

A kindergarten teacher was asked to have her class dramatise a fairy tale for a teacher's conference. The children chose *Cinderella*. "A good choice," said the teacher. "Everybody can have a role in the play. If you aren't Cinderella, the Prince or the fairy godmother, you can be mice, or guests at the ball." Soon everyone was assigned a part, except for Norman. The plump outsider. The teacher asked, "Norman, what character would you like to be?" "I would like to be the pig" Norman declared. "The Pig?" the teacher said bewildered, "there is no pig in Cinderella". Norman smiled and said, "There is now!" And so it was.

Norman designed his own costume. Pink long underwear, a paper cup for a nose and a pipe-cleaner tail. He chose a non-speaking role. The pig followed Cinderella everywhere mirroring her actions. If Cinderella was happy, the pig was happy. If Cinderella was sad, the pig was sad.

During rehearsals, when the handsome prince placed the glass slipper on Cinderella's foot. Cinderella claimed her power, saying, "The slipper is mine." Norman the pig danced on his hind legs and broke his silence. He barked. The teacher said, "Norman, pigs don't bark." Norman responded, "This one does."

The play was a smash hit and Norman the barking pig received a standing ovation. Subsequently during the preparation for an international teacher's conference the organiser approached the kindergarten teacher, "We hear you have a play." "Yes," he responded, "and it has a pig in it." The organiser looked confused. "You don't get a pig in Cinderella," he observed. The teacher smiled, "You do in this one... and what's more than pig barks."

My father's maiden sister Ivy lived in a residential hotel on Beach Road at the Strand. We holidayed in that hotel as children. Then, just as I left Rhodes dear Aunt Ivy died. 1965. She left my sister and I a few shares and a touch of cash. In my first teaching year the inheritance came through. When I shared the portfolio story with a colleague, he responded "Wow de Beers shares. You're rich." Then on closer look he observed "Oh, de Beers Preference shares… not so rich." Yet the cash enough to buy my first car – a white Ford Corsair 83. 1965 model in 1966 for R1600. A touch of bullet.

Once there was a Dorian

That car drove me though the Eastern Cape and on to Durban (sister Joy and bro in law Norman lived in Pinetown.) And finally, with everything I owned leaving King W end of 68. Meg, girlfriend, travelled with me in her car, also leaving to take up a Cape Town Post. She a good Catholic believed that French kissing was to be saved for marriage. Ivy, dear Ivy. I had known little of her life. Once I looked her up and found her name on an ocean liner passenger list. So here is part of a poem for Ivy Dorothy Haarhoff (1889-1965):

Dear Aunt

at the Timeless café
on Beach road, Strand ...
they play the old-time music
you listened to on
your crackle valve radio
in your room with its quilt,
cobalt blue bottles
and smelling salts
in the residential hotel,
close by, long demolished,
brick to dust to high-rise,
where you partly lived
your Strand spinsterhood. ...

when your blue eyes looked
out your tide-facing window,
were you gazing seawards
for the ocean liner that
carried your younger you
on a maiden voyage

Route 77

> in cruise mode across
> the Pacific, first class
> in an outer cabin,
> your trunk collaged
> with travel stickers –
> Philippines, Vancouver,
> Liverpool, N Y, Cape Town?
>
> Now, as a poet with a Parker pen,
> like the one your brother used
> to flourish the family name,
> I surf the incoming page
> towards you, towards the time lag
> when we stood smelling salt
> on the shore, ankles in kelp,
> my Ivy league travel aunt and I.

Amid the planning and plodding of the beginning teacher, including the futile scrawling of notes from the board, there were one or two moments of the teacher yet to be. Once I got a boy, Scottie, to hop around the classroom on one leg while he intoned a subject-verb congruence that he struggled with and so he overcame. Introducing movement and play into teaching. Ridiculous inspiration.

Amidst the school chores were the sports ones. Coaching rugby or cricket and on most Saturdays the long ride there and back to Queenstown or Grahamstown on the school bus. Billy the boss offered me a free bus driver's license but I chickened out saying my mother did not want me to carry such responsibility.

Dale teacher friends, Brian Harlech-Jones and I edited the school magazine – the official version and the unofficial one that entertained us, e.g. there were two pictures of the new gym. One of the outside and one taken inside. Official captions 'exterior view' and 'interior view'. In the inside photo there were boys bending over so the unofficial version it became 'posterior view'. Brian married Marie. When I visit, their dog objects to my guitar strumming. I was trying to strum a guitar left-handed. I still know my favourite song by heart, *The Wayward Wind*, Patsy Cline. A touch of me here – I, restless wanderer.

Later Brian offered me the senior lectureship at the Windhoek College of Education in Namibia. We were colleagues for twenty years.

Another Brian – Johnson, art teacher (I dubbed as Baj) arrived outside the hostel in his red Volksie, and friends we became. We had been at Rhodes together. Dry humour. One of his scholar report cards reads, "Johnny is a quiet pupil. Judging by his results he must be asleep." Another one, "He must stop this bad hobbit of tolkien in class". He moves to Cape Town the year before I do.

End of second year 1967 of teaching, Baj and I, in my tan Hush Puppies, off on a Trafalgar Tour. A kind of four week 'if it's Tuesday it must be Belgium'. Caledonian Airlines – London, Paris, Amsterdam, Vienna, Innsbruk, Saltzburg, Rome. Michaelangelo et al. Girlfriend Meg, indignant that I was off Europing with Baj instead of her, also booked herself, secretly, on the Trafalgar Tour to find out she was on a different one. We over-lapped one night in snowy Innsbruck.

And those dinner dances at the beach front East London hotels with live bands. (The Dealeans) *There's a kind of hush all over the world tonight* era – Deals, Kings, Kennaway. And hearing Max Bygraves in person sing *remember when we made those memories.*

In King, I joined Toc H, a Christian movement with an international presence. The name is an abbreviation for Talbot House originally founded in Poperinghe, Belgium, in memory of Gilbert Talbot, killed at Hooge, 1915, and is now a museum. Toc signifies the letter T in the signals spelling-alphabet used by the British Army in World War I. Talbot House was a safe place where all soldiers were welcome, regardless of rank. There were three levels – a games room, sleeping quarters, one floor up, and a chapel on the top floor. After the war, Toc H spread into a social welfare movement. I visited both Talbot House in Belgium and the chapel in the east end of London. A lamp like the Aladdin one kept burning day and night.

Toc H adopted the prayer of St Francis of Assisi. We recited in the dark, "Lord, make me an instrument of your peace." And then the candles were lit with the words, "Let your light so shine before men that they may see your good works and glory your Father which is in heaven." We took orphans from children's homes to sea resorts. We took the elderly on picnics.

Part of the Toc H attraction was the connection to the World War I. To Uncle Allan, killed in Delville Wood, 1916, days before his twenty-ninth birthday. Haarhoff the Glad Heart with a song for every occasion. WW1 poetry has always inhabited my heart. Wilfred Owen. Siegfried Sassoon.

Then mid-year. A public phone interview in the hostel corridor. Noel Taylor, Westerford head. Newlands. Cape mecca. "Are you a practising Christian?" Lead question. "Yes." True at that stage. Cousin Lil's friend in high education places put in a word.

1968 ends with Meg driving in tandem in her car, she too taking up a new post; us stopping en route at Herold's Bay, brimming with childhood memory.

THE FAIREST CAPE 1969 – 1978 (24-29)

Westerford High. A government school that behaved like a private one. Conservative Baptist. St Noel's I dubbed it after the Head's first name

– a place where for ten years I developed my teaching, poetry, my satire, faithful to the trickster archetype.

We'd end up in Foresters Arms (Forries) after a staff meeting and I'd read concocted minutes, collapsing two items the head had alluded to into absurdities via the slightest push e.g. Practising a fire drill protocol and a report on the misbehaviour of Beatrice, a sexy matriculant. The male staff are to take turns in rolling Beatrice up in a carpet. No wonder the authorities promoted me to write the annual staff play for the matric farewell. A send up send off… Sacred cows desacralised. Sent through the satirical dip. Dorian the licenced fool.

The School motto *Nil nisi optimum* Nothing but the Best (the Beast?) Taylor's wife Muriel wrote the school song and compiled the school hymnal. I dubbed that little red book *Thoughts of Maurial*. Here are a couple of lines from the original school anthem, circ 1960s. "An outpost stood… where brave souls manned the lonely beach twixt Cape of Storms and Africa savage hinterland."

There were three noticeboards in the staff room. Urgent Today, 24-hour messages, and Continuous Reference. Once a notice on the 24-hour reference read, "Urgent today. This notice is coming down in 24 hours." Who put that one up? We all had our pigeonholes for green-inked Noel T internal messages, needing instant response. My pigeonhole often criss-crossed with red tape. "This pigeon hole is temporally out of order."

Unwisely they put me in charge of the interns who came to practice teaching for a few weeks in November. Part of their duties, I told them, was to construct the Guy Fawkes, who'd be sacrificed in the flames on the top field during our annual 5 November fireworks display (a non-existent event.) This included surveying the top field and installing fire precautions. One year a savvy group of aspirants called me to come and view their straw creation. In a wheelbarrow, in a school uniform, a straw figure with spectacles who looked remarkably like Mr Haarhoff.

Bruce Phillips, a current friend and colleague of yesteryear, reminds me that on one 5 April, the day before the then van Riebeek public holiday, I phoned the secretary, impersonating the head of Van Riebeek Dairies. Westerford had been especially chosen for its extensive green fields so the Diary was donating a cow to the school. Could she please come outside and select one of the herd?

Teaching History and English. Friends were impressed when I told them the school offered Ancient Current Affairs and Modern Anglo Saxon. I decorated the classroom with, what else, quotations – "Education is not the filling of a pot but the lighting of a fire." – W.B. Yeats. I had not yet met the Buddha on the road – 'Your worst enemy is your best teacher'.

In the late sixties, Jackdaw UK, produced folders with historical facsimile documents. We got the matric history students to create their own folders (images, photos, letters, text) researching a subject close to them, such as a grandparent boarding a ship he thought was bound for Brazil but ending up in Africa. When I taught I held up two books – the official Fowler and Smit (Foul Smut) and Richards with cartoons. I'd say, "FS is your Bible. R is your hymn book. If you want an A, regurgitate FS. If you love history enjoy R. Don't confuse the two."

St Noels had a Christian Union. Yet many Jewish kids were at Westerford – imported to raise the IQ and matric A-symbols? When these students asked for a Jewish Union, the Head vetoed this as it "Would polarize the school". So these bright minds joined the Welfare Society. (Welsoc) I, master in charge, welcomed these students who knew how to do charity. An injection of energy. The unofficial Jewish Union. Christian and Jew and whatever, non-polarized, all working for a greater cause. We travelled to Namaqualand to paint a school, built a retaining wall for a swimming pool for an Anglican church in Clanwilliam and built squatter corrugated iron shacks in the Cape Flats. In a programme 'Each One Reach One' we adopted an elderly person from a nearby old age home.

My mother was matron of the sick bay at Avondrust, within walking distance, so an elderly supply provided. I sometimes linked the Welsoc to Toc H projects. The saying in Toc H matched, "service is the rent you pay for your room on earth". On Saturdays we drove the Kupugani (lift yourself up) mobile shop combi out to Ocean View (you'd need a periscope mounted on a telescope to see the sea). The 'coloured' Kalk Bay community exiled here. Cans of fish, reinforced nutrition biscuits on sale.

And a class party up at Eagle's Nest where I stayed in Stream Cottage. Some twenty-two late teenagers walk in the moonlight in the mountains on the estate. Two guys disappear. I'm up all night trying to locate them. Send a car-driving student to their homes. Nope. The next day two contrite presences at the staff room door. Meanwhile a diligent prefect had run to the headmaster. Drugs. The boys expelled. At a staff meeting I was at the end of finger wagging. I responded, "If you have the right to chastise in public, I have the right to explain why I acted as I did." So I spoke under the Head's red-faced glare.

I was given the U13A rugby team to coach. At this level all you need is an exceptional flyhalf, big for his age with hands and eye and boot to match, and a lineout jumper cum rucker, a fearless gatherer of loose balls. I had both. We often beat, to their bewilderment, the rugby Springbok producing schools in the area – Bishops, Rondebosch Boys. The other coaches wondered at this amazing coach. So, the next year I was promoted to first team coach. Disaster.

Route 77

Life beyond the school. Sharing Stream Cottage with Baj, arum lilies in the stream, an estate behind our backs, mountain view forests. Hymie Rabinowitz, the potter, up the hill (he the previous Stream Cottage tenant) a sweet especial rural scene. Driving to school down Rhodes Drive amidst the larney cars.

And Plumstead Methodist with a vibrant Guild. Tony and Chris (Will) becoming friends. Me teaching in the Sunday School. Falling for a fellow Sunday teacher who taught Latin at Wynberg Girls'. Elinore too fell for a while then returned to a theology student man to marry him.

Easter weekends. Some ten of us in three cars off to the Wilderness. Ebb and Flow, Touws River. On the way back on Easter Monday I drive ahead with a suspect clutch. It gives way so when the other two cars arrive they see me attempting to pull the car with a rope. Tony hitches me up to his triple carb modified Valiant and off we go on a short rope at 70 mph (112 ks). Has he forgotten he is towing me? I make several signs of the cross which Tony witnesses through the back window.

As we enter a bend, slowing down, I brake. No brakes. Burnt out as my foot had been riding the brake pedal for the last 150km. To avoid him I swing out around a blind corner. Luck of the gods no oncoming car. And the Tony rope pulls me back and I bang into the back of his car. No damage. Now how to go from here? Tony ties his front bumper to my back bumper. Down Sir Lowry's Pass, Corsair in the lead. Tony's Valiant in second place. A long funeral like queue behind. Darkness Autumnal descends. If that rope slips I be gone to glory. Dr Death chuckles, "Not yet Dorian." We abandon the car in Somerset West for fix and later pick up.

Shortly after that, car no 2 – Fiat 1500. Box like with heater and reclining seats. Also brand new the previous year's model. R1950. The last of the new cars. Mine a racing green.

Once there was a Dorian

1971. Lloyd Tristino. Fiat takes Tony and I to Durban one Christmas. En route I hold up an umbrella over the engine during a rain storm while Tony dries the sparkplugs. We board the Italian vessel headed for LM, Beira, Mauritius. Tony wins the fancy dress as Tevye in *Fiddler on the Roof*. Young women outnumbering us four to one. Tony had lived in Rhodesia and often drove to Beira. He tells all and sundry fellow passengers of the best prawn place in town. When we disembark and make our way to this prawn mecca, there's no room for us. The shipload is there.

At the end of the first Westerford year, Gill arrives. She understudies me in my favourite Std 9 class. We date. And I give up following this class as class teacher into matric and hand it to her and take over another Std 10 class – a rebellious bunch where there is this girl, Maryke, who will become my first wife, though I do not know it.

Meanwhile, I go for UNISA Hons, and we form a support group. In it is staff colleague Chris Horan, ex celibate brother, now married, who will die prematurely when a nose op goes wrong. Unisa Prof Hugo comes down to meet with us as we are active and vibrant. Spend an intensive at UNISA one holiday. I share a room with Manfred, a Natal teacher. We find lipstick love notes on our room mirror.

In my 20s and 30s I'm unawake and unaware around women. It seems I'm attracted as rescuer to maidens in distress, with suspect mothers. I, the knight on his steed, in whose presence the maiden will blossom. I'm reluctant to write of the ending of bachelorhood and my first marriage. We each have our stories, Maryke and I. She sent me a Valentine when in matric. Perhaps that started it. Us breaking rules, crossing boundaries. She matriculates at nineteen, having had meningitis twice, transmitted by a pet vervet monkey. I visit the hospital out of visiting hours.

Courting. Much hostility from her mother and father. Dutch immigrants who hobknobbed with Nat Party cabinet ministers. After

Maryke leaves school courtship is denied. Had her parents been strategic, and wiser, we might not have, in forced unity, faced this onslaught, united against it. Tony fetched her for the date, charming the old woman and I took over round corner. Daughter at twenty-one to leave home and stay with a friend. She has few women friends. A sign I ignore. Others send up caution. I ignore their advice too.

The day after she left home, sneaked out, I visited her parents.

Prof: If she wasn't twenty-one we have called in the police.

Dori: Why do you think I waited till she was twenty-one? I'm going to marry Maryke.

Mrs L: Over my dead body.

Dori: Don't tempt me (she did die of vitriolic old age).

June 1973. One rainy winter's day we marry. Tony and Baj two bestmen. I would later return that same favour for them. Clouded atmosphere, me twenty-nine, she twenty-two. In time, we discover our own reasons for separating, but don't then. If this were undone, then no Damian and Martine, whom I dearly love, who first taught me about love.

Enough, enough. I find in my reading of novels or watching movies, if the focus is on the relationship only, I get bored. All this navel gazing. There are wider realities that make for a fine story. Let in the seven deadly sins and the salvation of the gods.

WRIST AND RIB 1973 – 1978 (29-34)

1973. Sabbatical. New wife Maryke and I over the waters on the Oranje Castle. Days in London with British Toc H friends. Over to France on a ferry. Hitch hiking. Two French guys picked us up. They only knew two words in English that sent them into derogatory laughter – bully beef and tea. A walk through the WWI battlefields in northern France. I cut a birch walking stick from the regrown wood. Here are a few lines from the poem 'Stick Story':

> khaki bark wrapped round the handle.
> a notch angled the head to fit my palm.
> this third leg tapped its Morse code
> on many paths – Europe and Africa
> then on a mid 2014 hike
> in the Cape mountains,
> above a naval base, it snapped.
> no bone this, that re-knits
> in double strength ...
> around the corner above the bay
> I met another memorial.
> for the fallen 1914-1918.
> so I left it leaning there.

We also stay at the Toc H house in Popperinge. On snow days I read the history of the war and come across a competition for the design of a plaque to commemorate those fallen. This plaque hangs on the wall of my study.

Route 77

Medal, Allan Christie Haarhoff killed at Delville Wood, 17 July 1916

In France, we stay with an ex-pupil and family in the countryside outside Paris. Amsterdam Rijks, Rodin museum then to stay with Maryke's family in Appeldoorn. On to Germany. I regret not visiting Hamm in Westphalia where Frans Haarhoff lived before he, as soldier, then farm help, landed in the Cape in 1719. He ended up on a Huguenot farm near Stellenbosch.

An anecdote in the ancestor book. Frans Haarhoff, farm worker, marries Maria le Fabre who had buried two husbands, one of whom drowned. When in church they get to the 'any just cause why…?' a woman stands up, "He's betrothed to me." The wedding stops, the matter sorted and the bells ring so that Maria can become our maternal African ancestor.

Visit popular spots. Hofbrauhaus in Munich. Dachau. The death camp horror. *Arbeit Macht Frei* transcribed on the gate. Italy. Rome,

Once there was a Dorian

Michelango and da Vinci. Florence (still wear the market leather belt) and Assisi where the town glows pink at sunset. The Greek islands, Mykenos, Rhodes. As TS Eliot says, "There I have been but I cannot say where."

Back at school on 11 November I lead an Armistice Day assembly with slides taken of WW1 – images of the trip, and as a surprise from the back of the hall, I had arranged for a boy in the pipe band at Rondebosch Boys' High to trumpet the Last Post.

I begin to reconnect to poetry and to write again, some eleven years after the poem for my father. I begin in imitation of mentors. Sound like Hopkins, Keats et al, then find my own voice. The greats absorbed osmotically into cadences and rhythms.

I train as a Life Line counsellor. Am accepted. Then train others. Learn about listening 101. Paul Tillich 'The prime duty of love is to listen'. Nights spent in a seventh floor flat in Life Line's Roeland street hub. Francis, a regular small hours suicide caller. I learn about Carl Rogers, the Rogerian feedback… the reflection, dodging the 'what should I do?' questions, how in the presence of such listening a person begins to find their own way home. They know the answer so to lead them to that place via matching questions. Many have commented on the quality of my voice. I'm grateful for that gift. Some call me 'Mr Voice'. Thanks Ma, for sending this teenager off to elocution lessons.

Once at a Life Line do we put on a skit I'd written – a send up of all the don'ts of counselling – 'Wifeline knifeline, can I help you?' 'It's about time you pulled yourself together' etc etc.

I visit Ros de la Hunt (a wisewoman artist Life Liner) in anguish, self-trapped between two women, hurting both. The choice? She asks why I have come to see her. "To ask your blessing." Her response: "You need to become your own counsellor, friend, priest, guru, guide." Later

Route 77

I find that Ros was connected to Temenos in McGregor which becomes one of my spiritual homes where I still teach.

One night we're off to the drive-in with Bruce and Sue – two comrade teachers, in his vintage Rover. Of Bruce's laugh, folks said, "If it has puppies could I have one of them?" Then suddenly, not long after, his car ignites on the freeway to town. Bruce, his vintage car and his laughter burn to death.

Over many weekends we take to the hiking trails of the western Cape – a few staff and friends, Cheryl, Istine, Gregor, Tony. Overnighting in huts. Boland trail. Wellington. Rock pools below waterfalls. The skinny dipping age. On one Wellington hike we come across in an abandoned hut, a murdered young woman. As we leave to report, another group of hikers from another direction stops us, "Have you seen the body?" We point to the hut behind us. How do they know? "No, it's at a campsite up the kloof. Some five kilometres away. A young man stabbed." A double murder. An escaped convict had come across these two medical doctors camping. Killed the man, pursued the woman. Imagine her terror run. Trapped her in the hut. They later tracked the murderer down.

We move from Stream Cottage, alas. I buy into poor man's Rondebosch East. Later, in Plumstead. Often in a bright orange windbreaker on my Peugeot moped to work. Motorists see you not. Once, one whizzes past, scraping my wing mirror. I land on the tar.

Moonlighting, I become examiner for English literature in the bad old days. Coloured Affairs. Blood money. Heather, who is also marking will later become a colleague at the Windhoek College of Education. How to kill a poem? Set it as a question. One year it's TS Eliot's *Journey of the Magi*. In response to these lines 'At the end we preferred to travel all night, Sleeping in snatches' a few write, 'The wisemen had nowhere to sleep so they found snatches and slept in them'.

Once there was a Dorian

Through Toc H I begin to cross the group areas divide. We meet 'coloured' people. One, a cabinet maker, creates a pair of oak bedside tables. They will travel to many a place and still sleep alongside the bed. Four of us in brother-in-law Norman's generously loaned Peugeot 404 station wagon. Two 'coloured' guys and two 'whiteys', Sheena from Scotland, and Dorian set off to a Toc H Conference in Natal. They drive us through the night.

Back home, we build geodesic domes on the Cape Flats – a Toc H architect Graham's response to the housing crisis. He has built such an igloo in his garden. We make concrete and sawdust triangles with lugs at the three points. The dome never rises. The mixture inconsistent. The heavy triangles buckle the lugs.

Maryke is fond of dogs. We have two chihuahuas. One day I go pubbing after work to come home and find, as I open the back door, a gush of smoke. I'd left on the toaster and it had burnt through the wooden stand it rested on. Both dogs dead, still warm. *Mea culpa.*

Once on a road trip to Alice. To Lovedale to see old Dale College friend Brian who trains teachers there. Tony, Kathy his wife to be, Maryke, and others. We camp outside cousin Mike's A-Frames in the Knysna forest. A few days before we left Maryke had had a near accident when the bonnet of her Cortina popped up and blocked her view of the road. One eve in the tent, she falls over into an unwakeable sleep. This happens again when at Alice. So it's off to East London, Maryke lying in the back. Scary. The specialist diagnoses narcolepsy, injects her and she comes around. It will happen again.

And other women? What to make of trying to follow Nikos Kazantzakis, Zorba the Greek's advice, "If a woman sleeps alone it puts a shame on all men. God has a very big heart, but there is one sin He will not forgive – if a woman calls a man to her bed and he will not go."

Route 77

The marriage in trouble from both sides. I'm about to leave. Out of all expectation Markye falls pregnant. There is no way I can leave. I tell R, waiting in the wings, "I have to stay." "Don't leave me yet." Silence on the rest of this story. I will meet up with her in Joburg twenty-five year later.

And so Damian Christie Haarhoff is born, 25 May 1976. Noel, Westerford Head visits, in kindness, the Mowbray maternity. My son opens me to what love is. This delightful boy, quirky and confident. Emily Gabuza, our char, a holy woman, will help mother Damian. She puts him in front of the washing machine 'to watch TV'.

I'm stuck at Westerford. Applications to other schools; not to be. Ten years pass. 1978. Out of the sweet blue, Brian H-J overnights with us. He's travelling back to Lovedale from Windhoek where he has been appointed Head of English at the new teacher college opening 1979. We're off to Sea Point to the Winchester Hotel for an evening meal. In the car he says, "There's a senior English post going. Do you want it?"

An instant yes. Unequivocal. He phones the rector from the hotel, "I've found the man for the job." "Let him apply." So zap, in goes the application. The Head of Westerford pushing for a result as he has already lined up a more Westerford-fit successor. One of his men. Interviews at Rand Afrikaans in J'burg (the Univ oversees the college) then in Windhoek. The interview, not going well at first. A tight-jawed Afrikaner on the panel has serious doubts. This applicant has only a Hons degree. He's liberal to boot. At some stage – is it inspiration? I say, "I would like to train teachers in such a way that I'd be happy for them to teach my children." His face relaxes, I get this job. The rector shows me the house in Olympia that will be our home.

The relieved Westerford head says, "We did not know what to do with you." Some fifty days later, January 1979 we board the plane for Windhoek. Brian plus family, Maryke, pregnant, and young three and a

Once there was a Dorian

half year old Damian. Go north young man. I take with me my first self-published *Wrist and Rib*, 1978. Calligraphy by Glyn, sketches by Baj. Loose leaves in a folder inside a plastic wrap.

Route 77

> **WATER DIVINER**
>
> In grey stained trousers
> baggy in the fashion of the fifties
> gathered by a strip of belt
> he braces his workboots against a tuft of grass
> his body fluids call to water in the soil.
> With a calloused thumb he indicates the spot
> Working his metal pipes
> and cycling grey liquid through a tin bath.
> he sinks his shaft
> pushing through clay
> mating with water bearing loam
> rubbing sandstone in the cracks of hands
> So that he might grow crops to greenness
> like Moses striking water from a rock
> in a divine moment.

My first publication

WILD WEST LAND NAMIBIA: TEACHER TRAINER (1979–1983)

We arrive in Windhoek. The Sunday city is asleep, no taxi in sight. We walk along the Kaiser Strasse to Hotel Thuringer Hof. The next day we fetch railed cars at the station and move into our new house in Olympia next to the drive-in. Barren earth. I plant a wild plum with the help of two boys I'm teaching and their policeman father, and our dear Damian, nicknamed Duimps.

Some five kilometres away stands the Windhoek College of Education, a brand new building with an Olympic pool. Brand new staff, each of us at a desk the size of a queen size bed. Wooden bookshelves, built in. View of the veld. A white College but says the Rector, preparing to open. Brian and I share four lectures a week. Bliss. The rector asks for our suggestions for the motto and war cry. My suggestion whispered in the corridors is not accepted – 'WOK WOK OH FOK'.

Two mature teachers, Norman and Hannes, arrive for a fourth year qualification. Once we meet them for a late afternoon drink at Kaiserkrone. They both appear wearing shades as disguise. Brian and I, new to the town, have chosen, unbeknown, a hotel that doubles as a pickup venue.

So soon I'm into an MA through Stephen Gray at RAU (Rand Afrikaans University) on the novel set in Africa focusing on Gordimer and Mphahlele, who in some ways are predicting how South Africa will turn out. Reading and teaching African literature.

Drama department puts on a play. Andre Brink's *Afrikaners is Plesierig*. I play Skote Pretoors, the speech-making president. In top hat and tails I am wheeled onto a stage in a wheelbarrow. My friend Volker (German Department) plays the Communist, Brian the Brit. I'd get the role after Aldo observes me at registration. There are a few security police in plain clothes mingling with students and I pretend to be one of them, hiding behind a plant in the registration foyer.

Volker Gretschel, born near Dresden, escapee to Western Germany ends up in Namibia. He takes Brian and I, plus Kurt (Geography) into the desert in his 4 x 4. We camp at Bloodkoppies where the rocks glow sunset red. And in the Kuiseb canyon. Sleep under the stars. When the mosquitoes arrive I talk about Eine Kleine Nachtmiskiet. I reconnect with Volker in 2021 in Swakop and he still refers to this quip.

We recruit more English Department staff. Debbie from Knysna. Heather from my marking days. She was looking for a job in the Drama Department but the receptionist misdirected her to the English Department. I remember Heather, leaning in my doorway one day, asking, "What lies did your parents tell you?" Chris from Cape primary schools – had to fight to get him in. (qualification issues.) And Helen who substitutes for me while I'm on the Doctoral programme in York.

We often travel the 380km to Swakopmund. Stay in the A-Frame bungalows. Once Norman and Joy, with their children travel with us. Cape friends visit – Tony, Kathy, Willie, Helen. My mom and Emily, our Cape domestic, travelled by train and I meet them at the station with a trailer attached to the Peugeot 404 station wagon. (Mom a many-package traveller.)

Poetry pouring out. *Stickman* a publication with Marina Aguar sketches. One hot siesta afternoon lying prone on the office carpet, I looked up at the map of Namibia on the back of the closed door. This arrived:

Namibia

wild west land
holster in the hip of Africa
strung on the studded belt of Capricorn.

the sun lassoes the rain
tugged from the bare backed land
the rocks crack in pistol shots.

Once there was a Dorian

<blockquote>
yet on a sparse frontier
crossed freely, are
the cattle of the heart.
</blockquote>

1979. A week or so in Namibia, when one night Maryke begins to bleed. We drive around not knowing where the hospital is. Finally, finding it. Maryke aborts at five months, a baby girl, who would have been called Martine. Before the blessing of the arrival of next daughter Martine. The staff do not want me to see the fetus. I insist. There she was lying in a bare room in a stainless-steel basin.

<blockquote>
Little Astronaut

kicking too soon
before her time,
</blockquote>

Route 77

> this large head,
> these veined nails.
> thrush-shell blue,
> slipped through your cervix,
> warmth retreating
> from limpid sack.
> little astronaut
> dropped through space
> past a world of earth
> too cold to hold her.

Maryke soon falls pregnant again. Then, 10 December 1979 while on holiday in Cape Town, our girl, Martine Olivia is born. The Day of the Women. This time on our dawn rush ride, we do know where the Mowbray Maternity hospital is. I instantly love this daughter.

In the early eighties, one morning a car hoots, pulls in front. He's interested in my Life Line bumper sticker. Derek Puffit is wanting to start a branch in Windhoek. Well connected, he finds an old house. We begin. I meet a social worker, Manda Steynberg. We are the trainers of some seventy people. The big knobs travel for selection. They are still narrowly Christian based. I fight for Brigetta who is follows the Korean Sun Myung Moon (dubbed the Moonies). She is accepted. One night she and I go in the small hours to meet a suicidal guy on a bridge at the Station.

I am beginning to loosen ties with the Methodist Church, yet take up the role of confidante to the ministers Gavin, then Jimmy, who wrestle with the role in a divided political climate. A few friends current are priests or ex priests – hedging my bets?

Part of the thrill of Namibia was going to a country on the edge of independence. Early in 1979 the newspaper, *Die Republikein* proclaimed in a headline that filled half a front page, "All apartheid forbidden". Housing was desegregated. The mixed marriages act annulled. I saw Namibia as an experimental farm for South Africa, trying out the changes in a small country with a population of around 1.5 million. Wordsworth's words, ironically about the French Revolution in its first phases, echoing in my head, "Bliss was it in that dawn to be alive and to be young was very heaven." Maybe, at last, being a citizen of a country that I could be proud of? And then the process got stuck. Namibia's fate linked to Angola, Cuba, America and Russia. A ten-year delay, and a border war. We flew in low to the north to teach the nurses at Oshakati Hospital and drove into the town wrapped in wire. Undercarriage checked at the fox hole gate. And flew out again.

At the college, a fight between the right-wing Afrikaners and the extreme right. A group I dubbed the seven dwergies (dwarfs) plotted to overthrow the rector. The two liberal English lecturers, irrelevant in this bitter in-house conflict.

D.Phil. Towards the end of my time at the training college, we went off to the Centre of Southern African Studies at the University of York for ten months, staying the village of Heslington, just off campus. A row of cottages for international students. Our neighbours were Norwegian, Saudi Arabian, with an Irish domestic, and midst us, a family from Lincolnshire, first time out of their county.

Landeg White, my supervisor, had worked in Malawi. At the start he said, "A book here, let's work right through the thesis toward the book." So was born in the University library carrel, my nook, *Frontier Myths and Metaphors in Literature Set in Namibia*. From the first British travel writers through the border war to the first postcolonial writings. I carried on part-time back home.

Route 77

Enter stage left, right, and centre – a children's play. Dorian the playwright. Sandy Rudd produces. Retha Louise Hofmeyer creates the music. *Alice in Welwitschialand.* First staged in Windhoek and Grahamstown early 1980s (the train leaving from platform 28 on the night of the full Moon predates Harry Potter).

Arrogant Alice boards a moonlight train striped like a zebra bound for Swakopmund. She has lessons to learn. Zeb, the strange train driver, who later turns out to be the Wizard of Usakos, takes the train into the desert. We're in DMT – desert mean time – time measured by the blowing of the seven colours of sand, the length of the leaves on the Welwitschia plant, the curl on the Kudu horn, the drop on the desert bug.

In a court scene, Alice is charged with contempt for the desert and has to use her five senses to experience the desert before the train continues its journey. Kudu, whose school reports said, "Kudu could do better" acts as her guide. The cast includes Welly, the 2000 year old Welwitchia plant who sings the blues and Onymacris (Oni) (with his black bug for karate), who collects the condensing fog on its upside down body.

I learn some of the outdoor cowboy skills. Loading a kudu carcass into the back of the station wagon and a neighbour teaching me how to skin it, cut it up and make droewors and biltong with coriander salt and vinegar.

Houses. After an Education Department house in Socrates Street, buying in Schubert Street, the music quarter. Bach, Beethoven, Mozart Streets nearby. House came with flat and so an array of tenants. The most exotic, Professor Attia, an Egyptian statistician who predicts that Dominic will one day be a computer engineer.

Damian and Martine at Saint George's. Once I played Father Christmas, arriving in the fire engine. Martine on my lap in willing suspension of disbelief. Her father but not her father, who seems to know so much about her life. Then later, writing the new anthem for St George's and the first parody with it.

> Our school is built upon a hill
> beneath the aloe trees
> and every time we turn around
> up have gone the fees

After eleven years the marriage to Maryke ends. In those days custody to the mother unless you deem her incompetent. I'm glad I can be in the same city as the two children. X enters and an affair consumes us, with touches of the demonic. She often quotes, "Oh, what a tangled web we weave when first we practise to deceive" (Walter Scott). A mother, she dubs me Priest of Love (ala D H Lawrence – Frieda left her husband and children for him) and wishes us to run away. No, I will not leave the children.

In 1982 I become Head of the English Department as Brian moves across to the Academy, germ of the new university. Housed in the old German Maternity Home above the city. Where they flew a blue or pink flag for a birth. I follow him in 1983.

Tony, Cape Town friend, builds me a trailer – the back-end of a bakkie, cut off, and up north it goes. Mode of transport often a moped, Peugeot, then a 120cc Suzuki. Till one day a blow-out on the national road to the College. I wobble, somehow stay vertical. I decide, as in *Animal Farm*, 'Two wheels good, four wheel better'. Farewell bike.

Love the rain thunder when it rains...struggle in the plus three months of heat. I miss the sea.

Route 77

UNIVERSITY DAYS 1984 – 1997 (40-53)

How do you share thirteen years in some 3000 words? Select select select. A European rather than American movie. These surface from the moth balls, not in chronological order.

I move from College to Academy (germ of the new University). I read children's divorce books to Damian and Martine. Not your fault. We camp and adventure. Rained out in Sossusvlei driving through a shallow pan of water. Richard Aitken from University of Zululand, now a colleague, joins us with his children.

Six months solo in the Schubert Strasse house. Winter 1984. Eddie Black ex Glasgow, a colleague and I drive up north in two Peugeot station wagons, dropping students in Rundu then along Caprivi to Poppa Falls, then river crossing on a pont into Zambia where Eddie had worked. We visit a farm of one of his ex colleagues who has married a local woman. I pick peas off the pod in their garden. At a café two Italian woman approach us, having seen our SWA number plates they seek a lift south. We are leaving the next day so they need to get rid of Kwacha, the local currency. They meet up with two Italian men who swap currency.

The six of us end up that night looking at the Victoria Falls from the North side. Back at the car, armed drunk soldiers surround us. President Kaunda is at a nearby hotel touring market villages. "He will come and explain why we are arresting you." So the two Peugeots crawl to the police station under guard. There, the one in charge waves his AK at us. Talking of his sexual prowess. We're in a cell with a three-seater bench and a primus. Cold. We rotate through the night. The Italian men talk of the Italian police harassment. They blame us.

At dawn Eddie and I are interrogated. He first, while I wait in a Kafkaesque corridor with a naked dim light bulb. I know that people can disappear. Then my turn. It turns out Eddie's friend farmed next to an

ANC farm, so we must be SA spies. Story unfolds. In the night while we were in the charge office and cell, the head honcho had raided the friend's farm, finding only porn.

We were given our passports and told, "If you have not heard from us by twelve noon you can cross into Zimbabwe." We huddle outside the cop shop in a patch of sunlight. A white Merc sweeps past, a handkerchief fluttering out of a back window. Behold it is the President, come to explain our incarceration? Turns out that Eddie's friend supplied the police with cabbage (the Christmas turkey) and threatened to cut off supply unless they released us. At noon we crossed the long Zambesi bridge and sighed that sigh. The Italian women travelled south with us. I heard later from Eddie that the Sicilian fancied me. A story that never happened.

April 1985. Annie moves to Windhoek. I'd met her the previous September in Cape Town when friend Volker and I attend a UCT literature conference. Volker stayed with me in my mom's cottage in Wynberg. Annie was house sitting in Observatory Cape Town for mutual friends, Glyn and Cheryl. I dropped in to see them to be told they were in South America. She nearly did not open the door as she thought it was yet another tramp. On seeing me on the doorstep, she thought, "Oh, not him, that vain man." We'd met at a party a few years before. (Yes, Robbie Burns… "give us grace to see ourselves…"). But she asked me in for a cup of tea anyway. Many connections such as Rhodes, history with Winnie Maxwell. Four years behind me, so we missed each other there; also missed at Westerford, she the librarian. She did calligraphy and returned in the last decade of paper letter-writing, one of my poems.

Route 77

> Growth
> have you noticed
> in your sunwalk
> the knobbed tree
> that stood apart
> bare, awkward
> in the scented park
> among the bloombud
> and creeping foliage
> of springbegin
> how it has
> in this late season
> a pungent, urgent blossom.
> Dorian
>
> Anne © '84

So begins our relationship. We marry. Year end we take off to York for three months for the final alignment of my thesis, visit Crete while there, where we taste peasant dish *fasolia*.

And in due time arrive Dominic Rex (27 November 1986) and Adam Daniel (12 December 1988) into this world. Dom premature by two months, 1.3kgs. The pediatrician saves his life via a blood transfusion, drop by drop. He had jaundice and his bilirubin levels were too high.

Frustrated with academia, I begin looking for jobs. I am short-listed for director of the new Rössing Foundation Education Centre. An insider chosen. Annie and I end up editing the *Rössing Quarterly* magazine. One in-house and two out in the world articles, e.g. one on the salt pans off the Swakop coast.

My season of short listing continues. Director of ISEA (Institute for Study of English in Africa) at Rhodes. At the interview six men in suits at a long table. My ex Professor, Butler asleep; Malvern van Wyk Smith rooting for me. In the chair a friend of father-in-law Rex. He asks if I get the job what will be my memorial. Typical Grahamstown

Once there was a Dorian

question. I say start a Creative Writing Department. This is a good few years before my *Writer's Voice* (1998), also before other universities offer such a department.

Flying back to Windhoek via Cape Town, I overnight and next morning visit recommended psychic Esme in Kenilworth Road. She asks where I've been. I tell her about the interview. She says, "Not your job that." She lifts an object off her cluttered desk, a bronze eagle. "You'll see this object shortly and that will be a sign that your life will take off – not in Cape Town. Somewhere in the Western Cape. You'll land your bum in the butter." That afternoon I visit a sand tray in the home of a therapist that my friend Tom Smit had visited and played in. Lo, among the objects used in the sand play tray is the exact same eagle replica. And the house – in the same road as Esme, about 100 metres away. That evening Malvern phones. The job went to a Rhodes insider.

Tom. University colleague, Life Line counsellor, brilliant mind, bird lover, dry alcoholic, gay, headed a new college, then slipped back to drink, ending up in an out-of-the-way Namibian town and gassed himself. Martine and I assemble all the gifts he, her godfather, had given her, in a pile, light a candle and remember him.

For Tom:

Ex Libris

perhaps they should bury
a man with his books
in moulding earth,
or burn them,
set alight in a fire of words
on a Viking sea.
for what was left ex-libris,
bound in random stacks,

Route 77

inscribed your life
on an auction table.

a year after your dying,
I move, mourning you,
among this May day crowd
casting for bargains.
in these piles
the auctioneer's net
has trapped the fish-flit
of your swirling mind.

bird books flutter
light as levitation waves,
while fundamental education
sinks gravely in depths of mud.
exotic fish shudder through middle water –
pop psychology, ethics, gay renaissance,
poetry and oriental thought.
you underscored all clues
in a purple NB,
as you searched ever
in your five-decade drowning dive,
for the sunken galleon.

in this ocean of books,
your loved, oft-quoted poet
rises like a tide.
I flick the fly leaf
of your complete Blake,
to find you have reeled
in fishing-line hand.

Once there was a Dorian

> He ever will perceive a lie
> Who looks at truth with,
> Not through the eye.
>
> yet you snapped your own air-line.
> not even such perception
> could keep you spearing
> in the currents of this aquarium.

Among my friends, Brian Thorn's antique shop Camelthorn, serves as a venue for our men's group where we hold up objects – wall telephone, antique vase, and wrap them in our memories. In the lit shop, the red-light brigade walking past, gazing in at us. Our poetry group also meets there sometimes. USA Ruth, the Bishop's mother-in-law, Padda Padda, so named to jump away from the grim reaper who had taken off a few of his Tswana siblings, USA Jack, former angry Catholic brother, Brian and I.

And the antique shop is also the setting for *Shop Stories* that I scripted, constructing stories around the antique objects: an early Windhoek number plate, a taxi sign, creating the character who drove that taxi; the girl who inherited the doll. Aldo, drama lecturer, narrator in NBC TV's dramatisation of the stories. I also wrote an article on the shop for *Flamingo*. Air Namibia's inflight magazine.

1988. To Sweden to meet SWAPO as part of an Anton Lebowski delegation. He was a liberal lawyer who later was shot outside his home in the lead up to independence. They take two poets George Weideman and me plus journalists. SWAPO not much interested in the poets. Caviar and salmon in Stockholm, then to an industrial retreat complex on the Baltic. When we were not in session, the whiteys took to frolicking in the Baltic Sea, while SWAPO delegates huddled in meetings. We

Route 77

visited the Scania factory, and I came back with a toy truck for the boys. I borrowed a bike and went cycling solo through villages. High summer. No night darkness.

1990 Independence. As Head of English at UNAM I travel to link up with universities in SADAC countries. Botswana, Zimbabwe, Swaziland. I meet lecturers who will later become colleagues: Zak Malaba, Helen Vale. Foreign academics arrive – Kim Blank from Victoria, Canada. Laura Ootala from Uganda, Ismael Mbizi from Tanzania. And an academic 'father', Rajmund Ohly (a Pole) in African Languages, who took my poetry seriously. His favourite phrase when things go awray, *This is Africa*. So this for Rajmund:

Language Man Leaving

My academic elder
with a Falstaff laugh,
fills space and syntax
in our language corridor.
his lexical towers
rise like smoke beyond Babel
ringed and signed
by flying pidgins.

linguist of latitudes,
global in his gait and frame,
he wraps a tongue
round spoken hemispheres.
morpheme addict,
he hides several brands
in a folktale cave
where Alibaba's palate

Once there was a Dorian

shapes, open sesame,
treasures of speech.

when he craves a dialect draw,
he rolls paper in fingertips
and with a little spit
rounds his lingo cigarette,
flares a vernacular match,
inhales tobacco that glows
of his Polish home
then exhales Herero lions
and Holy Fires.

as you make semantic shift
back to the accents of Europe,
you transcribe your signs and signals
flapped in an African blanket.

I find friends across the divide:
(for Fanuel Muudja)

Friend Fanuel

tall as thorn, my fifties friend,
you walked St Barnabas class,
assembling children,
far from your Herero home,
driven to desert
in the abattoirs of war.

your grey-head humour,
static as cattle patches

Route 77

> along Botswana border,
> crackled current when power cut
> in skull-and-bone colonial days.
>
> then one summer with stagnant pools,
> after the birth feast of faith,
> you drove the reserve road.
> the insect that breeds in this tropic
> injected you sudden as gun shot
> into the cerebral heart
> with its spaces for craft and laughter.
>
> I still hear you on the wire line
> clearing throat in Katutura,
> your kraal-rasp voice
> cracking this English
> with its consonant pods
> and camelflower vowels.
>
> like Barnabas, communal man,
> apostolic father,
> gather your cattle
> in this great Namibian underearth.
> take to ancestral horns and hearth
> this static crack, this kraal voice,
> as the Holy Fire still flickers in you.

I take on Namibian citizenship. We all pretend the university only started at independence. Fun writing an anthem with more symbolic words, less blood of the martyrs. Obviously not in the running as this whitey is not a seasoned SWAPO member. Nor into national cliches. On one occasion in the State Theatre, in those confused early days, they started singing my same tune version – quickly stopped. Symbols and metaphors, such as trees, unwelcome in an anthem.

The cause betrayed. Christo Lombard in the Theology Department had visited SWAPO in Lusaka before 1990. The white right wingers dubbed him a communist. After independence he exposed SWAPO dealings with SWAPO D as brutal as anything the South African defense force threw at the border war. The Namibian President appeared on TV calling Christo a right-wing reactionary. My response? "Christo, amazing. You have switched sides in an instant."

1991 publications arrive. *The Wild South West* is launched, via Wits University Press and friend Eve the Director there. A poetry collection, *Bordering*, published by Nicholas Combrink at Justified Press, who later puts out *The Writer's Voice*.

Route 77

The cover for *Bordering* bears an Amy Schoeman photograph. For a year or so, Amy and I shared a two-pager in *Flamingo*. Air Nambia's inflight mag. Sometimes the photograph leading the poem or the other way around. In *Bordering* two sections: a general and a poetic history of Namibia. Including many of the traditional leaders pitted against the colonial might.

Here are three *Bordering* poems:

Coffee Break

it steams across the road
from the law courts,
a local Lincoln's Inn
hung in gingham green.
advocates sweep in,
gown frilled over arms
that clasp files
of fire-tight proof.
two men cross swords
on old cases and awards
and shift their spoons
like a chess mate move,
barristers down to their briefs.
a cop hovers over a cup
to see the end of the arrest
and meet the maid.
messengers fetch take-aways.
on the steps a woman,
tailor-dressed for court,
hugs a supportive sister,
shot of the bugger.

Once there was a Dorian

while Saturday's scandal sheet
flashes like lightning
through the drapes.
among these dramatic greys and blacks,
their car long ticketed,
their time thieved,
illegal lovers sip
black sweet mocca.

Battle of Waterberg (Hamakari)

a Herero in a uniform,
green as nature,
keeps gate at the rest camp.
his silent road-side wife
records, in floral costume
and blackhorn headpiece,
that this conservation place,
west of the desert,
was once Hereroland.
we walk footfall
along contours and come
sudden upon a graveyard
of a colonial war.

ironwork swings
on heavy hinges.
Schutztruppe dead
lie in stone rectangles
straight as a parade.
under the crosses

Route 77

>   the apparition that came
>   to teen and twenties men,
>   reads like the headstone print
>   of a gothic novel.
>   the graves are placed
>   under Waterberg
>   where a heliograph flashed
>   like a rising Christ,
>   the light of victory.
>
>   on Hamakari
>   the rocks are organ-piped,
>   red and ochre autumnal
>   and termites raise fingers of god.
>   a bone trail leads back
>   from the escaping desert
>   to this wet mountain
>   where blackthorns crown
>   with leadwood, wattle weep
>   and false umbrella thorn,
>   the root-entangled Herero dead.

Old Woman Brewing

in war days, she moved
as heady matriarch
on powder plains,
under an airforce sky.
she mapped her way
among the trees
her grandson climbed for her
to shake the seed

Once there was a Dorian

> for her windswept shebeen.
> when war evaporated like rain,
> she soaked the camouflage fruit
> of the makalani palm,
> and funnelled steam through stem,
> decanting from clay pots
> into old containers,
> discarded by the army.
> still she sits in roadside sun
> fermenting in sweat,
> and brews red-berried beer.
> the illegal glint in her eye
> shines like bottled fire.

And also in 1991 this Children's Book via Songololo Press (David Phillip) with Nicky Daly commissioning it. Book goes nowhere given the sepia unmatching illustrations.

Route 77

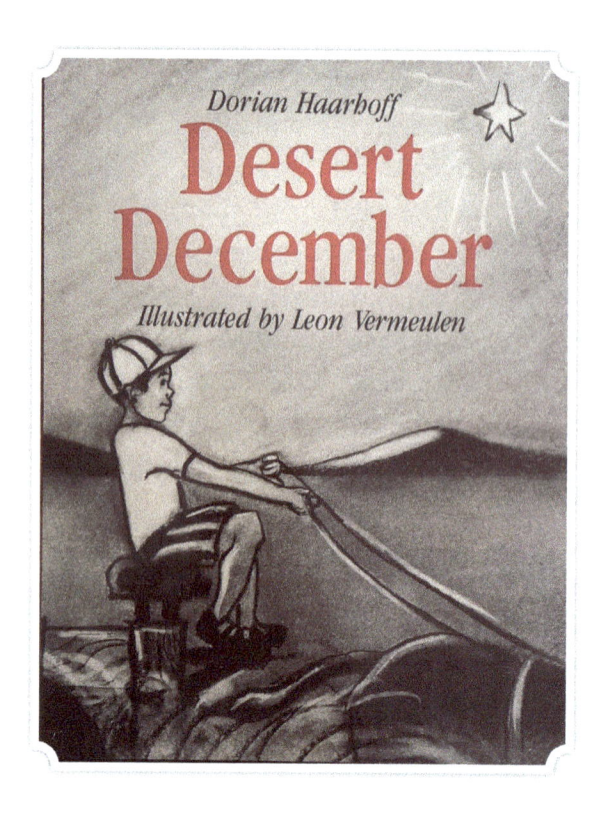

Dorian Haarhoff
Desert December
Illustrated by Leon Vermeulen

Other children's books follow: *Guano Girl* and *Legs Bones and Eyes*.

Conferences. One of the academic perks. I choose the Education ones rather than the English conferences as the venues were more alluring – Wild Coast, Port St John's, Magoebaskloof, Zululand. Never took the theory godmother too seriously, my papers, mostly send-up stories, messing with the current jargon – winery (binary) opposites et al.

Life Line hubris. Sometime in the early 80s an affair. The committee asks me to resign. I, the chairman, say, "It's not affecting my counselling. Fire me." They do.

Meanwhile in Academia. Beginning to feel like TS Eliot's dry man in *Gerontion:* I have lost my passion: why should I need to keep it since what is kept must be adulterated?

Once there was a Dorian

Frustration growing stronger. Once in Cape Town, visiting a career guidance psychologist for the first time, up came librarianship and psychology. Around the corner from his office, behold a UNISA branch. I roar around that corner. Registration closed the next day. I signed up for Psychology I and Psychology 2 and passed them. But then a colleague, Annemarie Heywood, came up with the idea of a Winter School. I do not know from whence came the words, "I will teach creative writing". And so I arrived at my calling, cultivated for some five years as a sideline.

Through my niece Estelle Jobson, then with a Swiss boyfriend, I met Carl Schlettwein from Basel. As a young man he had spent time in South West Africa. His philosophy? 'Pass it on'. This remarkable man suggested I put in an application to his Foundation to teach creative writing. So began a twenty-five year connection with Carl and Basel Afrika Bibliographien and the Carl Schlettwein Foundation. And then with his son Luccio, who becomes a dear friend. I offered students a life story and a poetry course and two edited books emerged, *Personal Memories: Namibian Texts in Process*, (1996) and *The Inner Eye: Namibian Poetry in Process* (1997), published by Basel Afrika.

Over the years, interspersed with the writing, I acted in university plays. Also once took a shot at director of Wilder's *By the Skin of our Teeth*. Never again – these amdram kings and queens. The set still being painted on the afternoon of opening night.

I go solo as Oom Schalk – learn seven Bosman stories by heart. Rosalie Truter is the PA of the College Vice-Rector. We became family friends. A cello player whose hands no longer obey the music within. She attended the first Bosman I offered in aid of Life Line in the Alte Feste, with Gunter on his concertina, me perched on an oxwagon in the courtyard. Boere kos. Thirty years later she arrived at an Oom Scalk Hospice fundraising in Somerset West.

Route 77

I write plays that are produced in Windhoek and at the Grahamstown Fringe Festival. Some of these are satires written around the edge of independence. In *Oranges,* a Namibian returning from exile has invented a way of altering the current off the Skeleton Coast by injecting electrodes into the ocean (the coastal desert barrenness compared to the lusher Angola coast is partly due to current flow). This brings rain to a triangle where oranges are now grown. The overseer reprimands a worker, sitting under a tree, taking a well-earned break, "This is citrus, not sit en rus". Wordplay abounds. SA is the chief export market for the Loftus Orange injected with brandy, sold to rugby crowds it is a winner. Fearing this plantation might make Namibia financially independent, SA send spy, van der Scrum to check this out.

Other plays are based loosely on historical events. *Guerilla Goatherd* on the life of Abraham Morris, leader of the southern Namibian Bondelswarts. In 1922 they rebelled against a dog tax. South Africa bombed them. Morris was killed in the mountains in a shoot-out with a policeman.

Terence Zeeman, drama lecturer at UNAM, who produced *Guerilla Goatherd*, edited and published three of the plays – *Goats, Oranges & Skeletons: a Trilogy of Namibian Independence Plays* (2000). We took another play based on the life of the Swedish explorer James Anderson to Goteborg, Sweden, to a winter festival, acting in front of an ox wagon in the museum.

Early 1990s. Canadian Kim returns to his alma mater. I follow a year later with family. An academic year at the University of Victoria, Vancouver Island in the Creative Writing and English Departments. We fly from Windhoek to Joburg, then Luxavia Airlines to Luxembourg, a bus to Brussels, flight to London and on to US east coast, then Seattle, and finally the ferry to Victoria. All this with a four and a two-year-old.

Once there was a Dorian

We rent a house, a bike ride away from campus, from a medical doctor and his wife who are to participate in the Victoria-Vanuatu Physician Project in Vanuatu for a year. His son-in-law, Rod Drabkin, becomes our local doctor, an-ex South African dodging army call up – he and I hiking companions on the island.

Family and I take in the lore of the northwest, the salmon stories, the Native American art and culture. Seafood chowder on ferry rides to Vancouver. Shoes off in homes, padding around in over-socks. Yard sales (garage sales) on Saturdays. Exploring the city via these yard maps.

Then arrives a Fulbright for three months to begin my *Writing the myths that make me* – a provisional title. I apply for Amhurst (Peter Elbow) and Stanford (Marjory and Jon Ford authors of *Dreams and Inward Journeys)*. The couple accept this maverick student so to Palo Alto I go. Faculty kindly hired a bike for me so off around the town and to the station, and by train to San Francisco, sans flowers in my hair. Finding, serendipity, a left-hand shop. Annie and boys join me halfway. So begins what will later be entitled *The Writer's Voice*.

I meet visiting physicist Brian Swimme at the California Institute of Integral Studies in San Francisco where he teaches evolutionary cosmology to graduates in the Philosophy, Cosmology and Consciousness programme. We talk stories. He, author of, among others, *The Universe is a Green Dragon: A Cosmic Creation Story* and *The Universe Story: From the Primordial Flaring Forth to the Ecozoic Era: A Celebration of the Unfolding of the Cosmos*.

While there, for my Fulbright free trip, I choose Washington DC where I meet Americans I had met in Namibia, now back home and then take Amtrak to Boston where I meet Namibian born Rob Gordon, anthropologist staying with a family, who researched the Bushman. Rob is there to run the Boston marathon. We travel to University of Vermont in Burlington, where I present wordshops.

Back home the children's lives unfold. Martine off to Wynberg Girls' High. Damian head boy of St Paul's. Namibian under twenty-one karate champion.

So I was a Prof for a while. Given Africa time, I only presented my inaugural address after I had resigned. Drawing on Matthew Fox's *Reinvention of Work*, Rupert Sheldrake on morphogenic fields, Meister Eckhardt, Campbell on mythology, Jung, I spoke from the fringe on how to put the universe back into the university. The Vice-rector's duty was to thank me. As he spoke he split into two distinct personalities. The sombre academic wondering how all this fitted into academic discourse. Then suddenly he shape-shifted to become an enthusiastic boy reciting long forgotten poetry, excited, animated, and then back, shrinking into his formal gown and then out liberated into possibility. Intriguing. The address was never published.

An ever-growing discontent with the university. Political, not academic decisions. Egos without substance. How to make the moonlighting mainstream? Time to jump at fifty-three. To risk. So what prompted a return to South Africa after twenty years? So much going in Namibia. Two words stick out – heat and dryness. Locals called October suicide month. Cracked heels, dried out nose. November to February upper 30 degrees Celsius. The sun flattening you. Also a wider market for work.

Annie and I explored the wetter, cooler places of the earth. West Coast, Knysna, then George beneath the Outeniqua Mountains. Some 11km from the coast, with an airport for flights to the big cities. George it was. Family went ahead.

Once there was a Dorian

I followed six months later at the end of the academic year. Those six months saw me presenting for the International school circuit in central, west and east Africa. Ivory coast… Kenya. By breakdown train to Mombasa and from Dar es Salaam, to Zanzibar by ferry to walk amid humid spices.

And via a visiting German lecturer at the University, off to Uganda, I offer storyshops with street children in Kampala (I had offered these through Petro Kimberg in Walvis Bay). We were busy with collages, pasting their stories in pictures. In my naivety, I provided glue sticks and the surreptitious sniffing began.

Workshop Kampala

they drew on sheets of
newsprint how they ended
on the streets.
stick figures, fists, banana skins
and cops hustling them along.

the teenagers nodded off
after their rambling nights.
so, after chicken and rice,
we built in a siesta.

I found a teen
under a tree
beneath the African sun
in open abandon
using his story sketch
as a sleeping mat.

Route 77

As I leave Namibia, I leave several school anthems behind. And return I will again and again for this is one of my tortoise shell-on-my-back-homes. I still spend three weeks a year storying there – a special place of the earth.

Rock of Ages

some young countries
hide their age
in a mass of foliage,
jungle green,
dripping with mist.

this Namibia lies
bones exposed,
a translucent desert gecko,
reptile on a rock,
crocodile on Kavango
with latitude and longitude
mapped on its back,
dust-coloured chameleon
with a tongue-flick along Caprivi.

elsewhere here is mammal land,
giving birth to grey shapes
that toughen under sun,
strung between equator
and quarter line.

here mountains rise
ringed in age,
lined long before

Once there was a Dorian

the tortoise built its shell
then crawled ashore,
or the first dinosaur print
was signed in stone.

Windhoek City Windhoek

Windhoek, City Windhoek,
/ Ai / / gams, Otjomuise,
an old person sitting on shifting waters,
memory a worn skin across two hundred suns,
recalling a veld patch in a drought land.
your springs seethe in caverns under earth,
your river roars in brief season.
thorn trees crown you, stones surround you,
guts of the country,
solar plexus of this land.

men have poured down your passes,
battle anger dying in a bone-cleft cry.
cattle post, mission post,
capital for Kaptain, herdsman and slave.
monks came with presses and vats
to watch the grapes of labour
struggle on the leaf.
trade tracks cross you
cut by wagon-men, cracking the ox-thong,
gunpowder and trinkets rattling at their backs.
now men stand on idle bridges
while sirens scream your streets.

Route 77

> and in the evening, sungoing,
> Windhoek, City Windhoek,
> / Ai / / gams, Otjomuise,
> as the falling light
> brings blue your mountains
> and the moon droops an old eye,
> I hear your underground angel
> troubling once more the waters,
> stirring, stirring,
> to bring minerals to our limbs
> and the breath of benediction.

LEAVING PROF BEHIND 1998 – 2003 (53-58)

When I resigned the professorship (1997), I took three vows – not the monastic vows of poverty, chastity and obedience, but rather that I would not teach conscripts anymore. When people are willingly present, they take responsibility for their learning. I would not teach towards an examination, for that so often corrupts the learning. The third, to stop asking questions that I thought I knew the answer to so that I could be surprised by the unexpected. Stories are about surprises.

These vows led me to my calling, working in creativity and imagination, twin sisters that bring healing, belonging. Showing people how to re-story their lives, acting as a mentor. The image for mentorship: A client dons one shoe and I the other. We set out walking through the chosen terrain – be it creative writing, work, development (UNICEF), academia or personal growth.

I have swum in the great ocean of stories with rural caregivers who mind children who are dying. Worked alongside narrative therapists, business leaders, embassy personnel, scholars (at Hilton College given the glorious title 'Writer in Residence') and academics – how to privilege stories in research. Shared Oom Schalk Lourens stories with audiences in Brisbane, Boulder, Wakkerstroom, Kloof and, and, and... The richness of my work? The stories people tell about their lives and how they tell them for this is ever a choice.

Guiding quotations? Here are seven stars in a countless galaxy:

1. *The first task is re-storying the adult… in order to restore the imagination to its primary place in consciousness.* (James Hillman)
2. *Why stories? Because stories are origins and origins are places that we walk out from. Because stories have many feet and travel several roads at once… because the story conjures the invisible.* (Deena Metzger)
3. *I am enough of an artist to draw freely upon my imagination. Imagination is more important than knowledge. Knowledge is limited. Imagination encircles the world.* (Albert Einstein)
4. *Enthusiasm is the first principle of knowledge and the last.* (William Blake)
5. *I asked myself, "What is the myth you are living?" … I took it upon myself to get to know 'my' myth, and I regarded this as the task of tasks…I simply had to know what unconscious or preconscious myth was forming me."* (Carl Jung)
6. *We are wound with mercy, round and round, as if with air.* (Gerard *Manley Hopkins*)
7. *When the soul wishes to experience something, she throws an image of the experience before her and enters into her own image.* (Meister Eckhart)

Route 77

    We buy a house in George. I enter the rhythm of my calling, working for myself, unlike my father who at seventy became unemployable and unpensionable and died the following year. Did his heart object? So I can't be fired. Now, favourite Herold's Bay close by. Wilderness. Lakes. Green, Rivers with water and sea surge. Hiking the Outeniqua paths.

Outeniqua Window

the African village print,
with grass huts, shields
baskets and women,
has kept us dream company
during dark hours.

we part the curtain
and let in the mountain.
today he stands etched in aura,
his hair illuminated
in a halo of honey cloud.
yesterday his brow,
touched with ethereal light,
shone blue as Mary.
tomorrow, as he ghosts in grey,
he guards the underworld
robed in mist rain.

Outeniqua, the elder,
wild man who gathers
the honeycomb and the herb,
throws his weather bones
and prophesies the day.

Once there was a Dorian

UCT Summer school. Port Elizabeth. Namibia. Johannesburg. I wander off like the Irish storyteller in Frank Delaney's novel, *Ireland*:

> In the winter of 1951, a storyteller arrives at the country home of nine-year-old Ronan O'Mara. The last practitioner of an honoured, centuries-old tradition, the Seanchai, enthralls his assembled audience running with narratives of foolish kings and fabled saints… until he is banished from the household. But these incomparable nights have changed young Ronan forever… as he pursues the elusive, itinerant storyteller. (Goodreads)

Here's a memory of Adam and Dominic, in a forest near George:

Kindling

off to find the night's firewood,
I link fingers with two sons
weighing their different gravities.

we track through twilight.
scuffed soles and new old shoes
run the forest floor and spin its spaces.

the younger treads a rhino path
his eye, a horn, prizes pine cones
from a camouflage of sticks and debris.

his brother follows the rustle of light,
a long-lashed giraffe, nibbling
where leaves are sweetest.

Route 77

>one with an armful of cone, stopped with earth,
>the other with wind laced through twigs,
>one drops, one plants the load for the fire pile.
>
>to raise the flames under first stars,
>in the hands of my fathering
>I take their gifts of earth and air.

As I trail my net in the lake of lost memories, I draw up another fish; me going to a hypnotherapist to work out the intricacies of a marriage. Out of darkness, much of it self-generated, comes an unexpected story within a story.

Derek Walcott's poem 'Love After Love'

>   you will greet yourself arriving…
>   at your own door, in your own mirror
>   and each will smile at the other's welcome.
>   Sit feast on your life.

influenced this one:

The Feast

>I have laid the round table
>and set the seven-bit candle stick, centre-piece.
>the hour is late. the chairs stand empty.
>the invited guests have not come
>nor sent regrets.
>
>I go into the streets of the old town.
>searching for discarded selves,

Once there was a Dorian

> calling them by name.
> the one in the ivory academy,
> sawn-off from heart.
> the one huddling in the alley
> where whores hang their red lights.
> the one whose face shows sea calm
> while the ocean churns in his gut.
> the one who sips jokes from a tap
> and does not divine laughter from the well.
> the one wandering the dry river bed
> his tears sucked by the sun.
>
> the boy who stood at his father's grave
> and wrote his first poem
> and who in middle years
> sat beside his mother's body.
>
> I embrace them one by one,
> breast bone to breast bone
> and I say
> The table waits. the candles are lit.
> drums strike the coming of the groom.
> the festival begins
> come and dine.

1999. On the shortest day, 21 June. My godmother Thora, who had been window-shopping with my mother when my father drove down Jones Street, phones. She lives in the same Avondrust home as my mother, "Come. Now. Your mother is dying." I jump into the car, travel at high speed into the sun and into the dark. Roadworks, I find myself at speed on a single lane bridge before I know it. Fortunately... no on-coming cars. Dr Death grins again. I stop at Riviersonderend,

Route 77

117km to go, and phone. Mom has died, and the mortuary contacted, "Please keep her body where it is." Reverse, ding a pole, race on to find her. Bonnet on head, the strings tied under her chin to keep her mouth closed, courtesy of Norman brother-in-law, who was with her when she 'translated', as a friend says. I sit a while pondering this mystery, after her long twilight senility. When both parents have died, the roof of your house is ripped off. This poem for her, she who was young once:

> A Mother's Death
>
> so she comes to brood
> and roost in the chorus
> of your memory.
>
> she, the dove, dwells in breath,
> light as a feather web,
> calling in your olive tree.
>
> in morning grey and in twilight,
> her milk throat sings
> the songs of the womb.
>
> she hovers in the garden
> of the Earth Mother
> in dappled shadow.
>
> she has crossed the deluge.
> now her voice
> wings its way home.

Patricia, my mother (1915-1999)

Meanwhile, work arrives from I know not where. Word of mouth louder than social media. Via a friend an artist in Mauritius, an ex South African invites me to teach there. I enjoy three visits to her centre. Local folk. Creole. Indians. One guy works for KPMG, so I do a day entitled 'Right brain stories for left brained people.' When I tell them this seventeen camel story some take out their calculators:

> An elderly man owns seventeen camels. He calls his three children to divide his inheritance. He tells them, "My Firstborn, when I die, you will have half my camels. My middle child, you may have one third. And you, you young scoundrel, you may have one ninth."
>
> The man dies and the children gather round to divide the camels. An impossible task. They visit the old wise woman in the village.

She speaks, "I am but a poor woman. But you may have my only camel."

Now the division is easy. The first born take nine camels (half) The middle six (a third) and the youngest two (a ninth). When they go to the camel kraal, they find that the old woman's camel is still there. (9+6+2=17). So they return the camel to the old woman and thank her.

I also do a day with the KPMG's Indian family, patriarch and all, busy with the process of dividing inheritance. They fetch me and drive to the south of the island.

Much later around 2019, I use the same camel story in a morning with Delheim, family-owned, working out how to incorporate the labourers. One says, "If the one getting half had been a little flexible, they could have worked it out without the old woman's camel."

Egoli

The only reason for me to leave the coast and venture inland to the highveld? I was looking in the wrong place at the wrong time for a woman, repeating unprocessed stories. I'm fifty-six she's twenty-eight – Larise completing her M in psychology, says her internship can be in the George area where her mother lives. So I can be back near boys. Not so. She wishes to marry, so after divorce, we do, on a ship in Mossel Bay. The woman photographer snaps her, in a traditional pearl wedding dress, clutching a battered suitcase with a look of alarm in her eyes, fleeing. Prophetic. We had spent a week preparing at St Francis Health Centre near Port Alfred, detoxing, trimming, tuning in. There I walked my first labyrinth.

The 2001–2003 years in Jozi – Dorian's folly. It wasn't the woman I married and lived with in Sandringham that endures. It's the three Jewish sage angels I met who have threaded my life with Shabbats, journeys, retreats to Leshiba in the Soutspansberg, Limmuds and progressive synagogues. I acquire the richness of a Jewish family, Ray and Lali Sher and Sybbie Barnett. The elders.

Sybbie who called herself my MBA – mother by adoption. She, so sunnyside up tiny, a rope hung from the car boot so she could close it. She lived at Randjieslaagte, which I dubbed Randjieslaughter. We travelled to Leshiba for retreats, here, where her granddaughter Katherine runs a heritage site, chalets based on Venda village design, where giraffes, twitching ears, watch us write away then us off on a game drive. Here where 11th century Arab beads from the trade route can be picked up off the ground. I praise poem these three glorious folk.

2001/02. Unexpected blessings arrive in people attending wordshops leading to two shared publication which included a story from each participant. One of them Sam Leyton-Matthews who will later bring me in to work alongside her with a Pretoria engineering company, Nine Dots. Friends with Anne-Marie Moore, calligrapher and teaching at their Rose Cottage home in the eastern Free State.

A sudden divorce from Larise's side. Many little bird reasons though the great eagle in the sky reason eludes me. Nor do I need to know. Had I my story-wits about me instead of floating in a romantic junkie cloud, I would have known that the way something starts predicts the way it ends. Such as her driving all night some thirteen hours to surprise me on a beach. Grief, the teacher, says, "What took you so long?" Enter Karma. I write myself out of the hole I've dug. Learn. Let a poem or three speak:

Route 77

Love's String

the kite flies free
in the heavens.
in bucks, dives, bobs,
swallow swoops, eagle soars,
rides sideways on still wings.
the kite's sure flight depends
on the tug of a string.

Second Skin

grief tosses me a hide,
stiff, raw off the animal.
I work its leather-wet death smell
through salts
to tan, soften and shape it.
I wear it supple
on my body.
it moves now, as I move,
breathing with me,
this sunburnt skin,
warming and adorning.

Time Slap

walking my birthday
along the cliff's edge,
on a bush-lined path
through a tree tunnel,

Once there was a Dorian

heel to toe I tread
on yielding ground.

fall into a birthday ago.
she, who withdrew her love,
between that moment and this,
sprayed gifts like waves breaking,
each gift reading how she
divined sea-need in me.

a branch slaps me sudden
across my shoulder, stings.
the monk prods
the dark-dreaming one
with his stick.
calls me back
to this path and
the motion of the sea.

Puppy Mind

the puppy runs wild
after the smell of rabbit,
sniffed down a hole.
whines and scratches
at the fluff beyond reach.

runs barking at the past
revisits a tree, leg-lifts,
then pants back
into the future,
drinking a mirage.

Route 77

> I must train this Labrador,
> call it to heal, to connection.
> to be where my feet shift,
> for it is guide dog
> and I am blind.

So the storysmous wagon travels south. Ahead of the pantechnicon. Somerset West. There are mountains, vineyards, quick to beaches, the boys four hours away in George, the Cape Town airport half an hour away. Should I have returned to George for the sake of the boys? All these roads not taken. I buy a Spanish town house with an elongated koi pond in the courtyard. I begin again. Jenny comes to join me for a year. Time spent on her smallholding in Broederstroom. But too much rebound on my side. So I hurt her too. So here I am under the Helderberg.

UNDER THE HELDERBERG 2003 – 15 (59-72)

The closer you get, the more to say, the more to leave ghosting amid words and lines. So a few random stabs at story through the decade of the 60s.

Somerset West. Helderberg Nature Reserve for evening concerts and hikes. Som West's own Kirstenbosch. Three hundred years of camphor trees at Vergelegen, land of wine and olives. Lauren Home: ford hikes. I often walk the Lauren Home: ford River upper reaches to the weir at Morgenster. On the R44 Avontuur, Eikendal, Somerbosch under the trees, the farm movie theatre Golden Eye, and studentville Stellenbosch or Stellies up the road. The wide Stand beach near by.

We form a U3A (university of the third age.) I give a talk, alluding to Jung. There's a man at the back of the venue taking notes. We are refused the same venue for the next meeting, Helderberg College, home of the Seventh Day Adventists.

Once there was a Dorian

I meet Elma across the Koi pond, as I need permission from Bridgewater Park residents to run wordshops. This begins a thirteen-year relationship. For my 60th birthday she organises a belly dancer. We co-buy a home. Error. Not listening to my intuition. Stories diverge. A fifteen year age difference. It ends when I walk away without my share of the home… Financial loss, emotional gain. I wish her well.

Katharine Ambrose artist, part of the Magic Carpet writer's group, offers me a thick-walled cottage at the back of her studio. Here I be for some seven years. Aneta and Gerda suggested I start this monthly Magic Carpet. 2006. Jos and Di, also faithful members. Still some ten strong. Leaving us for the happy hunting ground, Willemina, the crystal dame and Corissa-Maria, the artist and 'sabrager', opening a champagne bottle with a sabre. She slides the sabre along the seam of the bottle to the lip to break the neck away. We remember them.

Trips to the west coast Fossil Park near Langebaan. Dear cuz Pippa Haarhoff runs it. She also organises wordshops there. Picking up a handful from a tray, Pippa, the paleontologist detective, can detect what is stone and what is ancient miniature bone.

My legs take me on hiking trails. Cederberg. Tsitsikamma forest in the train. The Whale trail. Three visits to Boulder Colorado as storyteller.

Bruce Copley (Aha learning) invites all who had worked with him to a weekend at Shangrila near Mbombela (Nelspruit). Ray and Lali are part of this jamboree so I fly north and travel with them from Johannesburg. We all present a snippet of our work to the group. There I meet Igno van Niekerk, photographer and Liberty trainer. So begins a friendship with several visits to Bloemfontein to schools, to corporates, to psychologists.

Route 77

Photograph courtesy of Igno

While in Grahamstown for the festival, I launch *Drawing Water*. 2006. Ex Catholic priest academic friend-poet Cathal Lagan does the honours. I write poems about him:

By Pass

the old city within the walls
grew blocked with wheels,
throngs, animals, beggars,
merchants, mendicants.

above the cobbled streets,
roof tops leant heads together
shoulders jostled against stone walls
thick with muck and mudwash.

harvesting materials from
the outer limbs, they excavated

Once there was a Dorian

> an underground where the tube
> slid and whooshed in rush hour.
>
> city fathers built a ring road
> circling the four quarters,
> with a hospice for travellers
> and stable for horses.
>
> the traffic of your blood
> now lights streets lamps
> along pulse points
> and carries current round
>
> your cathedral of a heart.
> nave, organ and crypt
> illuminate the chambers
> behind your eyes.
>
> medieval man, minster man,
> you invite us in to share
> the wine that fills this vessel
> in the four quarters tavern.

2016. For a while – nine months – Maureen Shear enters my life. She is not well. Her Dr found a tick behind her ear so they did a dance of joy. But it was not tickbite fever. When we meet she is on the cusp of a cancer diagnosis. We live in hope as the cancer moves into bone, liver, brain. She dies in Hospice. Her son Chris and I remain friends. At the funeral parlour we share a belly laugh when asked a standard question, "Do you suspect foul play?" I took to the gym pool and swam seventy-two lengths, one for each year of her life. Three months older than I, she

Route 77

called me her 'toy boy'. I shared a letter and poems for her at the Poetry Festival, McGregor:

Dolphin in the Deep

length after length in water trance
I swim the Olympic pool
that windows onto the sea
framing the horizon sky.

I imagine I carry your light weight
shell of a body on my back,
your chin resting on my neck,
you arms around my trunk.

you who swam swifter than I
gold girl with gill lungs
who jack-knifed at pool end
and churned away, a flying fish.

now the dead cells swim in you
length by length along blood lanes
taking gold silver bronze
breast back crawl and butterfly.

would that I were the dolphin
who carries a soul through tides
to the land beyond this one
nuzzled on its mythic back.

Once there was a Dorian

Masked Ball Sonnet

when at the ball we dance in our glad rags
the stranger bows and asks for your slight hand.
I stand aside and watch his twirling cape.
he calls a tango number from the band
then whirls you in black cloak and giddy arms.
on your white hair he slips a bridal wreath
his toe cap glints beneath his swarmy charms
the blood rose gripped between his teeth.
so we plan, unplan, replan our dance each day
attend to what new tune your body asks
the dying cells foxtrot and waltz their way
in quick step time till midnight strike unmasks.
we hold each other's hands for one last jive
oh would the jailhouse rock swing you alive.

I lived on, daily thankful as the grace has it, for health and strength and daily food. And, yes, companionship along the seventies by way, detours that are not detours, leading to *Route 77*.

PRINGLE MINGLE BAY 2016 – 2022 (72-77)

Sometime, later, in 2016 I arrive in Pringle Bay to overnight with a friend Barbara Kennedy, also a friend of Maureen. She had cello-backed praise poems for birthdays and Maureen's funeral service. Barbara phones. She will be ninety minutes late. No problem, I, with a good book, park outside Pringle Mingle. And there she is, Annemarie, outside her accommodation complex, waiting for a guest. "I've been looking for you. I want to write my boy Tierre's story." Adopted age three when she was forty-nine. We share a bottle of wine and reconnect.

Route 77

Heartner Annemarie Breytenbach

I had met Annemarie at her on-the-rocks home, some ten years before when she hosted a Dorian poetry evening and a collage wordshop. She had moved from the Point to a four minute walk from the village centre. We will spend much time in the 345 Hangklip stoep sharing many bottles of the red. I come to write about this stoep. Here are two verses from,

All the Stoep's a Stage:

hidden in rows of undergrowth,
duiker, porcupine, mongoose
striped field mouse, lizard.
taaibos, disa, fynbos painted lady
blossom into audience
breathless with intent.

Once there was a Dorian

<blockquote>
bird high on the wire
in the cheep-cheep seat balcony,
franklin, ring-eyed dove, robin
all flutter to front row A.
they and the baboons some days
land on the flats to perform.
</blockquote>

The stoep is the hub of the wheel. We will spin out and run the rim, fly beyond the circumference to Temenos, McGregor, Turkey, Australia via Singapore, Windhoek and Swakopmund, 5500km road trip to the Limpopo River and Buddhist Retreat Centre in the Ixopo Hills. We will return to watch the moon on this stoep and with Omar Khayyám and his *Rubaiyat:*

> Here with a Loaf of Bread beneath the Bough
> A Flask of Wine, a Book of Verse - and Thou
> Beside me singing in the Wilderness –
> And Wilderness is Paradise enow.

The thou includes friends, birthdays, candles and fire. And Pringle paradise it is with mountain, sea, lagoon, fynbos. I park the car and often do not climb behind a steering wheel for five days, walking hither and thither to coffee shop, lagoon, beach, friends, local GP, keeping pace on foot with the ancestors, collecting firewood en route.

Ams's was a sea creature, daily diving with her friend Evette. Taught Tierre to dive too, so now he dives in the Mombasa harbour.

Route 77

Underwater Woman

wet-suited woman
with oyster catcher eyes
you read the deep
in wave pace and spume.
then masked, you float
on the surface mirror
half-submerged.

then descend lead belt
through seven layers
of water skin and bone,
sliding like a sand shark
playful as a sea pup.
your feet up flippers
flap like whale tails.

you bubble wide eyed
though levels of wonder light
to greet the changing blues
from silver to indigo.
like a jazz Ella Fitsg
you sing to the water weeds
that sway to the saxophone sea.

you greet a host of creatures
in the strobe lit sparkle –
the wise-eyed octopus,
saltwater chameleon
in kelp drag camouflage
gyrating to the beat,
mussel cluster, star fish,
oyster, alikriek and kreef.

Once there was a Dorian

drift among exotics
blend with bottom feeders
among rocks and wrecks,
so you snorkel and goggle
from the margins of
the mare incognotum.

you rise with gifts
to this above-water world,
a cornucopia of Agulhas
current harvest sizzle
served in earthen ware
you turned and shaped
on your circling kiln.

we sit on your sea-stoep
within soundsight
of the great waters
above the washed bay
of flapping whites
hung between two hangklips.

abundance surrounds us,
shells illuminated in solar light,
whelk, cockle, angel wings, clam,
wood carved gill, scales and fins.
your neck adorned winks
with a beaded periwinkle
soaked in your silvering.

anna marine, aqua woman
Thalassa, primaeval spirit
ever emerging, dripping
from the underwater origins

Route 77

>where we all crawled forth
>above the tide line.
>
>you read the sea in me
>see beneath this mask
>the tide ever in my eyes
>spring, ebb and turn.
>I feast on your extravagant
>wide, wide as the ocean love.

Part of us is Fiela. N2 rescue. A dog among dogs. Waiting out this lifetime in between Buddhist nun incarnations. She was our Just Nuisance, the Simonstown naval dog across the bay. Ams' stories of finding Fiela, nurturing her and other tales entranced me. Here are three verses:

>Love Song to Fiela the Faithful
>
>flea-black covered pup,
>days off a dry-nosed death,
>you dragged your stick body
>between township shack
>and the buzzing N2 highway.
>seconds later a car stopped
>offering synchronous salvation,
>sudden as a gust of wind.
>
>what was it that made
>a teenage boy, adopted,
>in a divine moment, see you
>from the back seat window?
>he edged on all fours

Once there was a Dorian

> through bush and litter
> to retrieve screaming you,
> shrieking at human approach.
>
> with seadog in your veins
> beaching, body boarding
> paddling among the diver boys
> kreef connoisseur, mussel cruncher,
> your seasoned soul evident
> in those tannin eyes, lagoon wide,
> coffee-bean brown, your body
> blending among the reeds.

Ams's mischievous childhood too arrives in verse. Ever the entrepreneur:

> Erasmus OK
>
> an idiom they had to learn
> proclaimed practice makes perfect.
> so first she traced the lines
> and squiggles with her finger,
> gleaned from the dotted line
> in reports, letters, cheques
> and official documents.
>
> then while teachers
> sawed and jawed
> the yawning lowveld air,
> she pencil practiced
> the way he signed his name.

Route 77

> she also tried it upside down
> in the colour ink he used.
>
> her tongue wove round
> the way he shaped the initial E
> of their sevenletter surname
> (happened to be her lucky number)
> then noted how his pen
> slid across the page
> over the r a s m to the final u s.
>
> proud of the name they shared
> with the renaissance scholar,
> by grade seven she'd near enough
> perfected her father's scrawl.
> a graduate in forgery
> she, in two seconds flat, scribbled it
> on slips of permission paper.
>
> these she sold at break time to
> playground truants who slipped
> the school gates bound for the town
> for cigs and chappies, their coins
> and the headmaster's solid signature
> bought at a tickey a time
> clutched in their mitts.

Ams so connected to nature as presence. And yes, in Pringle, the wind – south-easter and north-wester bringing rain.

Once there was a Dorian

Pringle Wind

it's easy to believe, here,
in a Kansas tornado tale
that swirls house Dorothy and Toto
and drops them in an image land.

roofs fly off a runway funnel
like a plane lifting then
crashing in crumpled metal
on the teeth of the sea.

it whip-winds Hangklip breast
then sucks the nipple dry
as milk clouds skid, shudder, sour
in a shadow south-easter sky.

thunders through the crab claws
of the bay, dowsing all in spray
and surge, save for at either point
lighthouses that signal the storm.

in isiXhosa *umoya* is word
for wind air breath and
the whooshing Biblical dove
descending on our unsuspecting heads.

and yet, and yet what if
we allow this fury to shape-shift
the insides of our skulls
in a dervish whir?

then the wicked witch wind
of the south-east can curse and roar

Route 77

> while we still spin on a point
> in an inner-wheel spirit whirl.

Pringle Bay (Photo by Dorian)

And the walk, the walks from Pringle to next village Rooiels along the coastal path. And Christmases here:

> Pringle King
>
> imagine the child born here
> where the wind whirls around
> the Hangklip hung in sun.

Once there was a Dorian

on such a night the stone nipple
ringed in aerola mist
ghosts beneath the Milky Way.

the stable might have been
the lighthouse near 'no room' hotel,
and the donkey, a duiker
somehow bearing the woman.
the cradle strewn with fynbos,
pincushion, lemon finch feathers,
and a Mary blue disa, awaits.

the lighthouse signals
to the southern cross,
beaming its own star
across the water breaking
to phosphores the angel fish
and mussel cluster clinging
to the rocks of faith.

the whale thrashing her bulk
gives birth in the bay,
dolphins croon and cuddle the shore.
a baboon with baby clung to her belly
leaps down the mountain side
to escape the Herod Alfa male.

as dassies, otters and swallows
come to adore, owl keeps watch.
the franklin, myrrh-maid
and golden eagle arrive
riding thermals and surf
with gifts of veneration,
pain and begin again.

Route 77

> the fisherman father,
> his line hooked into
> this heavenly haven,
> reels in. greets the wild sea.
> from a sand dune
> above the kelp line
> where blood beak oyster catchers
> hatch their Yuletide chicks,
> he plucks for his firstborn
> a fullbloom protea King.

Here, since I am the friend of disillusioned priests, I meet splendid Gerald Steward in search of the holy in poetry. His library a monastery beacon in the dark ages. He is part of our Poetry Moments group, some dozen of us who meet monthly. And in Somerset West play dates and sleepovers with Bob and Peter once every four months. Books, sharing wine, conversing.

2019. Then the fire came one new year's midnight. Someone shooting a flare. Gerard, a neighbour, produced a fire book. He chose my offering as the opening:

What in us needs burning?

The sky broke like an egg into full sunset and the water caught fire.
   (Pamela Hansford Johnson)

Early January 2019. Swimming upstream in the Buffels lagoon in Pringle Bay through black ash water, I passed a house the index finger on the flaming hand of fire had singled out. Three days before this the holiday makers and I had waved to each other as I floated past. The other lagoon-side houses stood as witnesses.

On the other bank above the scorched reeds and nests the odour of ash hung in the air – the 300-year-old milkwood forest cremated. Above that, the charred mountain with pythons, dassies, buck and tortoises incinerated. The charcoal mounds smoked where only yesterday fynbos had flourished. A woman died smothered in the smoke. Eight days later the fire spreading far and wide, wind driven from the Helderberg to Grabouw, Bot Rivier closing roads.

One man sending a flare into the New Year's eve sky. We stood on the stoep at 345 Hangklip at midnight as that flare shot into the sky. In an instant a rose cloud billowed into the heavens. Eleven days later the fire galloped on the back of a fiery north-wester steed, kicking its heels, stampeding through some fifty houses and a church whooshing through Betty's Bay. Pringle and Betty's Bay joining a litany of fire loss – Hermamus, Knysna, Wupperthal, Grabou, Signal Hill and…and…

Many stories rise from such ashes. One of a buck. People thought her so tame as she stayed in their garden only to discover that all four hooves were burnt. A friend counselling an extended family where nine people died. A girl rescuing thirty tortoises. People trying to ascribe meaning through beliefs and desires. And what do people thrust into their escape bag? Apart from the obvious – passport, cell, documents, laptop. Some grab sturdy shoes, five litres of water, a hair dryer, diary, a favourite book, trinkets.

I do not know the intention of the 1 Jan midnight man. Celebration? Entertaining children? Even if benign, *King Lear* leaps to mind, "Oft with the best intent we incur the worst." We are a destructive species. And what of deliberate human destruction – as in fire bombing?

Route 77

Fire as image, symbol and analogy has pursued writers through the ages. The soldier, Billy, POW in Kurt Vonnegut's *Slaughterhouse Five*, survives a night in a slaughterhouse in 1945 during the firebombing of Dresden. 130,000 dead. And Hiroshima? Paradoxically, sometimes all we have are words to express the inexpressible.

The local recovery began. Some embittered… some hopeful. Stories of resilience, good neighbourliness and rebuilding emerge. As in the tale where a young Hiroshima girl with atom bomb induced leukaemia folds a 1000 cranes for world peace. This book contains some of these stories of choice and creative response. Healing is born from the parents, Creativity and Imagination.

Some years ago I was part of an early morning silent walk through fynbos months after another fire. Here are a few lines from my poem "For the Love of Gravity." They record the challenging words of the one who led the hike, words that offered me the title of this piece. Words that leave us with a question.

>we traipse though veld.
>He speaks. after fire, the fynbos
>seeds lie like stars
>on black earth.
>he asks what in us
>needs burning?

The great sea of unknowing (*Mare incognotum*) I am drawn ever towards the close-by ocean… walking, swimming in summer. In winter I take to the heated pool in the local gym and swim 1000 metres most days, meditating, concocting stories as l move through the water.

After ten years of no poetry publication, *ZenPenZen* arrives:

Zen – Chinese *chán* 'quietude… body-mind…being present ….simple… dropping illusion

Pen – Latin *penna* 'feather'… for writing or drawing…the tapering internal shell of a squid…a playpen…to compose

Yen – 'calm'…a yearning for…Japanese currency… a swift bird known for creating edible nests in swallow nest soup

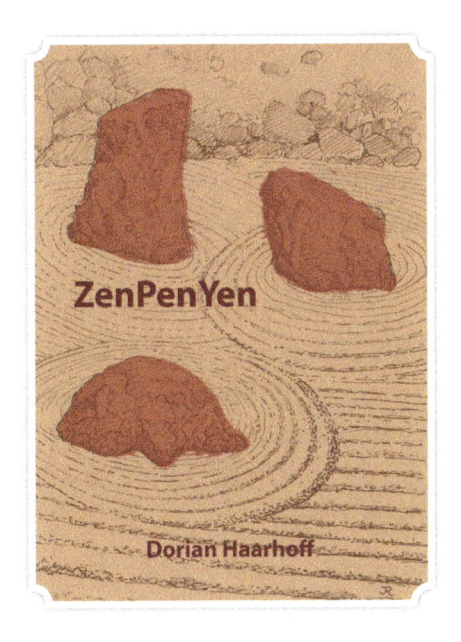

8th poetry collection

Route 77

And when I pass beyond this vale, I'd like my ears to brim with one of the *ZenPenYen* poems:

Two Women Laughing
(for Ams and Martine)

my beloveds outlaugh the hyena and the hadeda.
like Anansi the spider keeper of the skygod's stories
they spin their mirth from their abdomens
and catch me in a tickle web vibrate strong as silk.
they crack up time with teeth and tongue
shell the pistachio and swallow the nut of it.
switching to esophagus so they don't choke
they guffaw up and down the air pipe in gusts
belly to back teeth then ring the changes in gales.
break up storm weather scudding across skies to blue them.
their ten second bursts aerate blood and cell dawn to dusk.
they cackle in delight at foibles failures
and unfortunates that take
themselves serious serious. exercise forty plus face muscles
they twin cities across oceans, shoulders shuddering
they echo all joy. heartner and daughter
explode stress time into holy moment
in the fizz of Hafiz the Sufi who hears God laughing.

Here's the zoom version of the launch, courtesy of Igno van Niekerk
https://adilo.bigcommand.com/watch/h1EulWxu

Then the green-eyed Maizy with pointer paw, husky eyes, chocolate lab body joins us. Now we are three again.

Here endeth the chronology of the first cycle of seven.

2

Edge Moments

So that's the chronology – less than a 30% weight of this book. Here are eleven of many alive moments, thumb print incidents, rising from the years. When epiphany expands within tick-tock time, 'eternity in an hour' (Blake.) A random selection… perhaps the heart of this Route 77?

ACROSS A CROWDED ROOM

2012. He's dressed in a charcoal-striped suit, black shirt, red tie, a leaner man than his father, fine-boned. We drive – he, his mother, Annie, and I onto a farm track, home of his singing teacher, Elisabeth. It's the old 'around the piano' tonight, some twenty of her students to sing their chosen song. Rows of chairs face an upright walnut piano and a digitised one, for notes that need to be transposed a tone up, a tone down to match the singer's pitch.

No electricity… the power line soldiers, passing current along the wire hand to hand, have gone awol. Dominic, three days off 26, is No 14… but the programme might shuffle for his song needs digital accompaniment.

The singers respond to the teacher's call for the warmup of voices. They hum and chant, ha ha ha ha. The trickster in me waits for the hof hof hof. Dominic shifts from foot to foot. Not a good sign, whispers

Route 77

his mother. She has brought his medication and water – in case. Dosed him a little during the day so he can be tranquil. Not pace up and down … scrub his hands twenty times. When he returns to his seat, she asks, "Dom, are you OK?" He nods yes. Is he?

The concert begins. Some students are A plus Eisteddfod, others beginners. Dom's been with Elisabeth only a couple of months. A young ten-year-old lifts her voice over the lectern. An MBA man sings Schubert. A woman with lithe lips offers a folk song. An older woman in the Lisa Minnelli hat, red lipstick sings Handel's *Where 'ere you walk*. A Sesutu man from Lesotho sings a German lied.

I who have driven 400km today to hear this young man sing, wonder can he hold himself and the note? As I travelled, I sang aloud to myself the verse I soloed out in the church choir at age eleven. Will Elisabeth need to rescue Dom? This boy born at seven months, six weeks in an incubator, his first auditorium filled with his voice.

The lights arrive. Then it's his turn, this handsome Gandalf wizard of a man. Cool is this Asperger's man with possible schizophrenia. The psychiatrist says, "It's like a seizure. His brain can go walkabout at any moment." I look across at him. No flicker of panic. "Who can explain it? Who can tell you why? Fools give you reasons, Wise men never try.…"

As he walks up to the piano, I think of his great-uncle Allan, marching through the desert singing "I'll tell Tilly on the telephone." The old blind woman, Mrs Stoops, in the nursing home where my mother was matron, knew Allan and my father in Kimberley in the early 1900s. She told me of their fine voices ringing out at evenings round the piano, such as this one tonight. Allan was the baritone of baritones. My father sang to me as a child. Gilbert and Sullivan's "Willow, Tit-Willow" from the Mikado.

So the man with these genes in his chords stands before us. Elisabeth plays the opening notes and out of the mouth of Dominic comes this pure voice, this larger-than-life baritone, unfaltering, a Rogers and Hammerstein South Pacific lyric – *Some Enchanted Evening*.

Then suddenly, mid-stream, mid-song, the piano stops. Dominic holds the note, holds the note, a smile on his face. Playful. "There's a page missing," mutters the pianist. Our Dom is not thrown. He walks from lectern to piano. They rewind and his voice takes up the song again. Then the teacher takes his arm, "We have to have that song over again." She finds the errant page. And so the evening is once more enchanted as this son balances on a songline.

I reach out for his mother's hand. Half this boy's lifetime ago I left the marriage home, and now it's a year to the day since this man was found pursued by ghosts. Ah yes, the show is not over while this man sings. Nor after. The audience and ancestors applaud. Your songline, beloved son, carried through you, reaches from death to birth to beyond on this, ah yes, enchanted evening, the first anniversary your life calling you across a crowded room.

EATING WITH THE TROLL

I have met Morten, a helping angel, thrice. One Christmas a speaker defaults so they ask me to stand in at the last minute. A garden function up Hell's Hoogte next to a dam. There I meet Linda of the olive oil Costa family who knows Morten of Norway. He's in South Africa to promote his nine body type work. We meet in Gordon's Bay and he invites me to tell stories at one of his seminars at a cross country ski lodge north of Oslo. Morten was the trainer of the Olympic Norwegian cross country skiing team. At the seminar I drop in stories where relevant, for example, while the clients receive a body massage. *Morten has the power of presence.* He merely prods you with a finger and you collapse on to the rubber mat that covers the seminar floor.

Route 77

A couple of years later from Morten the invitation to hike the pilgrim path up the spine of Norway. July 2014 just before I turn seventy. I fly via Istanbul. Three days there. Then on to Oslo. My role? To tell a story to walk with and talk about every morning. One morning it's

The Rabbi and the Clown:

An exhausted rabbi, travelling late at night, arrives at an inn. The innkeeper apologises, "I'm sorry there is no room." "I am desperately tired and must leave early in the morning. Do you not have somewhere where I can lay my weary head?" "Well," says the innkeeper, "There is a clown sleeping in a double bed. You can share the bed with him."

Early in the morning the innkeeper wakes the rabbi. He dresses in the dark, pays his way, thanks the innkeeper, and steps out into the street. As dawn comes, he notices people giving him peculiar looks. Then he catches his reflection in a shop window. He is dressed as a clown. The rabbi exclaims, "That stupid innkeeper. He has woken the wrong man."

On that morning we set out. Looking up at the mountain I sigh, "We have twenty-two kms to walk today and most this is uphill." Morten responds, "Ah… the Professor is with us." Minutes later I enthuse, "Look how the light breaks through the clouds." Morten responds, "Ah… the poet has arrived."

Edge Moments

The youngest and oldest pilgrim with a troll

On another stretch, this:

>Eating with the Troll
>
>along a pilgrim path
>past forest, lake, farm
>and Middle Age burial mound,
>a fellow pilgrim regaled a fairy tale.
>neither she nor I had walked
>this Norway stretch before.
>
>the king offers the old carrot –
>the one who kills the Troll wins
>half a kingdom plus princess.
>the two oldest brothers, Per and Pal,
>set forth with bread in their packs.
>when en route the hag asks for sustenance
>they say they carry shit so shit it becomes.

Route 77

>Espen Asheladd, the unassuming,
>no Viking he, shares
>his crust with the witch
>who guides him to the Trolls' hovel.
>the tip about the ogre's Achilles heel
>rings in both blond Espen's ears.
>he and Troll, taking up spoons,
>sit down at table, head and foot
>to a gruel duel and shovel away.
>slinging his backpack to the fore
>like a cow's second stomach,
>Epsen spoons the porridge into it.
>
>the challenge hangs on a knife edge.
>one-eyed troll, stuffed, looks on amazed
>as Espen clutches a dagger and slices open
>his stomach bag then carries on stuffing face.
>he slides the blade down table to Troll
>who hari-kari slits his own gut.
>
>all day the story walked with us
>like the Emmaus mystery third.
>so we came ankle weary to a lodge.
>as we entered for our evening meal,
>painted red on the dining door,
>seated at a rough-hewn table
>with steaming bowls before them,
>sat blue eyed Espen and bearded Troll.

On another night we arrive at an inn. I look around the room where we gather. An ancient room with a mighty fireplace in one corner and a grandfather's chair in the opposite corner. Storytime.

Suddenly the story asking to be told arrives. A woman on her violin accompanies me after our fellow hiker opera singer has sung "Nella Fantasia" composed by Ennio Morricone from the movie *The Mission*.

The House of the Fathers

A traveller is lost in the forest. Night is falling and with it snow. He thinks, "If I stay in the forest tonight I will perish." He sees a light in the distance so makes his way through the trees to a cottage. There he finds a thirty-year-old man outside chopping wood. The traveller asks, "Night is falling and with it snow. If I stay in the forest tonight I will perish. May I spend the night in your cottage?"

The man responds, "It is all right with me but you must ask my father." The traveller enters the cottage and finds a sixty-year-old man sitting at the table looking exactly like the thirty-year-old outside. Except that he is smaller and greyer. The traveller asks his question and the sixty-year-old responds, "All right with me but you must ask my father."

Next to the fireplace sits a ninety-year-old man, even tinier, more grey. The traveller asks his question and the ninety-year-old gives him the same answer, referring him to a one-hundred-and-twenty-year-old man sitting in the corner. Who refers him to a one-hundred-and-fifty-year-old man, who in turn refers him to a one-hundred-and-eighty-year-old man, each one getting tinier and greyer. Finally, the traveller is referred to a figure who is so tiny that he is resting in a hunting horn above the fireplace. The traveller asks, "Night is falling and with it snow. If I stay in the forest tonight I will perish. May I spend the night in your cottage?" And the tiny tiny man says, "Yes."

There is something in the eyes of my fellow pilgrims and the locals – recognition. "That is one of our Norwegian stories." I did not know that. Synchronicity grins again.

For part of the way a pilgrim priest accompanies us from Nidaros Cathedral in Trondheim. He shares with us a set of beads that the Lutherans adapted from the Greek fishermen's worry beads. I construct a set of story beads based partly on his set – a 24 bead clock. Gold for Alpha and Omega at 12, black for dark night of the soul at 6, green for the creative 3 and blue for imagination at 9. Eight tiny turquoise ones around 12, 3, 6 and 9. For 8 different kinds of silence. Holy, angry, writer, reader silences. I sometimes wear and use this in wordshops as we create our sets and hang our stories on a string of story beads. And with each stringing I recall the Pilgrim path.

IMAGES, TRIANGLES, YOU AND ME

The tale is often wiser than the teller

In this edge moment a few stories run into one. Become one. During 2021 and 2022, I was storytelling in Namibia engaging with therapists, teachers and cousellors who work with children at risk – courtesy of the Carl Schlettwein Foundation. The theme: How creativity and imagination offer a path to healing.

In one of the exercises I offered one of my ballads, *Night Flight*, unpublished, illustrated by Erna Buber. The guiding question – how could you use this with children? Here is the poem and one of the images.

Edge Moments

Night Flight

Last night as I lay dreaming
a Zebra came to visit me.
I jumped upon his stripy back.
We soared towards our tree.

The tree grew near the window
of our house in Donkeydraai
It rose so high above the ground
its fruit reached to the sky.

"What is your name?" I asked her.
"And why did you come for me?"
"My name is Zeb," she answered,
"and just you wait and see."

Just as we passed the branches
Zeb picked an orange with her teeth.
"If we are travelling all this night,
we'll need a bite to eat."

"Now you must keep this orange."
She rolled it on her back.
I caught the juicy orange moon
and put it in my sack.

I held on to the Zebra's mane.
As we rose, I stroked her pelt.
I could not see our donkey
who grazed the nearby veld.

We rose above the village
where people sighed and snored.

Route 77

Up away in the cool night air
Zeb flapped his wings and soared.

"I think dear Zeb you chose me
because my shirt is striped?
My granny made it for me
in rows of black and white."

"You are so kind to the donkey
that lives in the village below.
By the time that morning comes
there is a lot that you will know."

The moon was full and golden
as we rose up through the night.
"If we get any nearer, Zeb
we'll soar beyond its light."

As Zeb and I jumped the moon
she wore a smiling face
"Molo, dear sister" we greeted her
"Tonight you shine in space."

Then we flew back above the veld
near river, jackal and hare.
"These are your family too" Zeb said.
They all looked up to stare.

So we flew on in silence
as I peeled the orange moon.
We made up a song to thank the tree
And then we made up the tune.

Edge Moments

Just as the sun was rising
we landed at Donkeydraai
I still could not see our donkey
we dropped down to land nearby.

"The spirit of life is in everything,
in the tree, the moon, the hare."
And as Zeb spoke she vanished
and the donkey stood right there.

And as I climbed back into bed
in the village of Donkeydraai.
I opened my arms to my family
in the river, earth and sky.

Night Flight with Erner Buber illustation

Here are some participant observations that I had not been conscious of. This is the mystery of the writing process. The story begins with an isolated child and ends with him being connected to a wider family. It connects the child beyond other human beings to a river, the full moon and creatures. This breaks down the sense of loneliness as the child belongs to a wider reality.

The child identifies with the zebra as they are dressed alike. It is a ballad (in this story zebra and boy make up a song and a tune) and so it is easy to choose a tune they know and sing it. Singing raises our spirits. Participants also discovered that the zebra is intentionally both a he, and a she. People also spoke about the mysterious identity of the zebra who might be the donkey that the boy befriends. So the story also speaks to the possibility of transformation.

While in the story the moon, orange and tree are all objects, they are also symbols that speak to us beyond rational understanding. We spent time exploring how images connect us to a larger conversation. When a child looks down-hearted and overwhelmed, a therapist could talk about a tree in a time of drought when leaves and roots have withered. This connects the child to nature cycles. It can help move the concept of my suffering to the suffering. The child is part of a wider cycle.

I introduced them to Chuang Chou and Coleridge. In a dream the boy enters the world of Chuang Chou. "Once upon a time, I, Chuang Chou, dreamt I was a butterfly, fluttering hither and thither, I was conscious only of my happiness as a butterfly, unaware that I was Chou. Soon I awaked, and there I was, veritably myself again."

And Coleridge?

> What if you slept
> And what if
> In your sleep

> You dreamed
> And what if
> In your dream
> You went to heaven
> And there plucked
> a strange and beautiful flower
> And what if
> When you awoke
> You had that flower in your hand
> Ah, what then?

Can a therapist and child both be a flying zebra for each other?

I also engaged with therapists around another one of my stories "Hannah's Kist" – an adult fairy tale:

Hannah's Kist

When she arrived she came with a cedar wood kist. The trunk was as long as a broom handle and as wide as your finger tips could stretch. The couple found it on the beach with her perched on it. Brought by the tide. Her name was carved on the kist in a bold scrpt. Hannah. And a gold key hung from the handle tied with a length of silver thread.

Her parents dragged it to their house near the sea. They struggled it downstairs to the basement. Her father knotted the thread and hung the key around her neck. And the kist lay there collecting dust. Before Hannah could speak she would gaze intently at the basement steps and try to crawl there but they blocked it off with a low wooden door.

Route 77

In her early years she asked for her kist. "When you're older," said her mother. Then one day when she asked again her father responded, "What kist? There isn't a kist Hannah. No Father Christmas and no kist." So Hannah forgot all about her kist. She lived for a while near the sea and played like a mermaid. One day she moved inland. The key still hung round her neck and she never took it off. If anybody asked her about it she said, "My parents gave it to me when I was born."

Soon Hannah found herself in the tug and tide of living. She loved, lost, moved on. One year both her parent died. There were illnesses enough to count on two sets of fingers. More losses, some laughter and a measure of joy. Then she met a man who said he loved her. One day he asked, "Give me the key." Hannah shook her head. "Then at least take it off when we lie together in the bed. "No," said Hannah. The man left her that very day.

That night Hannah had a dream. She dreamt of the sea and something tossing in it. The next night she dreamt of a box-like thing on the shore. Then the third night she dreamt of the basement. Then Hannah remembered. She took the first train to the sea town and wandered among the ruins of her childhood home. She came across the entrance to the basement under a pile of rubble. Hannah cleared it away with her hands and climbed down the steps lighting her way with a candle. In a corner under cobwebs and coated in dust lay the kist.

Hannah took it home and put it in her favourite room – the one with the fireplace. She cleaned it till the cedar wood glowed and the handles shone. Then Hannah sat on the kist, knees drawn up and wondered. Should she open it. What if all horrors leapt forth from its intestines. What if? What if?

Edge Moments

She took the key from around her neck and put it in the lock. But she did not turn it. A day passed. She turned the key. Her heart knocked in its cage as she heard the lock spring open. But she did not lift the lid. Another day passed. And then, taking a breath from her abdomen to her head and back again she lifted the lid. A little rusty in the hinges, a little arthritic. The smell of cedar rose to meet her.

Hannah gazed in wonder. Her kist was brimful of parcels. Somebody had wrapped each one in linen cloth and tied a label to it. Each was marked in an ancient script. A litany of labels from A to Z and back to A. She read the names – Dreams, Art, Music, Memory. Attention. Bliss. Imagination. Creativity. Loving kindess.

In the suceeding hours, days, and years she unwrapped the parcels and placed the linen wrap back in the kist. And she savoured each gift. Hannah lived to a ripe age. Queen of Joy. Mistress of Bliss. Keeper of the deep places. On the day she died she unwound the last parcel. Hearts-ease.

Her friends wrapped her body in the linen cloths and placed her in the kist. It fitted as if measured for her by a caring carpenter. They carried her back to the sea side town as was her wish. Her friends placed the kist at the edge of the low tide line. The waves curled round it. And in the morning Hannah's kist was gone.

Route 77

Hannah Swart illustration

I spent time looking at how when we set up, what I call triangles, the therapy experience is enriched. The trio of therapist, child plus story is one example where the therapist and child communicate through the story which creates the third part of a triangle. Looking through pictures together also creates the same triangle effect as therapist and child communicate via the picture. This offers a child safety for through the image he/she reveals information difficult to disclose.

A childhood memory drawing based on a piece of material also creates a triangle. They are present in the room while being present in the memory and interacting with me at the same time. People also created characters from found objects bound together with elastic. In groups of three they created stories. Here is an example:

> Once there was a shiny red car that was abused by a driver. The car became rebellious. If you put it in first gear it reversed. If you turned to the left, the car went to the right. If you put your foot on

> the brake, the car accelerated. One day the red car knocked down a girl. The red car began to cooperate and rushed the girl to the hospital in time to save her life. After that the people honoured the red car.
>
> When the town got a new fire engine and ambulance, the shiny red car led a procession through the streets and everyone applauded.

In a powerful moment, psychologist, Lorraine, offered this red car story to another participant, Hubert, who had been in prison for eleven years. He had been a gang leader who did a 180 degree turnaround. He started CODAC (Coastal Drug Awareness Campaign) while still in prison and now works in community and in schools as a motivational speaker.

In *Crow and Weasel* (Barry Lopez) two creatures travel farther north than anyone had ever gone, farther north than their people's stories went. Their return voyage brings encounters with Badger, who teaches the youths to tell a story well, "The stories people tell have a way of taking care of them. If stories come to you, care for them. And learn to give them away where they are needed. Sometimes a person needs a story more than food to stay alive. That is why we put these stories in each other's memories. This is how people care for themselves."

One of my favourite Biblical stories – *The Emmaus Road* journey when a mysterious figure joins the two disciples, creating a third illuminating presence. This too is the mystery of the story triangle.

Stories travel to a place in the psyche where most needed. Story can be used as a medicine that once taken can remain and act within the psyche...long after the last word has been spoken.
- (Clarissa Pinkola Estes)

Route 77

LEO

For my daughter Martine.

    So you chose a name for the child. Leo. Your husband and your father are Leos and it connects you to Africa, where you were born. A fertility route baby, for Duncan, who with two teenagers, has long been tube-tied. For Martine, at thirty-five, this to be your first child. Due April 2015. To be born on Australian soil.

    I recall you at twenty-five sitting at a Cape harbour on False Bay, sipping coffee, unfolding your choices. I wrote this poem for you then. The MacNeice quote accompanied your birth notice in the newspaper in December 1979:

Sea Worthy

You're alive beyond all question
like the dazzle on the sea my darling
Louis MacNeice

we meet at a seawall café,
you in your mid-twenties
soon to marry.
yachts bob at their moorings.

you drop the words
into my coffee cup
and into the breeze:
I don't want children.
you unfurl the sail
of how you arrived
at such an island.

Edge Moments

our conversation compass
turns in its glass.
we plot direction –
a line of mothering
breaking in rough seas.
how, in your harbour days,
I cut the rope to drift
from your mother's craft.

how you tacked
into au pair harbours,
learning how to sail.
saw men sailing solo work-seas
while wives, bundle in arms,
waited on the shore.

we swing the compass.
the ear of my cup points north.
the coffee tide falls.
we talk of grown children
who sail beyond blue.

I turn the rudder of our talking
to how it was to wait for you.
how my champagne joy
slapped the bows,
how I feared gales might capsize
your boat, rip my sails.
how adult love can be murky,
but in loving you I saw the ocean floor.

I recall the MacNeice
Births column quote
and an Irish mystic's

Route 77

> safe passage prayer.
> my boat so small, the sea immense.
> we leave the jetty
> and the coffee dregs.
> you have acquired sailor's legs.
> eyes shine in sea light.

So you stepped out of an ancestral line of compromised mothering to become an au pair, still connecting to children who left your care years ago. Here's an email from one, four then, now thirteen: "To who it may concern: There is a lonely girl called Caitlin (also known as Lulu-belle) who is asking for a Skype conference to discuss important things like weather soon." I remember another time, drinking seaside coffee with you with your charge in her stroller. Now years on in Australia, anticipating the wonder of this child. What a mother you will make.

When you became pregnant you heard of volunteers who transform wedding gowns into baby shrouds (NICU Helping Hands Angel Gown Programme – Australia). And who, like the elves' shoemaker, make clothes for babies born lost. Though these women service all of Australia, they happen to be down the road so you dropped off your wedding dress.

The tricky months pass. Sighs of relief. At work a boss-man (one of those) declares you redundant. It's the pregnancy, though he won't say so. Gone the maternity leave. Unfair dismissal.

At four months, time to visit the specialist. Boy or girl? You and your dear man go with open hearts to the sonar. Going well, going well. Then the surgeon speaks, gravely. "The baby has Spina bifida. Literally a 'split spine'. A fault in the spinal cord and surrounding vertebrae with paralysis of limbs and probable brain damage."

Shock. The two of you make a choice no one else can make. The grieving begins. An injection to stop Leo's heart. A weekend of waiting with the dead child inside, then on Monday 1 December 2014 you go into hospital to deliver Leo, the foetus/baby. While you pack, Duncan packs as well. "Where are you going?" you ask. "To hospital," he replies. He takes up residence in the hospital room, unfolding his camp bed. You have been married just under a year.

In the waiting room you walk past the buzzing edge of expectant grandparents and mothers about to deliver. Christmas and the birth of the Christ child hovers like a star in the air. A box arrives 'for Martine and Duncan' in the name of another child lost before full term (Toby Gordon) from an organisation, Precious Wings. It contains a baby shroud made from a wedding dress, a teddy, clothes to fit him and a butterfly. The box also contains a photo frame, a candle, a journal with butterflies on it and 'forget me not' seeds of hope.

Time passes twice round the clock. Contractions. You, the parents, are led to the birthing suite. Duncan is at the birth, stroking your hair, holding the 'barp' bucket… Calm, you give birth to Leo on 2 December. A strong heart, four beating chambers, all toes and fingers intact. An umbilical large as Leo's legs. Son of a soccer ref, Leo already has a club foot. There would have been no womb kick. 2 Dec. Leo's born at 21 weeks (26 cm, 410 grams.)

Hospital staff talk to Leo as they dress him. There's a cap to cover his head. "Now you will be warm. Now you'll be ready for your mom." Trish and Claire, Mater Mother's Private Hospital midwives (angels?) who hold intimate knowing of bereavement births, paint Leo's feet powder blue. They tread his footprints onto a card, stenciling in his name. They shed tears. They take photos. They can't remove all the paint so they smile. "He's his father's child. He can go to heaven with grubby feet."

There's a butterfly on the hospital room door. The symbol indicates 'There is grieving in this place.' Some butterflies only live for a day.

Route 77

Martine, you and Duncan spend sweet-sad time with Leo, diving down into sorrow. You do not try to dodge suffering. You enter the gates of loss and write:

> I woke up just after midnight last night... Feeling such deep, profound sorrow and I don't know how to be here. I can't breathe and can't seem to imagine that the pain could ever subside.
>
> I've looked at photos of Leo and he looks different to what I remember from yesterday.... Yesterday when I held him, he looked perfect and so peaceful, but in the photos somehow he looks so frail and not nearly as perfect. My neck barely feels strong enough to support the weight of my head, nor my chest cavity strong enough to hold the weight of my heart... I wish I could just sleep for as long as it took to heal and wake up with my heart intact again and my soul restored.
>
> I am so grateful to you for being my Dad and for your support throughout my life, especially now, and I graciously accept your invitation to bring my heartache to you, knowing that I am loved and cherished. I am grateful for Duncan who has not left my side … and for everything I had to experience in my life to get to him. Grateful too that somehow I am worthy of his love and devotion. (4/12/14)

While this is in motion many time zones away, I light a candle, as do my friends. I'm reading an autobiographical novel *The Family Orchard* by Nomi Eve. A couple give birth to a child with retracted limbs. They hear of another child in the same condition who collects butterflies. They discover their own child is brained damaged. No butterflies.

Edge Moments

Martine, you hold up baby Leo to the Skype screen so I, his grandfather can see him. We cry and bless him in the presence of a woman who conducts a ritual:

> Leo, your name is written forever on the hearts of your family and held in the heart of God....
> Martine and Duncan, may the creator of all life surround you and your family today with love and peace. May you treasure the moments you have shared with Leo. May your lives be transformed into a wellspring of promise.

> Love must birth love
> And we can be its face....
> A butterfly lights beside us like a sunbeam
> And for a brief moment its glory and beauty belong to our world
> But then it flies again

We are in the presence of this mystery and the ever-echoing not answered 'why?' This grandfather remembers your mother, before your conception, miscarrying at six months. She lay alone in a cold room in a metal basin. She too was named Martine (poem offered elsewhere).

Back home you hang a butterfly next to the star on the Christmas tree. This only days before your thirty-fifth birthday and your first wedding anniversary. You create a box in the name of Leo to be passed on to another mother and child. You have joined the random family of loss. Your face has taken on another beauty – a knowing one. At the cremation you choose to hold Leo again. You tell me, "When I first held him it was as if he should be alive, but wasn't. Now when I hold him, he has gone." Like the Egyptians, you place in his coffin a teddy and gifts that his siblings, Duncan's children, have given him. You close the lid and place your hands on it. Other gifts you pack around the coffin. "I don't want him to be squashed," says this mother. Like a Viking Leo sets sail on a burning sea.

Days before the sonar visit, you had applied for another job, and had your interview the morning of 'injection day'. The woman was impressed. Then you told her about the pregnancy gone awry. She offered you the job. Later, she told you that she too, twenty-five years ago, swam through a similar sea.

Such is your strength and courage Martine, and the loving presence of the man you have chosen, second time around. Leo, we will remember you, alive in our pulses. And, yes, Martine, you have acquired sea legs. Like the dazzle on the sea. Your eyes shine in sea light.

HO SPICE

Where do I and Ho Spice (Hospice) begin? Is it in what the Ozzies call Opportunity (Op) charity shops? Me the ferreter, once finding Chinese stress balls in the hands of the Ho Spice seller behind the counter. Yin-Yang pattern. She asks, "What are these?" "Don't know but come to daddy." And those book treasures. Aladdin's cave.

Or does it begin with friend Peter Fox? Joy introduces me to this man and we meet in his office – he, who around 1998, the spiritual director of St Luke's Ho Spice Kenilworth. Then arriving in Somerset West and through Sue, facilitating a Helderberg Hospice counsellor story training. 2004. The gift of the dying. Throw a story bouquet over your shoulder like a young bride for the living to catch it. Before they too marry Dr Death. Hospice carols at Vergelegen picnics on grass beneath the giant three-hundred-year-old camphor trees.

Enter Oom Schalk for Ho Spice fundraising. With the Stellenbosch concertina player, Henk Cerfontein. Stories in between boerekos courses.

That was a marathon remembering. You delighted the audience with all his foibles, which so accurately mirror our own. You had us all captivated from the first yank of the trousers and snort of the nose, even before you put your hat on. Not only did you provide the inspiration and impetus for the evening, and not only were you the chief drawcard, you also set to with the waitering as well. And so aware of the needs of the audience… the little lady at the back who might have struggled to hear didn't escape your attention. And a mouth organ maestro as well – a man of many parts. (2015 Patricia McNaught Davis former Events, Media and Marketing, Hospice Somerset West)

Then at the Strand Pavillion, Maureen and I dancing, some few months before her death. At a farm off Winery Road. Then at Sage and Thyme. And Mau, entering the space with her. First the Hospice home carer visits, calling after she collapses in the bathroom, then she is admitted. I'm the AGM speaker in the hall not far from her bed. If I raised my voice she might hear me. I share the *Dolphin in the Deep* poem with the audience. For another fundraiser in memory of Mau, an afternoon concert – Barbara on cello. Chris, Mau's son, on French horn, Bruce Copley on his array (he drapes cloths to adorn the podium) and Dori on poetry.

And then lucky draw – I who have invested possibly some R25000 (R100 a month over the years) win the R10 000 jackpot and low, the new Lenovo lap top arrives… a daily Ho Spice reminder.

In 2019 Aneta Glenister, chorister, invites me to MC the Voices for Hospice in Somerset West. My ballad interweaves with a programme of songs and music:

Route 77

The Songs of the Hospice Helderbirds

as daylight fills this Bright Street church
musicants tune their keys and strings.
Hospice singers spice up their songs
for the music festival now begins.

the birds from trees descend to rest
on the staff of wire lines and space.
between two poles that form the score
they become the notes of sound and grace.

throbbing bodies pipe organ notes.
their wings and feet sign crotchet and quaver
tail feathers shape clefs – treble and bass.
their melodies ecstatic set us aquiver.

feather light from the Hospice garden
sugar birds frit frit through scented air
the reed finch lauds its lemon splendor
a turtle dove coor-cooor-coors the hours of prayer.

here's a three beat Piet-My-Vrou –
some call this shy one Be-Here-Now.
it pitches his tone so wind chime pure
through throat and beak its praise resounds.

this trilling measures the beat of hearts
as it plays with octaves this spring day.
thrilling the twilight with evensong
these Hallelujahs take our breath away.

Edge Moments

Items include a traditional 17th Century Irish lament, a Bach snare drum viola da Gamba combo, and nine-year-old Elena Monvois on, oboe, violin and piano. Bevan Sylvester, minister and musician, a new friend, ends with an organ and bag pipes finale. "Highland Cathedral" resounding as two bag pipers, man and wife, march down the aisle.

In the audience, Hospice volunteer Audrey, turning eighty, asks me to write her a praise poem. And Bevan and I meet to jazz about collaboration. Who knows where this will go.

Hooray Ho Spice and Gail the CEO who lost her husband and moved from volunteer to boss. Ho Spice, handmaiden to Dr Death. And of late, meeting up and working alongside the Cape-based Soul Carers Network (end of life doulas). How to help the dying leave their stories as gifts, as a legacy. Here's part of a flyer:

> The Library Inside: Leaving a Legacy, Leaving a Gift:
> A Storyshop Retreat
>
> The communication of the dead is tongued with fire
> beyond the language of the living (TS Eliot)

Stories are gifts we leave behind. A wise elder once shared, "The graveyard's an interesting place. Full of untold stories. Make sure that by the time you die, you have shared yours." Every death is a double death for when we die, the library inside our head and the stories in our heart die too. Unless we have shared them. When we share the stories of those who have died, they come alive in the telling. This storyshop is about rediscovering and sharing our stories about our loves, lyrics and losses.

Route 77

THE SAME RAINBOW'S END

In Bosman's *Ox Wagons on Trek*, life imitates art. So our reading can offer us responses that generate art from life and death. In Naomi Shihab Nye's poem *Kindness* (1952) these lines:

> Before you learn the tender gravity of kindness
> you must travel where the Indian in a white poncho
> lies dead by the side of the road.
> You must see how this could be you,
> how he too was someone
> who journeyed through the night with plans
> and the simple breath that kept him alive.

Here's my parallel journey from the early 2000s:

The Same Rainbow's End

once on an overnight no-moon train,
coastal Cape to City of Gold,
we slid early morning
into a small town siding.
as I dropped the shutter, an ambulance
on the platform reversed past the window.
I jumped the steps and followed
to where it halted a dozen coaches down.

I sole watcher, witnessed two men
load a body bag into the back.
a woman in gloves, a detective glint
in her eye, emerged from a compartment.

she brisk clipped diabetic attack...
mid-fifties... got on midnight at Kimberley.

as a paramedic raised the tail gate
I stepped forth. I'd read days before
of a mortician who sang to cold slab corpses
hymns and serenade songs – abide with me,
you are my sunshine, moon river.
I spoke. I'm a priest... will say a word.
well, a poet is a sort of one.
ask Lawrence DH
whom folk dubbed 'priest of love.'

to quizzical heads I sang to one
who embarked from my birth town
and around same age, died in transit,
bound on the same rail to
who knows where, a journey song.
two drifters, off to see the world...
we're after the same rainbow's end,
nodded to bemused medics
I walked back to the compartment
still whistling beneath my breath.

GALWAY BAY AND BILLY COLLINS

If I were to select the big five in my poetry game park, Billy Collins would be one of them. He says the opening of a poem should not need breaking and entry, hacking through the forest to get to the princess, but a welcome mat for your reader. One of my favourites, a quirky poet and Laureate of USA – as in Forgetfulness:

Route 77

> The name of the author is the first to go
> Followed obediently by the title, the plot,
> The heartbreaking conclusion, the entire novel
> Which suddenly becomes one you have never read…

I hear of a Billy Collins poetry seminar in Galway Bay. I send sample poems. And am accepted. The University gives me R5000 towards the workshop. British Council rep Jasper Utterly, who funded me a Cambridge British Council writers' seminar in the mid 90s, regrettably can't add pounds alongside this as it's not Northern Ireland. I fly to London then train to the west coast of merrie England. Dublin ferry, train across Ireland. University of Galway residence. To join the fourteen all-American poets who have come with Billy, many like he, Irish shamrock Americans.

Light of heart he attends to our offering as we take turns. Plying our craft. He, like so many, can't pronounce 'Nambibia.' Outside the seminar visits to the west of Ireland – grand poetic tradition… Yeats' tower. The Arran Isles by boat. The waterfront pubs. Three of us, two lasses and I, bus trip then walk through the countryside.

Ah the humour of the Irish. Once I'm walking in the countryside when our bus stops to pick me up. "Africa?" I ask as I board. Bus driver, without missing a beat, "The next bus." Then as we leave, I, bound for Dublin by train, the rest of the poets off to Shannon airport, I hurl a misquoted Yeats line into their bus, a parody of the opening line from Yeats' *Lake Isle of Innisfree*, a poem my mother so loved that I had it calligraphied and framed. Not "I will arise and go now to Innisfree" but "I will arise and go now to Duty Free." Billy C sends me a parody of the poem, taking off from that one line. I alas, no longer have that parody.

I found in Ireland everywhere, something of Annie's ancestry (or as I imagine it - poetic licence?):

Edge Moments

Tracing your Face

I kissed you 'stay well' in Africa.
but travelling on this island
of stone and clover,
found you here, before me.

your freckles bridge the cheeks of the girl
who runs along the riverbank.
here the same ungovernable shrub
thatches the adolescent's head
and turns fox in late light.

tribal knuckles and thumbs
that knead the earth for small yield,
work the craft of the unsung.
fingers that trace fine the pagan text,
the calligraphy of kells and saints,
entangle you in a kin of fingers.

you span this ancient
mothering and Mary brow
and stride in the stubborn nun.
you're the aged Gaelic face
croning holy at the woman's well.

fed by a grandmother's blood
you flow in the myths of place.
here the quarter Celt in you
increases to a feast of folk.

Route 77

WALKING ON WATER – NORTH AMERICA

Some several trips in the 1990s – 2000s. No, not New York. No great pull. To San Francisco, Seattle. Taking the Amtrak with observation car from California through to Washington State. Meeting on the same ride, a Mormon whom I had converted to mythology ala Joseph Campbell before our destination. Then the Stanford Fullbright.

2000 – 2003. Ah yes. Boulder, Colorado. Jim Palmer thrice invited me as storyteller at annual April Conference on World Affairs. For a glorious week, we are hosted by locals. Boulder houses Naropa, the Buddhist University, a city of bookshops, health stores and high altitude minds.

I hear conscious luminaries such as Jean Houston who says, "At the height of laughter, the universe is flung into a kaleidoscope of new possibilities" and, "We all have the extraordinary coded within us, waiting to be released." I enjoy Patch Adams the physician clown. Roger Ebert the film critic. I listen to Don Campbell talk on The *Mozart Effect*, tapping the power of music to heal the body, strengthen the mind, and unlock the creative spirit.

I enjoy in conversation the generous mind of surgeon Leonard Schlain who gifts me a copy of his book *Art and Physics: Parallel Visions in Space, Time, and Light*. His thesis: Art interprets the visible world, physics charts its unseen workings – making the two realms seem completely opposed. Yet, you can track their breakthroughs, side by side, throughout history to reveal a correlation of visions. Then there was Barbara who wanted me to facilitate a storyshop in Italy as part of her cookingshops. Alas this did not happen.

At one session I'm sharing the story stage with a young African American woman and we end up talking of our grandmothers. I mentioned how my grandmother of thirty-three grandchildren, (that we know of – there was a black sheep son, Stanley who disappeared) me near the youngest end, bent over the cradle and spoke, "This one has healing hands." When I added that I had not used my hands as a medic to heal, a man in the audience stood up right then and there. "I have to interrupt you. The way you orchestrate your hands when telling a story is healing." It was that kind of audience.

After one session a woman came up. This was our exchange:

"I was married to a Haarhoff." "My ancestor came from Hamm in Westphalia in 1719 to South Africa. His name was Frans." "That was my husband's name and he came from Hamm. Our son looks a little like you."

I become friends with the organiser Jim Palmer who, after one session, in his thank you echoed a story I had shared: "A Rabbi, Priest and Dominee are out fishing in a boat. Rabbi climbs out, walks on water and catches a fish. Priest climbs out, walks on water and catches a fish. Dominee says, "It's my turn now." Into the water he steps and sinks. The other two pull him up. Sinks again. Third time nearly drowns. As they haul him up, Rabbi passes behind hand comment to priest. "I think it's about time we showed him where the stones are."

And Jim's generous response? "When Dorian tells stories he walks on water."

And then there was the International Poetry Festival in Medellin, Colombia, City of the Flowers. Luminaries there too. Spend time with American Sam Hamil, translator of Japanese and Chinese poetry into English. In a café he draws on a serviette a stick figure. Next to it two lines and squiggles. "A man standing next to his words, the Ideogram for integrity." A few of us take the funicular up the mountainside. Poems rendered in Spanish and English to vast crowds.

Going on to Damian and family in Houston. (In 2005, after a conference in Banff in the Canadian Rockies, Hurricane Ike had prevented me from travelling to see them.) On return, via Florida, losing a suitcase never found. Later back to Boulder as Jim's guest, Athenium Fellow to lecture in his Film and Jung Studies Department.

And in 2019 working alongside Catharine Anderson in North Carolina at the St Francis Retreat Centre adding stories to her soul collage work. Nineteen vibrant women present.

LIVING THE STORIES I TELL: THE FACES OF BULAWAYO

Billy Robertse, the church organist in Bosman's story *A Bekkersdal Marathon* feels that when his fingers fly over the keyboards, his hands pull out the stops and his feet press the pedals that send the bass notes though the pipes, "He could play all day." I feel that way about storytelling. One day Billy is put to the test. I shared this story in Bulawayo one September. Then I, too, was put to the test in a night marathon.

2015. Cuz Judy, one of the Zimbabwe Haarhoffs, and her husband Mike Carter run a charity, Bulawayo Help Network which supports destitute Zimbabweans who have lost farms, investments et al. They invite me to work with these elderly folk to encourage them to write their stories. I stay with these dear newly discovered cousins. We open our life stories to each other. They instantly become family.

Judy and Mike also arrange other events – an Oom Schalk evening round a fire, a visit to Whitestone School with children and staff, an 'open to the pubic' creative writing wordshop. A storyshop with trainers who were affected by the 1980s genocide in Matabeleland. (Gukurahundi – the rain that sluices all life away). They wish to use stories to reach other people processing trauma.

I enjoy the presence of all I meet. Their spirit. Their courage. I tell many stories. One is of the Rabbi who goes to the synagogue every day to pray. One day a policeman accosts him, "Where are you going?" "I don't know," responds the Rabbi. "What do you mean you don't know. Now I'm going to throw you into prison." And as the cell door clangs shut the rabbi calls out, "You see I told you I don't know."

I also talk of our choices and responses when the dark night arrives. We can choose how to interpret what happens to us. I tell of Ryokan who when thieves stole his one bowl, one cushion and one plate from his hut, wrote, 'The thief left it behind. The moon at my window.'

I arrived on Sunday, due to fly out the following Monday. On Friday late afternoon, half an hour before ending a wordshop with sixth formers, two immigration officers arrive and cart me off. I ask someone to phone Mike and Judy and they meet me at the Immigration office. Four people doing the interview. Immigration and Security.

The questions begin. "Why are you here?" "Who did you work with?" "What props did you use?" Magazine pictures, rags, elastic band, drawings. Passed around these become exhibits. "What stories did you tell?"

I tell the immigration folk this story:

> A woman's baby dies. She cannot find it in her heart to bury the infant. So she approaches the great healer in the village. He sees her coming and responds, "I know why you have come. Give me the child I will bring her back to life."
>
> The mother is ecstatic. As she hands over the dead baby, he says, "There is one thing that you must do for me. Here is an empty cup. Go to any hut in this village and bring me a cup of rice." As she leaves he calls after her, "By the way, the rice must come from a home that has not known grief or suffering."

Route 77

> The woman goes from hut to hut to hut. Eventually she returns with the empty cup and says to the healer, "Give me the body. I will bury my baby."

Judy points out a sign stuck on the wall of the immigration office. She asks if she can snap it. No objection. "This is not a police station," offers one of the officials.

> The Most Beautiful People we have known
> are those who have known defeat,
> known suffering, known struggle, known loss
> and have found their way out of the depths.
> These people have an appreciation,
> a sensitivity and understanding of life
> that fills them with compassion, gentleness,
> and a deep loving concern.
> Beautiful People do not just happen.

Judy grasps my shoulder and tells them. "That's what my cousin has been doing here." I had told wordshop folk, "There's no straight story. Irony, ambiguity, paradox and contradiction accompany each tale." These four sisters sit with us now.

Inscrutable faces. Phone calls to higher authority. To and fro. The verdict. "We are detaining you tonight and deporting you tomorrow." Official reason. "We could prosecute you for false declaration." I had ticked the entry box 'visiting relatives' and had been volunteering stories. Unofficial reason – the day with the genocide survivors. A perpetrator, then say twenty-five, would be late fifties now. Still around. Need to pee. The plain clothes escort offers these words, "Pity we had to meet in these circumstances."

Edge Moments

Mike also wears another hat. He is an opposition senator in the Zimbabwe parliament. Judy mentions this, "Can't we keep him tonight? We will deliver him to the airport tomorrow. He is seventy-one." I try to look seventy-one, and a half.

No avail. I am taken to the Hillside police station. "Lucky," whispers Mike "that you are not going to the main one." Stripped of shoes, socks, spectacles, tissues, watch, neck chain. Into a cell I go in pants and shirt. Concrete floor. Rough, grubby blankets. A broken toilet bowl. Grubby brown and white walls. High, barred windows, solid door with a peephole. No bunk, no light, no water, no food. I wonder what the holding cells at the main station are like if this is the soft option?

One mercy. I am alone. Another mercy. Loving family know where I am. Third mercy. I was picked up with only one wordshop to go. Fourth mercy. I am not beaten up. In the next cell riotous young men perform all night. Banging away. Louder than the kitchen in Willem Prinsloo's *Peach Brandy* – one of the Oom Schalk stories I had told.

I pull the books inside me off the memory shelves. Grateful that my calling rests and rises on reciting by heart. All night I tell all the Dorians locked in together, a ream of stories. Out loud. The four walls in this Zen minimalist space echo in fine acoustic. About the 'don't know' Rabbi. "The Cup of Rice." Fairy tales long and winding that lead me to my door. "The Chinese Tapestry." "The House of the Fathers."

I sing songs. *Some say love it is a razor that drowns the tender reed* (my favourite, on son Dominic's CD). Hymns. *God moves in a mysterious way / his wonders to perform / He plants his footsteps on the sea / and rides upon the storm*. Quotes. *I could be bound in a nutshell and count myself the king of infinite space*. (Hamlet) and the monastic *Go into your cell. It will teach you everything you need to know*. Word play. *Do I have a cell by date? Was there a sellout in one of the groups?* Poetry. *I have walked through many*

Route 77

lives / some of them my own / and I am not who I was / though some principle abides / from which I struggle not to stray… how shall the heart be reconciled to its feast of losses? (Stanley Kunitz) My poems also shared during the week.

I practise breathing, listen to my heartbeat. Offer the Buddhist loving kindness meditation. Hold the people whose names are scratched on the door in that circle: 'T-shirt man was here.' No nail or sharp stone to scratch 'Storyteller was here too.' Practise chi gong moves – rotating the ball of chi … loosening the arrow, holding up sky, pressing down earth.

I think of all the travelling beds I've slept in this year. A recent one in a chalet, up in the mist, looking over the Ixopo valleys at the Buddhist Retreat Centre. The one I'm on tonight is by far the largest – 4 x 4 metres. It takes up the entire floor. I track the block of meshed moonlight across the ceiling. Thank you Ryokan, now I get you. I am not alone. A lone mosquito keeps me company.

Judy traces and phones Annie and Dominic in George. They chat for an hour. Adam and his wife Jo are there too. Annie says, "He will write away all night." "He has no book nor pen." "Then he'll make up stories in his head." Later she tells me a Zim friend says they watch the Carters and their guests.

At dawn a policeman allows me out into the fenced enclosure. Mike and Judy greet me with water and snacks. They too have been up most of the night. Later Judy tells me this story, "The night you were in jail, Mike and I were woken by a strange scraping noise outside. We opened the back door and there below the steps was a moving crate. Diego, the cat had put himself in a jail crate and he became a Cat Tortoise in sympathy with his Ascending Master. Since then, he has slept on your bed." (Diego did not come near me the five nights I slept in that bed.)

Back into the cell. Clanging door echoes. Time passes. I know it's long after Immigration are due to fetch me for passport pick-up and airport transfer. I think, 'Will I be here all weekend?' I'm troubled now. I bang on the door. No response. At last they arrive. The metal door shudders open.

Judy has packed my bag. "Like packing for my brother", she says. Rush rush rush. I change at the airport. "Pity it has to end like this," says cuz. "Perhaps it's not the ending," I respond. (I had also told stories about that – the show's not over until the anorexic man sings.) Mike looks at me, "Now you are one of us." This is the sense I arrive at during the long night. In the minutest of ways, for one night only, unscathed, I am subject to what the people I have worked with all week have endured for decades. Theft. Torture. Murder.

A young immigration man escorts me onto the plane. I feel his empathy. I'm asked, "Will you come back?" No hesitation. "If allowed in, yes." "Beautiful people do not just happen." Well done Billy Robertse. And I'm still waiting for the anorexic man to sing.

PETTY THIEVES AND ANGELS

I enjoy four days in Barcelona before facilitating a writing and healing wordshop as part of a holotropic breathwork week in a forest near Llostera near the Costa Brava. Courtesy Luccio Schlettwein from Basel at his brother's country home.

My friend Brian Thorn's caution, plus Airbnb host, "Be careful of *ladrone*, pickpockets in the metro and on the beach." People with luggage are the special targets of the army of Romanians, Pakistanis, North Africans, or even southern Spanish who hold their annual Pickpocket Championships in Barcelona every summer.

Route 77

I wish to swim in the Mediterranean, so one evening with bus ticket, ten euros and house keys all in a black zip pouch in a sling bag, no towel as I can drip dry, I step onto the sand in front of the restaurants. There is no someone with whom I can leave my bag. I line up a spot in the sand. There is a yellow notice near the restaurants... over to the right where the rocks begin, a pole... over to the left, some distance away, a beach hotel. I dig a hole and bury the treasure.

Now what to do with T-shirt and sling bag? A couple arrive and settle a few paces away. I walk towards them measuring my steps. Twelve. After a bout of sign language arm waving, I work out they are from Kiev in Ukraine. They are not swimming and yes, will look after the bag. I drop the sling bag with them, so might as well retrieve the buried bag and leave it with them too. So retrace twelve measured steps. Falling onto my knees I dig and dig. Nada. No bag. Only a Med's worth of sand. My chest says, "And now? How do you get back?"

I look up. The Ukrainian couple watch this digger. What is the frowning in their eyes? Ahead is a metal detector beach comber. I'm saved. I run up to him. Wave my arms, point beckon. He follows, taking sweet time muttering "*Ladrone, ladrone.* They only need two seconds." I mark the cross. He runs his machine on high, shows me the settings. Nada. Nothing. Goes over the territory again. Spectator sport for the Ukrainians. He shrugs his shoulders and leaves.

I keep digging. Nothing. I spy another metal detector beach man. He tries, going over the spot marked X. Higher, lower, side to side, with the concentration of a priest at prayer. The Ukrainian man digs too. Nada.

I sigh. If my heart were a metal detector could its hum find the metal key? I ask, "Help, guardian angel." I return to my digging and my hand clasps the treasure and raises it. I, no Catholic, make the sign of the cross to the bemused second metal man.

After a Med swim I thank the now beer-swigging couple and walk off drip-drying into the narrow streets of La Ribera district. I come across in a square, Santa Maria del Mar, a Gothic cathedral built in the 1300s when the Mediterranean tide ran close in the days of Catalonia's maritime pre-eminence. The organist perched half way up a wall, practices filling the vault with Bach. I light a candle to thank guardian angel.

HIKING HAIKU

I like to wash
the dust of this world
In the droplets of dew
(Matsuo Basho)

How many roads must a man walk along? How many paths? From my twenties onward I have hiked. Hobbiton on Hogsback. I wrote of the Wellington Hike and the murders earlier on hiking in Westerford days. Boland Trail in snow in the seventies. Then in Namibia the Fish River Canyon thrice in the eighties. Once friend Tony tried to catch a fish with his line and hook. I thought if I were a fish, what bait? So a piece of biltong on the hook and soon we were cooking the silver fish in foil on the river bank.

On another hike, friend Stuart and I brought along two unknown colleagues. Victor and Jan the Belgian. The hike begins with a steep decline to the bottom of the canyon. Then in four/five days you walk out the eighty odd kilometres to Ais-Ais, the hot springs. Victor begins to shake – fear of heights. We take his backpack. He, weak-kneed, we end at the bottom. Now we have to walk, cajoling him, step by step. No way out, only on. A hike from hell. One morning the Belgian is gone with

Route 77

half our food. No idea if he is OK. Turns up back in Windhoek. So it goes.

Back in SA, Tsitsikamma forest in the rain. A woman and I walk and talk so much we lose the turn off. Walk on for hours in a deteriorating track. Back track in heavy rain, slip sliding. Arrive to meet concerned fellow hikers. That night I dry boots near our fire. The toe caps set solid so I have to cut them off. On we go. Luckily it's slack-pack.

St Olaf's Norwegian Pilgrim Path shared earlier. And then the Whale Trail. The Score? Hikers six, whales ninety-nine. In all states of grace and poses close in to the coastline. We cross a narrow ridge in high wind and rain and then fan out onto the beach south of Bredasdorp. Such stone huts. One of our party is Hettie, the masseur. Aah those massages after a day's hike. Slack-packing. In her black box ferried daily to the next site, she hides a surprise:

Essentials on a Hike

at the first hut at the head of the track
black boxes wait, looming large
against a stone wall, to be ferried
daily ahead of us on this Whale Trail.

sixty litres seems a lot to leave behind
on a slack pack hike, until you squeeze in
sleeping bag, that gravity jacket
and each morning and night's meal
to the power of five.

it's a little like shedding for death.
I pack, unpack, repack, discard
a ball of string, tin of tomato,

Edge Moments

>boots, shaving kit, novel.
>sit astride the lid to clip it closed.
>
>I'll be a bearded readerless sandaled man
>these days, light of heart.
>another hiker straps her box with
>the grin of a secret hid inside.
>
>with a daypack slung with water
>energy bar, avo sam, hot flask,
>we trudge through mist and angled rain
>along a rocky mountain saddle.
>then through high tide ankle sand
>into the northwester, shirts flapping.
>arrive on the third evening at the beach hut.
>
>she unstraps her box and smiles
>and suddenly there she is alone at sea edge
>with the kite rearing like a breaching whale,
>arms outstretched like a diver.
>
>she holds this wild horse, Pegasus,
>kicking into the wind,
>cantering light across the sky.
>and she rides it bare back
>soaring, soaring.

Once on one walk, way back, focusing on the way my leg muscles and joints moved, how ankles flexed, I walked myself into the present out of an unhappy trapped time. Here's Kierkegaard, from a letter to his favourite niece, Henriette (1847). 'Everyday, I walk myself into a state of well-being and walk away from every illness…I know of no thought so burdensome that one cannot walk away from it.'

And from the wordshop annals – *Walking with Your Story: A Creative Retreat* (Betty's Bay 2009)

> What did the grass below the koppie say
> Stranger, the yellow grass, when you looked around,
> Then hastened on? Of shadows on the ground
> the long grass spoke… (Veld Secret : Bosman)

We walk to waterfall, dark wood, mountain, grotto, lily pond, beach and dune. We draw from these places the images, symbols and themes for our life journey. There's a Latin phrase *solvitur ambulando*. It is solved by walking. Perhaps it is equally true that it is solved by writing – *solvitur scribendi*.

Matsuo Basho the Haiku master, set out in the spring of 1689. His *Oku-no-hosomichi* (*Narrow Road to the Deep North*), a travelogue in poetry and prose, charts his 2,400km journey. And so a haiku to thank, to honour these legs:

> I walk mountain bliss
> each hike an Emmaus road
> meeting the stranger

Edge Moments

Footnote: Gift from Evette Weyers sculptor, friend and wordshop participant. She loves metaphor as much as I.

3

FAITH

In the middle of my life I found myself in a dark wood. The way was wholly lost and gone…My will and desire were revolved, as a wheel that is equally turned, by the Love which moves the sun and stars.
- (Dante: beginning and end of Divine Comedy)

THE PLIABLE ECLECTIC BUBBLE

Annie Haarhoff, linocut and calligraphy

Route 77

A pilgrim travelling to a shrine arrives bone weary, lies down on her back and crosses her feet on a statue. The custodian rushes out crying, "The statue is holy. Remove your feet." Looking up at him, she responds, "I will Father. But can you please place my feet on some place that is not holy."

Here are eleven hints and guesses at how Faith arrives in its disguises. For years I have offered a 'Writing your Spiritual Journey' course. As Rumi reminds us, "there are hundreds of ways to kneel and kiss the ground." We journal about our changing beliefs and find the stories around those moments of insight. When like the snake we shed a dead skin… lived through that dark night… opened the prison door to a larger world… stepped into the great unknown. We ask many questions as we travel, invoking the image of the pilgrim, path and journey.

This echoes my own travails and travels. I was born into literal dogma. Level one. We are told what to believe – for me Christianity, the one and only true faith. Within that Methodism. A teenager wanting to be a missionary. Then a minister. Later a Sunday school teacher. Then beginning to encounter those within and those without in the fold that speak in metaphors. Books. No wonder authoritarians burn books.

An early insight via a book title – JB Phillips *Your God is too Small*. Later to find this echoed in Meister Eckhart, 'The idea of God is the final obstacle to God… The eye with which I see God is the eye with which God sees me.' And David Steindl-Rast, 'We all know that the religions have a tendency to become doctrinaire, dogmatic, moralistic and ritualistic. Forgotten what the ritual is all about but they do it. How can we rescue that with our heart, our whole human person?' Rast says we have an experience of the luminous and want to repeat it so we set up the conditions when it happened. That is the birth of dogma, the map. The group forms. As the landscape and seascape changes, the group

Faith

mapmaker calls us back instead of changing the map to accommodate the shifting rivers and coasts.

Enter in the eighties Joseph Campbell on mythology. Matthew Fox's creation spirituality. And then encountering similar stories in other faiths – virgin births, child saviours, dismembered bodies resurrected. Aha, so Christianity is one of many stories and the paradox makes its stories true on the inside.

So I entertain and entrain a belief bubble. Not shaped by literal truth but by metaphor, by story. If an idea asks for entry and it leads me to greater compassion and less judgement, I let it in. Discard what no longer serves.

Here is an early exploration in search of imaginative truth:

Two-sided Christ

if Gabriel,
double-winged and daring,
had split the chromosome
and annunciated
sibling twins,
double x, xy,
and Mary's womb
magnified a duet
in her magnificat,
and wise men brought west
gifts for shaking bones…

one Christchild could have
prime-died, crucified
tasting death splitside
as sacrificial prophecy

Route 77

>and celibate
>centrepoint on the carpenter cross.
>
>the other,
>like a Donne love compass,
>could have run circumference,
>done the birth splits,
>savoured till the tongue buds
>mislaid taste
>and lived on the point
>when, lying pierced
>by a calcified side,
>she hears the cell dying.

And salvaging the stories in this tradition:

>Expecting
>
>from the outer rim of worlds
>known, unknown,
>they come, circling
>towards the stable.
>on camel routes, sheep paths,
>angels wing on invisible tracers,
>oxen unyoked, plod to shelter,
>a woman blue-wrapped on a donkey,
>a man walking in sandals,
>hiding prophets in his beard.
>a tavern of innkeeper children.
>at the earth's core they gather,
>here at the edge of themselves
>where stars shine brighter,

> straw breathes its pungency.
> and a child cries
> sharper than a sword.
> they step into a halo story, where
> any herald thing can happen
> and turn expectant faces.

Enter myth. Enter paradox. And to holding contradictions. And beginning to wonder what Keats means when he proclaims the tenants of his faith: 'I am certain of nothing but of the holiness of the Heart's affections and the truth of Imagination – What the imagination seizes as Beauty must be truth'. I search for personal meaning in this.

A MYTH? WHAT IS A MYTH, GRANDPA?

Mythology beats at the heart of my faith. I only began to find my mythic ways in my middle forties. I am rich through twelve grandchildren (Leo included). If they were to ask this question, this would be my response. I've pitched it ahead of them. May they grow into it even as I do.

I love your question. To try to answer, I'll tell a story. You know what a story is? It's a make up on the outside with several truths hidden on the inside. Which then changes the outside. Perhaps Rilke's insight can help us here, 'I am circling around God, around the ancient tower, and I have been circling for a thousand years, and I still don't know if I am a falcon, or a storm, or a great song' (*Book of the Hours*).

Stories are about goddesses and gods, about parallel worlds and realms, where trees speak, birds become people and sea monsters devour the unwary. Choosing our paths. A story is about what never happened but always has, over and over, dressed in all the cultural costumes of our world. Here's Horace, the Roman poet: *Mutato nomine et de te fabula*

Route 77

narrator. Change only the name and this story is about you. Change the place and it's about you too.

A tale is like the flower, Yesterday, Today and Tomorrow. It unfolds in time. Yet it also blossoms and decays in the reverse order. Like an inter-penetrating gyre that spins and coils out from both ends at the same time. It's a didgeridoo player who circles sound through the cycle of in-out breath. Like the Okavango River in Namibia that flows both ways.

Many have sought to solve the riddle of a myth. To sing its mystery, moment and mysticism. One of them, Carl Jung, carved a Latin inscription above the lintel of his home. *Vocatus atque non vacatus dues aderit* (Invited or not God will be present). Another, Joseph Campbell, spent his days and nights trying to understand myth. He believed 'a myth is a metaphor for the individual journey in our lives...so follow your bliss'. In big words how do we live a mythology not a pathology?

Are you lost, children? So am I, for we are trying to express the inexpressible. That's why I'm writing in metaphors because an image takes us as far as language can go before we enter the silence beyond tongues, the echo of don't know, We enter the cloud of unknowing.

Imagine – now that's a quintessential word. Imagination, our highest faculty says Coleridge the poet. When Joan of Arc stood on trial, one of her accusers taunted her, "You say you hear the voice of God. How do you know this is not just your imagination?" The Saint to be, retorted, "How would God speak but through the imagination?"

> Here's a made up story:
>
> Imagine twins, a girl and boy. Asleep on their reed mats, curled up in a dream in a thatched hut near a stream. In a cloud kingdom above and in a cave below, a goddess, who is in both places at the

same time, weaves a tapestry from spider web, lama wool and silk thread on her loom high as seven mountain ranges, wide as seven seas, rich as seven kingdoms.

The goddess shuttles and creates seven thousand images that play across the flickering lids of the twins. Filtering into their individual and collective dreams. An overarching rainbow refracts their lives into seven shades. Like the seven chakras. The chakras are like a rainbow inside us but can't be seen with the naked eye.

Creatures frolic and inhabit her shuttle screen – the bees buzz, the squirrels chatter and the lemon finch whirr-weaves amongst the invisible creatures of the forest heart. Big five, minute five, hybrids, centaurs, unicorns roam the landscape. The big and small sea five dive the deep.

Now the goddess adds to the woven design the stories she and the god know by heart. 70 x 7 fairy tales, ancestral legends and narratives of origin end and origin. Remember Einstein? When a woman approached him, asking, "What should my child read to become a famous scientist like you?" he answered "Fairy tales." And when she added what else? he said, "More fairy tales." The goddess must have whispered this in Einstein's ear when he was awake asleep.

And before the children wake, the goddess takes up a fountain pen dipped in the endless river and writes in invisible ink all these images lightly on the children's skin. It filters through seven layers into the organs and tissues, bones and muscles, into the third ear and eye. Stories seep into every cell in the breezes of dawn.

When the twins rise and dust their eyes, the girl and boy go about their separate way and together tasks of hewing wood and drawing water. As they finger each image in each in-out breath, they inhale the mysteries of big picture belonging. They hear through each da dum beat of their hearts the gurgle of the stream, where they dip their buckets, and also the thunder river from source to ocean estuary. And along their waking-up journey the twins begin to live a doubled life, bringing in the images of the tapestry into the everyday and everyday into the tapestry. It spirals in the labyrinth of their lives.

As they move into womanhood, into manhood and encounter Shakespeare's 'thousand natural shocks' they become witness to their own and each other's tales, watching not with judgement but with compassion. They know by heart the mystic wisdom of all faiths. Like Elizabeth Barrett Browning they know 'Earth's crammed with heaven, and every common bush afire with God; And only he who sees takes off his shoes; The rest sit round it and pluck blackberries.'

They pick born-into stories off the tree that are not theirs and hold them to the light. Peel off the clinging husks of dogma and eat the ripe fruit of experience that appleglows their cheeks. They learn to tread lightly and follow Hildegard von Bingen, musician, mystic, who one thousand years before their earth time, sought to be 'a feather on the breath of God'. And with lightness arrives its twin – laughter. So the twins keep playing for they too have read blind Milton, 'Sport that wrinkled Care derides, And Laughter holding both his sides.'

They remind each other daily, "don't get ahead of the story"… for story is a trickster figure that subverts expected endings and outcomes – fair or foul. The twins follow the be-here-now bird chirping the moment. They live in daily thank you, for as Meister

Faith

Eckhart reminds them, 'If gratitude were the only prayer, it would suffice.'

That dear grandchildren is a hint of what a myth embraces, energises and enfolds. To the power of seven as we seek to live a storied life.

Love from your grandpa who inhabits and wanders beyond the age 7 x 11. And who longs to grasp the hermetic, medieval truth: 'God is an infinite sphere, whose centre is everywhere and circumference nowhere'.

So as you sail to the edge, 'there be dragons', take three sailor seasoned companions with you – Image, Metaphor and Symbol.

LISTEN WITH THE DEEP EAR IN YOUR CHEST

Take breath and read with your ears
(Gerard Manley Hopkins)

I return to listening – an art I don't always practise. While teaching a ZenPen retreat at the Buddhist Centre near Ixopo, one of the teachers, Sue Cooper, whom I taught at Westerford way back when, reminded me that the word 'silent' with the letters scrambled is the word 'listen.' And then I read Mark Nepo's *Seven Thousand Ways to Listen*. And Cathy Anderson, teaching a photography and meditation retreat, gifted me with Krista Tippett's *Becoming Wise, An Inquiry into the Mystery and Art of Living*. Her interviews with many known and unknown luminaries and bearers of wisdom, are available on onbeing.org. Among the six double columns of names at the end of the book, I find Karen Armstrong, Desmond Tutu, David Stendl-Rast, John O'Donohue, Wangari Maathai, Thich Nhat Hanh. Plus plus all the others I'm meeting for the first time in her text.

Here's Rumi:

> ….the branches of your intelligence grow new leaves
> in the wind of listening. The body reaches a peace.
> Rooster sound comes reminding you of your love for dawn.
> The reed flute and the singer's lips.
> The knack of how spirit breathes into us becomes as simple
> and ordinary as eating and drinking…. As brightness is to
> time, so are you to the one who talks to the deep ear in your
> chest.

Robert Frost said, 'The ear is the best reader'. There are levels of listening when we approach as an 'ears alert' the reader. If we read aloud, we hear the voice of the writer perhaps from a different time and place. A vibration echoes in the present, in the resonating chambers of the body and in the cave of the brain. Here's Yeats in the *Lake Isle of Innisfree*:

> …for always night and day
> I hear lake water lapping with low sounds by the shore…
> I hear it in the deep heart's core.

When we write we're listening to that part of us doing the writing. As Ray Bradbury, the science fiction writer intuits in a poem, 'I do not write. The other me demands emergence constantly.' We are listening for that other one who comes perhaps from our consciousness not from our rational brain. When we hear a word, a phrase, a line, the words create chemical and electrical impulses that tingle down the spine, that raise the hairs of our arms. It's the ear in the cells. The body as instrument.

We're listening as Ganesh, the elephant god in the Hindu pantheon, listens. Here is my version of this myth. The poet calls on Ganesh to take dictation of the great Maharabarata, the song of India:

Faith

Elephant Pen

the sage called Ganesha,
of the two tusks
and ink-pot belly,
to earth a poem
long as the Ganges,
to capture its currents,
the washing of bodies
and the floating candles
set alight in paper boats.

they agreed to unbroken motion,
matching the rhythms of the lyrics
to the flowing script.
the sage intoned and Ganesha
stroked volume on volume
across cascading years.
then mid-stream his pen split
in a river of words.

without skipping a beat
Ganesha snapped his right tusk.
friend of scribes and writers,
he inscribed in ivory
the immortal verse,
the sacred song of India.

As writers we listen to the subject that has chosen us, entraining with it, picking up its vibrations. We're also listening to the conversation around this great subject – the conversation recorded in other works. We're listening to how the words might sound to our future audience, our reader. We're listening to silences too. To the great silence around the subject, to what is not being articulated for 'whoever is silent touches the roots of speech' (Rilke).

Emily Dickinson spoke about a 'noiseless noise':

> the words the happy say
> Are paltry melody
> But those the silent feel
> are beautiful.

Many poets celebrate such a silence. Here are a few lines by Hopkins:

> Elected silence sing to me
> And beat upon my whorled ear,
> Pipe me to pastures still and be
> The music that I care to hear.

During the Truth and Reconciliation Commission hearings in South Africa, a young man who had been blinded when a policeman shot him in the face at close range, spoke, "Now it feels like I've got my sight back by coming here and telling my story."

This simple act, requires attention. Being present. Creates relationship. Generates faith.

Faith

INHABITING THE CITY OF SYNCHRONICITY

The seemingly haphazard, random, and arbitrary events that comprise the story of our lives begin to form a coherent and purposeful narrative when we view them from a divine perspective. With the wisdom of retrospective insight… coincidence is but God's way of choosing to remain anonymous.
(Rabbi Benjamin Blech)

We all live in a city called Synchronicity. The streets, edifices and green spaces of our lives form an interconnected pattern. Our internal and external narratives are in constant conversation. Ancestral cities lie beneath our feet. We delight in seeing through the visible world (title of Jungian Jean Singer's book) as we tug at the web of belonging and feel it vibrate in our fingers.

Synchronicity is an ever-present reality for those who have eyes to see (Jung).

A woman patient shared a dream with Jung. She was given a piece of jewellery, a golden scarab (beetle). While she was relating the dream, Jung heard a tap at the window. He opened the window and in flew a beetle which he caught in his hand, its gold-green colour resembling that of the golden scarab in the dream. Jung handed the beetle to her, "Here is your scarab."

Jacob Needleman, my favourite philosopher, discusses the uncanny symmetry displayed throughout nature's ecological web:

> In a universe without a visible center, biology presents a reality *in which the existence of a center is everywhere implied*. Synchronicity hints at a coordinating agency of unimaginable scope and subtlety whereby all the coincidences and correspondences of the world coalesce as if threads in a grand design, and within which our lives

are holoscopically nested. Seen in this way, the synchronistic event can be seen as affording us a passing sideways glance, as if through a glass darkly, into the mind of God (Needleman, J. *A Sense of the Cosmos: The Encounter of Modern Science and Ancient Truth*).

Indigo Mind, a group exhibition (2015) celebrated the work of neurologist Oliver Sacks. Indigo Mind relates this mental state to that of the artist's creative process: clarity, expansion, and focus; an elevated state of energy and movement where objects and ideas come into synchronic being.

Stanley Kunitz is one of the great poets on my Parnassus (a mountain near Delphi, in Greek mythology, the home of the Muses). His father took his own life before Kunitz was born. In his poem, "Quinnapoxet," he shares a synchronous dream about an instinctive use of sign language which he did not know. He was fishing when a bullhead 'gashed my thumb with a flick of his razor fin.' His parents arrive in the dream, 'they raised, their cloud of being / against the dripping light.' Behind his mother was a man:

> with his face averted
> as if to hide a scald,
> deep in his other life,
> I touched my forehead
> with my swollen thumb
> and splayed my fingers out
> in deaf mute country
> the sign for father.

A story: Joey Riklis, from Ohio visits the Wailing Wall in Jerusalem after his father, a survivor of the holocaust, had died. His father was an

Faith

ardent practitioner of his faith. Joey had rebelled so the two men had been alienated. Feeling remorse, Joey went to Israel to explore the heritage he had spurned. People were inserting scribbled notes into the crevices of the Wailing Wall. People believed the stones were so holy that requests placed inside would be blessed.

Joey wrote his own petition, asking his father's forgiveness. There were notes crammed all over the place. He finally found an empty crevice and inserted his small note into the crack. As he did so, he accidentally dislodged another that had been resting there, and it fell to the ground. He was about to put it back when he was overcome by an impulse to open the note. He read: "My Dear Son Joey. If you should ever happen to come to Israel and somehow miraculously find this note, this is what I want you to know: I always loved you, my beloved son. And Joey, please know that I forgive you … and only hope that you in turn will forgive a foolish old man." Signed, Adam Riklis, Cleveland, Ohio. (Halberstam and Leventhal, Small Miracles: Extraordinary coincidences from everyday life)

And a personal story: Annemarie (Ams) and I are reading. I open a page with a poem about Adam, my son. She asks me about him. We swap books. She reads the Adam poem while I read the book she passes to me. Literally a line later I read that one of greatest Mathematicians of all time, the 18th century German genius Karl Frederick Gaus, proclaimed, 'God arithemetises'. Adam who practises a rooted belief in God is a passionate mathematician. And the book I'm reading? *Synchronicity and You*. And the name Adam gave his cat? Gaus.

I have already referred to the pilgrim path where a fellow Norwegian walker told me the fairy tale of Espen which we found that evening the image of Espen and the Troll was painted on the door. When synchronised in heart, mind, spirit, we enter this synchronous flow.

Route 77

GIVE US THIS DAY OUR DAILY QUOTE

In search of spiritual literacy, I find quotations lining the way, the cairns that those further down the path have left as beacons.

John Roome sketch in ZenPenZen

Give us this Day our Daily Quote

some days you can live
off a poet's quote, a catch
that flaps your way
in the early morning.

bright scaled, surfacing,
it reaches you
as you stand knee deep
in a sea of reading.

Faith

> this linefish lands
> splashing at your feet.
> offers its flesh, saying
> take, eat, remember this.
>
> the author follows
> the fishbone arrow
> as he listens to the voice
> of the dawn stranger.
>
> the one who whispers
> after a night of empty net,
> cast on the other side
> of the vessel.
>
> through noon and tide,
> sun slant into twilight,
> sliver by sliver
> each flake feeds you.
>
> as beach embers glow
> suddenly you see
> the miracle of teeming fish
> caught in the writer's mesh.

When distressed as a teenager, when fear knocked at my heart, I turned to my exercise (well-named) book to the list of quotations this leftie had transcribed. I read these mantras aloud, intoning over and over till they entered the heart and stilled the storm. Calmed the beathing, suffused my body with hope. Quotes make fine company. Sometimes they stand alone or embed themselves in stories:

An anthropologist, stalking through the forest in India, comes across an ancient sage dancing in a clearing. He watches from behind a tree. The old woman strokes a tree then bathes herself in moonlight. Unable to contain his curiosity, the anthropologist steps from his cover and with a puzzled look on his brow asks, "Pardon me old woman but what are you doing alone in the forest?" With an even more puzzled look the sage replies, "Young man, what makes you think I'm alone?"

At a rural gathering a famous actor is invited to recite Psalm 23, The Lord is my Shepherd. He recites it perfectly. At the end there is applause. Then one of the locals points to an elderly woman, "She also knows that Psalm." After much persuasion the old woman gets up and recites in a quivering voice, making the odd mistake. As she ends there is a holy silence. Someone asks the actor, "What was the difference between your recitation and hers?" The actor responds, "I know the Psalm. She knows the Shepherd."

Then, Biblical quotes in the King James poetic cadences, Old and New Testaments intermingled. 'But the fruit of the Spirit is love, joy, peace, long-suffering, gentleness, goodness, faith' (Galatians). 'But they that wait upon the Lord shall renew their strength; they shall mount up with wings as eagles; they shall run, and not be weary; and they shall walk, and not faint.' (Isaiah). 'Let the words of my mouth, and the meditation of my heart, be acceptable in thy sight, O Lord, my strength, and my redeemer.' (Psalms) And Methodist hymns rousing, uplifting the spirit, suffusing this mortal frame with energy. They still set me aglow. Poetry as music. Our youth Guild hymn brought the dawn of imagery. Good 'ole Charles Wesley:

Faith

> O thou who camest from above
> the fire pure celestial to impart
> kindle a flame of sacred love
> On the mean altar of my heart.

Macbeth too part of my memory chain (Matric prescribed). 'I'll fight till from my bones my flesh be hacked'... 'Blow wind, come wrack. At least we'll die with harness on our back.'

These were rootstock to my quotation tree, as in Norse mythology, binding in an eco-cycle earth and heaven. They ferret beneath the ground and bring forth the sap and ring the ever-expanding trunk in the garden of the beloved. Poets, mystics, mythologists, philosophers wander in the orchard shade of these pages.

I often preface poems with a guiding quotation. This one also ends with a quote:

The Meeting of Head and Heart

The heart has reasons that the reason knows not of
(Pascal)

head who had long been estranged
from heart and her ways,
sharing nothing, accepted
an invitation to meet
to see what they held in common
since he inhabited the same village.
no harm in a cup of tea.

my place? suggested head.
heart laughed. let's meet

Route 77

in the middle somewhere
so we both travel some way
along the roads of the body.
head risked driving down face freeway
to the Palate Palace
and chose a table near the door.

as they sipped from steaming cups
heart spoke of a cook book
with zen aromas, flavours spices and herbs,
seducing head who warmed
towards this generous friend.

they walked on hand in hand
down neck alley
to the Vocal Chords café
for another cup
then trundled back.
since life was short
it made a huge sense
to share this cell intelligence.
so they sat around the table tongue
and chanted om mani padme hum. *

*the jewel of the mind in the lotus of the heart

Rumi: 'Lovers don't finally meet somewhere. They're in each other all along.' Hafiz: 'The sun never says to the earth, "You owe Me". Look what happens with a love like that, lights the Whole Sky.'
And and and....

Faith

THE FEMININE FACE OF GOD

God creates Eve and tells her, "I now will create Adam. But we need to let him think he was created first. Agreed?" Eve smiles and nods. And God says, "This will be a secret between us girls." In the Old Testament Creation story, all is inert, stationary. The story does not start until Eve moves and introduces us to time and death.

First Bite

did the snake offer Eve
the fruit from his mouth?
or did she pick it,
as the creature curled
around the stem,
reaching a hand heavenward,
cradling it in her palm,
then the downward tug?
or did the crop drop
to the lightest touch?

was she in love with colour,
edengreen, sungold, rose
as the flush of her throat?
did Eve ask its blessing,
before her teeth pierced the skin
and the crunch crisped the garden,
her saliva rising like sap
to mingle the pulp on her tongue?

did she watch the pectin
browning the core,
and as she counted pips,

Route 77

> say A is for Apple,
> in this alphabet of tastes?
> and did blossoms ring her hair
> the day she tasted God
> in the first bite?

Years ago, via my sister Joy (bringer of many books) I encountered a shape-shifting book, *The Feminine Face of God*. Women from different persuasions sharing their encounters with the Divine. One tells of intuition stifled as a child, appearing in later life. In the Jewish Rabbinic tradition this wise one is called Shekhinah from the word shakan, which means 'to dwell'.

I heard a story about the little girl asking her mother, "Where was I before I was here?" The mother responds, "You were in my womb." So arrives the next question. "Where were you before you were here?" "I was in Granny's womb." "And where was Granny…." The Same answer. The child's observation? "It looks like we're all in one big womb, and that womb is God."

A litany of mystics leads me to St Teresa of Ávila whose Little Way chapel graces the garden at Temenos. Julian of Norwich, Mechthild of Magdeburg, Hildergard van Bingen (1098–1179).

> Hildegard and the Abbot
>
> once you buried a man
> in consecrated ground,
> one whom father church
> with its heavy ring finger
> had indicated intern
> outside the walls.

Faith

> when the Abbot demanded
> that you exhume his bones,
> you refused for you felt
> the sphere of his repenting.
> his body had been anointed
> and oil adorned him.
>
> when the Abbot ordered
> his troops to do the digging,
> you removed the cross
> and smoothed the mound
> on the grave with your spade,
> slapped flat as Mr Abbot's world.
>
> out trumped with other texts,
> the official imposed silence
> on you and yours.
> so you dug deeper into that gift,
> into the under-soil
> of all forgiving.
>
> the silence slipped into
> the Abbot's stopped ear.
> he recanted, lifting the ban.
> and there was Edensong
> and first bird twitter
> gracing that green garden.

And those Jungian mentors. So many. Evocative in title and text. Here are four that have shifted the ground. Helping make all ground holy, not only where Moses stands before the burning bush:

- Marion Woodman, *Leaving My Father's House: A Journey to Conscious Femininity.*
- Clarissa Pinkola Estés, *Women Who Run With the Wolves: Myths and Stories of the Wild Woman Archetype.*
- Caroline Myss, *Entering the Castle: An Inner Path to God and Your Soul.*
- June Singer, *Seeing Through the Visible World: Jung, Gnosis, and Chaos.*

They open to the parallel world of the mysteries of the not-yet-known or the unknowable. They offer a way to the inner kingdom and a key to open the 'doors of perception' (Blake). It's women mostly in the last third of the lives who arrive at my storyshops and retreats. They too are my teachers.

RABBINICAL MYSTERIES

Once at a fair a tarot reader offered a reading in exchange for *The Writer's Voice*. Past life cards proclaimed I had, as a Roman soldier, been taken out for bucking authority (this fits) and that I had twice in previous incarnations been a rabbi (fits too).

So attracted, not to orthodox dogma, but to progressive Judaism, to traditions (wish I'd encountered early a matchmaker of my own), rituals, stories, a spiritual tradition, jokes. So many of my favourite mensch are poets (Stanley Kunitz) philosophers (Jacob Needleman) scientists (Albert Einstein) spiritual storytellers (Rachael Naomi Remen) and Jubus – Jewish-Buddhists (Jack Kornfield) and wise Rabbis. Rebbe Nachman of Breslov, for example, who lived in the 18th and early 19th centuries and was known for fusing kabbalistic elements with in-depth Torah scholarship, promoted the practice of *hitbodedut*, an unstructured, individualised form of direct communion with God that lends itself to various silent meditation techniques.

2001 – 2003. In my brief sojourn in Sandringham, Jozi. I have mentioned Sybbie, Ray and Lali: my Jewish family, who all feature in a life story publication. Once, four of us stood on a balcony at friend Kari Ritchie's' home in Linksfield, looking down on the life I had lived there, diminished, shrunk into a view.

See the praise poems *Achilles Heal* at the birthdays for these three blessed Elders, turning seventy, eighty and ninety. And the Shabats in Killarney. Going with Ray and his son Stephen to offer a ritual for his grandson at Stanford Village farm. Lali involving me in Limmud (Jewish Festival), thrice – 2014-2017. There, some dub me a holistic Jew. At one Limmud session on spirituality there's a woman rabbi, Adina Roth, Hassidic rabbi, Charles Mendelow, an American one, and Ray, with me in the chair. I share the God and Eve story and ask them to respond. I share other stories and ask them for their take.

Here are two cornerstone stories I share in storyshops:

> People approach the young Rabbi with their questions. They come one by one. "Why did my child die?" "Why did my wife run away?" "Why is there so much hatred and anger in the world?" "Where can I find work?" The Rabbi is not able answer such questions, so he approaches his teacher, the great Rabbi who says. "I will come and answer their questions." There is a great buzz in the community. On the Saturday morning the synagogue is packed. The great rabbi arrives. He bows to the Torah, the holy book. Then he bows to the people.
>
> He sits down and says, "Ask your questions." He listens intensely to the first question and then says, "I won't answer now. I'll wait until

everybody has spoken". People look at each other in amazement. How will he remember? One by one people ask their questions. When everybody has spoken there is silence. The Rabbi begins to rock his body, humming a *niggun* (a chant to induce a prayerful attitude.) The people wonder what the great Rabbi is up to so then they begin to sway and hum as well. Then the rabbi stands up and begins to dance. The people dance too. After the humming and the dancing, the rabbi faces the people. There is silence. He bows to them, then to the Torah. The Great Rabbi says, "I have answered your questions" and he leaves.

The Baal Shem Tov was getting old. He called his disciples and allocated them their life's work, their vocation. "Gabriel, you will be a story-teller." Gabriel asked, "How will I know when I have told the Big story?" The Baal Shem Tov responded, "You will know."

The Baal Shem Tov and Gabriel set off on their travels telling stories in many villages. Then the Baal Shem Tov died. After many years, weary of travelling, Gabriel heard of the rich man in Sienna who offered good money for untold Baal Shem Tov stories. Gabriel made his way there. The excited host called his family and neighbours to witness the story.

That evening Gabriel stood up and opened his mouth. But not one story emerged from it. Gabriel could not remember a single Baal Shem Tov story. The host's face was a picture of sadness. Yet he encouraged Gabriel. "Perhaps it is because you are weary of travelling. Come tomorrow when you have rested." The next day the people assembled and Gabriel once more stood before them. Not a single story came forth. He could not remember a single Baal Shem Tov story.

Faith

The host's face was once more a picture of sadness. As he headed out the town, threading his way through the streets, Gabriel came across a house in the outskirts with the shutters closed up. Suddenly he remembered a Baal Shem Tov story that he has never told. He hurried back to the mansion to find the rich man weeping out his eyes. Without asking the source of such grief, Gabriel plunged into the story.

"Years ago the Baal Shem Tov and I travelled to outlying villages. As we descended into one village, we could feel the fear lining the walls. The houses were all shut up, doors and windows barred. A voice called from within, "You must leave. It is not safe here for Jews. The priest in the village square is inciting hatred against us." The Baal Shem Tov gained entrance and sent me, Gabriel, to call the priest who surprisingly came. They were closeted for thirteen hours and when the priest came out, he was weeping copiously. Then he disappeared.

The rich man of Sienna stood before Gabriel, shaking, clutching his shoulders and looking into his eyes, "Do you not know who I am? I was that priest. I was born Jewish then converted to avoid persecution. To be safe I became a priest and to be even more safe, I started persecuting Jews. When the Baal Shem Tov called me that day in the square, something in me made me come. We were closeted for thirteen hours."

The Baal Shem Tov said to me, "Go back to your roots. Go back to who you are." I asked him. "When will I know that I have been forgiven?" and he said these words, "You will know this when you hear your story in the mouth of someone else and their big story and your story become one."

Route 77

I find in this Jewish faith Eight Levels of Charity. In reverse order:

8. Donations given grudgingly.
7. When we give less than we should, but do so cheerfully.
6. When we give directly to the poor upon being asked.
5. When we give directly to the poor without being asked.
4. Donations when the recipient is aware of the donor's identity, but the donor doesn't know the identity of the recipient.
3. Donations when the donor is aware to whom the charity is being given, but the recipient is unaware of the source.
2. Giving assistance in such a way that the giver and recipient are unknown to each other.
1. The highest form of charity is to help sustain a person before they become impoverished so as to make it unnecessary for them to become dependent on others.

The word '*sukkot*' means 'booths', like the shelters the Jews lived in when they were travelling through the desert, or the shelters farmers use while gathering the harvest. During *Sukkot* (booths as in a desert dwelling) families build a temporary shelter in their yard, called a sukkah. The roof covering made of palm leaves or bamboo sticks, and the walls made of any material that can hold up to wind. Families decorate their huts with leaves, fruit and vegetables, along with their kids' artwork. It is traditional to eat meals in the *sukkah*, and some people even sleep in them during the week-long celebration. Rodger Kamenetz's book, *The Jew in the Lotus* (playing off The Jewel in the Lotus) centres on a historic dialogue between a group of rabbis who went to meet the Dalai Lama. Another rich grafted tradition. And so many traditions, so many reminders. This leads me to midrash.

Faith

CREATIVITY, IMAGINATION AND MIDRASH

For the unfolding of the universe your creativity is an essential as the creativity in the fireball... the fireball was a cauldron of creativity.
(Brian Swimme)

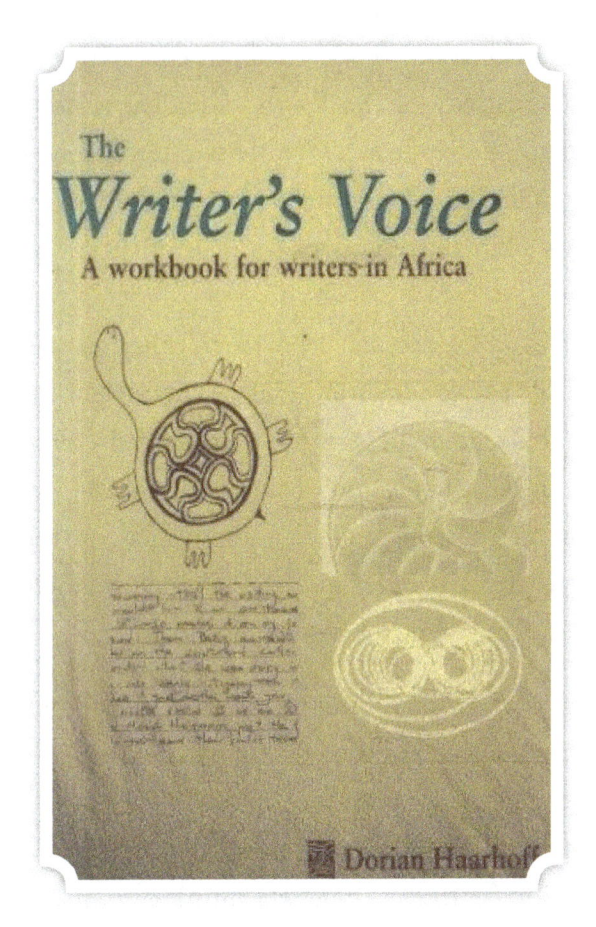

This entry is adapted from *The Writer's Voice*. Creativity is bedrock. The therapist Otto Rank understands neurosis as the resulting from our failure to entertain the artist in each of us. The theologian Matthew Fox concurs. 'We are whole and healthy only when we create' (Creation Spirituality).

Route 77

But how do we create? Perhaps part of the answer is not to colonise the imagination. Creativity is larger than our personalities. If we try to own it through our egos, it eludes us. It is in the air.

Brian Swimme believes that ever since the explosion of the first star, the universe has been ablaze with creativity. Human beings are the youngest manifestation. 'To learn about creativity we must begin to understand the creativity of the Earth.' Creative is not something we become. It's what we already are. Creativity often involves shifting from our fixed ways of seeing – standing on our heads, looking through our legs. Creativity's siblings are enthusiasm, curiosity, insight, connection, imagination.

Betty Edwards, a Californian art teacher, calls creativity a chameleon concept (*Drawing on the Artist Within*). A chameleon merges with its surroundings. This image suggests that creativity is rooted in everyday existence. It's not only a question of thunderbolts and lightning. Here's Betty Edwards on the stages of creativity based on the work of the German physicist Herman Hermholtz, a French mathematician Henri Poincare, and an American psychologist Jacob Getzels:

1. Insight into a problem (asking different questions)
2. Saturation (steeped in the idea, researching)
3. Incubation (mulling over the problem)
4. Illumination (the moment of insight)
5. Verification (putting in concrete form)

Thomas Moore, in *On Creativity*, believes that creativity is not restricted to the spectacular but lives in the ordinary. He stresses the idea of creator as maker and doer. Making a pair of shoes is a creative act. The ordinary can be accomplished in creative ways. Abraham Maslow argues that the ordinary is sacred. Moore also suggests that when thinking about creativity, we over-stress originality. Much creativity involves recovering a lost tradition and applying it anew to our time and place. Jung was highly creative, yet many of his ideas came from the Greeks and can also be found in Romantic poetry, written a hundred years earlier. In the same way there might be something creative in the mediaeval art of alchemy or in tribal society that is lacking in our ailing modern societies. In connecting to this wisdom we become part of an ancestral creative tradition.

Creativity lives in the image, in the combination of two words, ordinary in themselves. But when these word-sticks spark they make fire. We all reveal our creativity in our dreaming. We conjure up images that delight us and make us tremble as they interact with other images.

Here's an imagining while at a rainy retreat:

Walking Meditation

the bird calls. we rise
from mat and pad
and follow its path.
robes swish and sway.
a light wind runs along arms.
step in single file,
circle the Buddha who sits
unmoving in the middle,
bird perched on a branch.
round the labyrinth
silent at centre
we shape an outer ring.
hoop the zen garden
where bird lights on a rock.
wing and feather led, we

Route 77

> loop back to the hall
> where we sink onto mats
> still as the candle wick.
>
> and all the while, between gongs,
> we have sat here like stones
> under rain on the roof.
> yet we find Buddha.
> labyrinth, zen garden
> all inside us now
> after the imagined
> ankle flex, arm swing shuffle
> follow of the bird.

Enter Midrash.

The work of imagining God takes place in community, and each person has her or his share in owning and shaping a theology. The plurality of perspectives creates a many-sided living midrash.
(Peter Pitzele)

Midrash – The imaginative fleshing out of an Old Testament story, supplying details that are not recorded and adding a personal interpretation. Fleshing out the bare bones. Midrash = Jewish exegesis derived from verb *'darash'* – to search… investigate… seek something undiscovered. Midrash – a ritual evoking the Divine through dedication, emotional involvement and expectant inquiry.

Rabbi Akiva (50-135) heard that his student Ben Assai was expounding the Torah surrounded by a nimbus of flashing fire. He hurried to investigate. Was his pupil attempting a dangerous mystical flight to the throne of God? "No," Ben Assai replied, "I was only linking up the words of the Torah with one another and then with the words of the Prophets and Prophets with the Writings. And the words rejoiced as when they were delivered from Sinai, as sweet as at their original utterance."

Akiva's fame had reached heaven. Intrigued, Moses came down to earth and attend his class. He sat in the eighth row behind the other students. To his embarrassment he could not understand a word of Akiva's exposition of the Torah as revealed to him, Moses, on Mount Sinai, "My sons have surpassed me." Moses reflected ruefully, like many a proud parent, as he made his way back to Heaven.

You have already met my midrash poem on Eve. Here's my attempt at putting midrash flesh on Mrs Lot:

The Salt of the Earth

...and Lot's wife looked back
and was turned into a pillar of salt.

the couple stumbled from home
as directed by angels,
leaving wickedness, relocating.
the man set a steady compass,
heady with divine injunction.
body angled on a crow line
he flies from quake and fire.
the woman following,
like Orpheus before her,
reneged on forward story.

her eyes circled the city of Sodom
that had been hearthstone.
they swept like the reed broom

Route 77

> wielded before leaving.
> she hunted under the sleeping mat
> for a memory shaped
> by the weight of their bodies.
> she searched the wilderness.
>
> and after the brimstone bolts,
> he pressed on alone
> while her salt-lick tears seasoned
> the diet of the wild.

And a great midrash read – Peter Pitzele's *Our Father's Wells: A personal encounter with the myths of Genesis.* In an attempt to understand himself, his heritage and the dilemmas of manhood, Pitzele looks to the legends, parables and fables in Genesis. Pitzele recalls his own quest for spirituality and his leadership of a psychodramatic group, in his re-telling of the major Genesis stories through interpretative fiction. He journeys back from his various odysseys in alternative faiths to search out the roots of his own birthright.

Scripture is full of dramatic possibility. The great cast of archetypal figures – Adam, Eve, Cain, Abraham, Sarah, Isaac, Jacob, and Joseph – are given a fuller dimension in his rendering of their stories. Woven throughout are threads of Pitzele's own personal history, demonstrating the relationship between myth and experience, between the profound images of the Western spiritual tradition and the life of a man who wrestles with his roles as father, husband, son and brother. The Genesis stories, Pitzele writes, are 'slippery, quick, powerful, alien, intense, unremitting. They grip me, and I grapple with them'. Pitzele suggests we dig anew the ancient wells that our fathers dug.

So I dig, I dig.

Faith

A BUDDHIST FLOWER

There is a lovely road that runs from Ixopo into the hills. These hills are grass-covered and rolling, and they are lovely beyond any singing of it.
(Alan Paton, Cry the Beloved Country)

For more than a quarter century I have been teaching at the Buddhist Retreat Centre in these hills. One of the special places of the earth. Teaching a men's group, poetry, ZenPen, Healing the Family Tree, Journaling. Qigong in the dawn, swim in dam in the cool afternoon.

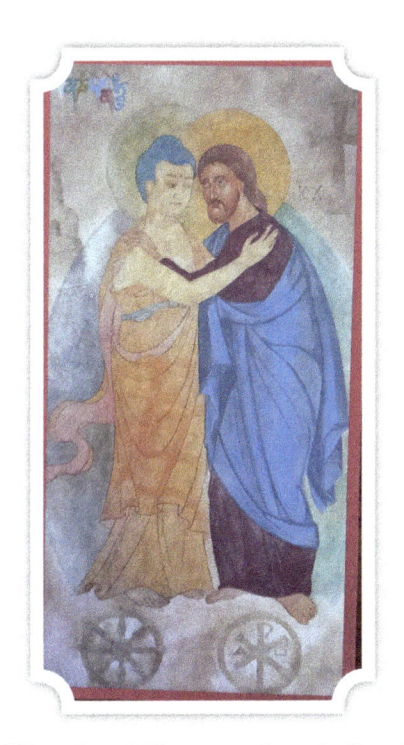

In the Little Way chapel Temenos: icon by Brother Maidwell

I come here via experience rather than dogma, letting breath and heartbeat lead. I'd fail an elementary exam on noble truths and pillars.

Route 77

The Buddha asked the meaning of his name, responds, "I am awake." In his first sermon Buddha held up in silence a flower. This echoes Angelus Silesius, the mystic – 'Sin is not noticing a flower grow'. Mystics like him are into koans too (riddles that bypass intellect). I love his:

> God, whose love and joy are present everywhere,
> Can't come to visit you unless you aren't there.

Here, in Ixopo, poetry pours forth. One morning I had eaten out of a white bowl but had the day before bought a blue bowl from the BRC shop with Buddha sitting at the bottom. I inserted this into the poem, trusting the imagination. I shared the poem after breakfast and one of the participants smiled, "I'm so glad you did that. I made that bowl."

Poems find their way into BRC recipe books *Quiet Food* and *The Cake the Buddha Ate:*

A Long Loaf

I bite into a slice of Ixopo toast
spread with butter and marmalade.
each mouthful stretches a long way.
do the ancestors lick their lips
at the mark of my teeth in the bite?
and the rhythm of my circling mouth?
there are as many of them watching
as there are crumbs in the loaves
rising from today's baking.

each bite is for the hunger
of my mother and fourteen siblings,

Faith

    my grandmother and her hunger
    and thirst for righteousness.
    for all the forefathers
    who hungered for enough,
    such as my grandfather
    who looked through a bottle
    at the kaleidoscope of his life.
    I chew for my father's line –
    his brother killed in war,
    his sister dying in infancy.

    this butter is not scraped thin
    but lies thick as curd.
    the rind and peel bitter-sweet,
    layered rich as an autumn stream,
    spills over the edge of the bread.

    come ancestors, dip your fingers
    in this syrup, lick them clean.
    share the gold crust, this family manna.
    may you taste fragrance
    in lemon and orange blossom.
    I bite this bread for all of us.

Then teaching at Emoyeni for the past five years, near the town with pretty woman name, Mooinooi. Poems pour out there too:

    Tree Wrap – Emoyeni

    here at this retreat centre
    a tree rises and rests
    between talk studio and

thatched meditation hut
the beams draped in quietude.
its limbs shade the green leaf wall
where we move through an archway
between two modes of being.

as the trunk ascends
above ground
it splits into two, branching
into bough then twig.
bronchi in both lungs
breathe in and out the sky.
the leaves bow,
windbrush and whisper
while the roots tunnel
under round rocks and earth.

both belong to the studio conversation
while offering silence to the hut.
as above so below,
the tree reaches across
and wraps speech and silence
in its curved arms.

Encounters with people drawn there, who become lifelong friends. One of whom is Kosheek Sewchurran, Director of the EMBA at UCT Business School who invited me to present to his executive students the ZenPen offering. I have done this for seven years and helped midwife his book on leadership. Yes, Dalai Lama, may my religion be kindness.

INDIAN MYTHOLOGY

The Upanishads, Hinduism's oldest sacred text, offers the notions of the self and afterlife. We live in an illusionary world which perpetuates the cycle of death and rebirth (*samsara*). The myths of the Hindu pantheon speak in the same tongue.

The Child God

once he played in the sand
filling his head, hands and mouth
with its grains, sticks and leaves.
his mother prized open his lips
to clean the grit from his teeth.

her mouth opened in wonder.
she beheld in the great cave,
milky way and morning star.
the tongue, a great whale,
frolicked in the spittle tide
that swirled round molar rocks.
the earth rotated on its axis
and the sun and moon balanced
on inner lips and palate.
an arch opened to the heavens.

and then the boy as gently
placed his sandy hand across her lids
and closed them, drawing blinds.
and when she opened her eyes again
she saw only spit and sand
in a small boy's mouth.

Route 77

Then the joy of working alongside Rajie Tudge (also met at the BRC) over some four years and the emergence of her memoir, *Teaching the Canna Bush, My journey through apartheid and beyond*, rich in Hindu mythology. I wrote praise poems for her and Brian her husband when invited to their celebration. Here is part of the poem:

Rajie Woman of the Moment

All hail Rajie with stories wrapped
in the folds of her sari and academic gown,
rich in shade texture and adventure.
How shall we sing of travails, travels and triumphs
of a barefoot girl who wrote of an imagined shoe,
sang full throated Tagore's anthem
stick in hand, instructs the canna tree?
An unauspicious beginning when
The astrological almanac
predicted the gundohs. a hard life.
a life of service
She who grew up in Ganesh street
prayed early to Lord Ganesha
remover of obstacles friend
of scribes and writers.

In Hindu scripture there is a text: Two birds, each the friend of the other, perch upon the same tree. One eats the sweet fig while the other looks on without eating. We are both participator and witness to our actions. The paradox is that when I watch (witness) myself with compassion, I am more intimately involved in the moment. Like watching myself on a movie screen.

Faith

Here's to life, to faith so rich in myth. Here's to the lore of India.

MYSTICS AND GNOSTICS

God is the breath inside the breath

Mystics point fingers to the great mystery. Don't look at the finger. The above quotation could come from any one of the faiths. It happens to be Kabir, 15th-century Hindu mystic poet and saint.

I have heard Tim Freke speak in Cape Town and in Boulder. In The *Jesus Mysteries and other works* he claims that early Christianity originated as a Greco-Roman Egyptian mystery cult. He explores parallels between Jesus and Osiris-Dionysus. So no historical evidence of a person but a mythical figure to induce the Christ consciousness in us. My metaphoric belief bubble can take this in for the power is in the story.

Enter the Gnostics later in my life. Reading though the night Elaine Pagel's *The Gnostic Gospels*. Feeling like Keats "On First Looking into Chapman's Homer."

> Much have I travell'd in the realms of gold,
> And many goodly states and kingdoms seen…
> Then felt I like some watcher of the skies
> When a new planet swims into his ken…

and like ee cummings:

> here is the deepest secret nobody knows
> here is the root of the root and the bud of the bud
> and the sky of the sky of a tree called life which grows
> higher than soul can hope or mind can hide.

Route 77

All these Gnostic gospels did not make the first team. Contemporary texts suppressed. *Gospels of Thomas, Mary Magdalene et al*... Here is my lineage. Individual interpretation rather than orthodoxy:

The Red Earth Jar

in the sweat of December '45,
when I was one,
a peasant led his camel
to the mountains of Jabal.
he dug up sabakha, top soil,
at Hammadi Caves,
for his garden.
his steps echoed
in the chambers
of buried Egypt.

his blade intoned a strike.
he scraped the contours
till an urn emerged,
half the measure of a man.
he traced its neck and buttocks,
wondering. his blood-beat up,
he raised his mattock
and smashed it to starry shards.
he resurrected no gold, no silver,
but papyrus, Coptic script,
caught in loose leaf and leather,
one embossed with an ankh.

his camel carried his find,
dumping it at his mother's oven.

Faith

she fed straw and shredded leaves
to the fire. the rest she gave
to the village priest
who passed it to a reading one.

so, word by word,
the news spread throughout the land.
as Ali al Samman's mattock
unstopped the Gnostic gospels.
from a 2000-year sleep,
the jinn leapt from the red earth jar.

This is the *Gospel of Thomas* with two of the sayings of Jesus:

If you bring forth what is within you, what you bring forth will save you. If you do not bring forth what is within you, what you do not bring forth will destroy you.

When you make the two into one, and when you make the inner like the outer and the outer like the inner, and the upper like the lower, and when you make male and female into a single one…when you make… an image in place of an image, then you will enter the Kingdom.

So unlike Luther, I'll keep shifting my stand according to how the earth moves and light falls. In this story the mystics are here there and everywhere, hiding in vowels that breathe the divine. I have written of these who reflect divine light unlike Lucifer who fell from heaven for he saw himself as the source of his own light. Stephen Spender's poem applies:

> Who wore at their hearts the fire's centre.
> Born of the sun, they travelled a short while toward the sun
> And left the vivid air signed with their honour.

Another is Julian Norwich (1343 – after 1416), an anchorite who wrote the best known surviving book in the English language written by a mystic, *Revelations of Divine Love*. The first book written in English by a woman. He said, "Not 'Thou shalt not be tempested, thou shalt not be travailed, thou shalt not be dis-eased." But he said, "Thou shalt not be overcome."

It might be fun to compile an alphabet of mystics – R for Rumi, K for Kabir, E for Eckhard, T for Theresa, H for Hildegard and so forth… No wonder the 3-M trilogy of words, mystic, mythic and mystery are in English so close.

4

VOCARE

TORTOISES ALL THE WAY DOWN – WHY I DO WHAT I DO

Here are eleven of the many balls I juggle in response to the great question, "What is your work in the world?".

A man dies and finds himself in a pleasant meadow. He thinks how wonderful to have a house here. And low and behold, a house appears. And what about a river? And a boat? These also appear. And so he wonders, well, a family too. And the family arrives. And so it goes. Until one day he goes to the organiser and says, "I would like to work." And the organiser responds, "Nobody works here." So he says, "Then perhaps then I'll try hell instead". The organiser says, "Where do you think you are?"

1994. At fifty, restless with Mickey Mouse academia, apart from our English Department (Brian Harlech-Jones, Helen Vale, Richard Aitken, these three be Quakers – William Hofmeyr, Annemarie Heywood, Ishmael Mbisi, Laura Otaala et al) and a scattering of enlightenment in a few other Departments such as German, Biblical Studies, Library Science. This among a cacophony of pseudo academics with ostrich egos and minimum creativity.

Route 77

At that first winter School at UNAM, I offer a writing course. I discover my *Vocare*, my calling. In response to a question from friends, "Why do you want to teach writing and write a book on this?" I write this ballad:

Ballad of Fathom Fifty

I dreamt I lost a sailing ship
Deep in the psychic sea.
My ship went down beyond the sound
In infant history.

It seemed I went adventuring
Beyond known latitudes.
Map-maker hands had faltered there
All charts were rough and rude.

Before we sank we must have sped
In primary colours bright.
Our sail unfurled in mighty wind.
We tacked through waning light.

The waves that cracked her ribs
Were made of pirate: and of storm.
And then she struck a hidden reef
In tropic currents warm.

She lay so long that I forgot
She lined the ocean floor.
No diver ever saw this hulk
No shanty sang the lore.

Vocare

And barnacles encrusted her
Fish monsters made her home
Beneath the jagged white shark tooth
Beneath the great whale foam.

Through waves that roll in from this wreck
I slowly know its awe.
Now I am bound to salvage work
Through rhyme and metaphor.

I dream I find ten thousand balls
So I can see her float.
Each one an image rich in air
Deeper than anecdote.

I dive deep down in fear of bends
Hair rises in my nape.
The cage of story carries me
I feel its treasure shape.

As I inject her hulk with breath,
She rights and rises like a fin.
Our hull and mast ride now the wave
The poet's galleon.

While staying in a home of a Pretoria artist friend, an ex Westerford colleague, Penny Bailey, I read a book on healing family patterns. I come across an aha. Trained as a teacher and training as one, the constant debate – are you nature or nurture, genes or environment – never satisfied me. Then in this book I see a Chinese triangle of influences. Shaped we are through *Chi* (environment), *Jing* (sexual energy or genetics), and the third, maverick wild card *Shen* (vocare).

Route 77

In the Platonic myth, the Lethe flowed around the cave of Hypnos and through the Underworld where murmuring induces drowsiness. When the souls of the dead passed into the afterlife, they had to drink from the river to forget their past life and be ready for reincarnation, forgetting why they had come. Our task is to find out why we are here – our calling. This time round this is why I am here. Yes, William Hutchinson Murray (attributed to Goethe) you speak true:

> Concerning all acts of initiative (and creation), there is one elementary truth that ignorance of which kills countless ideas and splendid plans: that the moment one definitely commits oneself, then Providence moves too… A whole stream of events issues from the decision, raising in one's favor all manner of unforeseen incidents and meetings and material assistance, which no man could have dreamed would have come his way. Whatever you can do, or dream you can do, begin it. Boldness has genius, power, and magic in it. Begin it now. Whatever you can do, or dream you can, begin it.

End 1997, age fifty-three, I jump into the pages of the *The Writer's Voice* to live them. To live by Faith. Farewell pension, medical aid, housing subsidy, end of month cheque. The book is launched at the Durban Country Club early 1998. And all I've done with the first fifty-three years will feed the adventure. Teaching, reading, Life Line, travel, dead ends, errors…

> Nothing,
> is lost, sweet self
> Nothing is ever lost.
> The unspoken word

Vocare

>Is not exhausted but can be heard.
>Music that stains
>The silence remains
>O echo is everywhere,
>the unbeckonable bird.
>(Lawrence Durrell)

The teenager en route to minister (his 14-18 certainty) is to become a metaphoric one. So say many friends. St Francis leads the way:

>Lord, make me an instrument of your peace:
>where there is hatred, let me sow love…
>where there is despair, hope;
>where there is darkness, light…

So I fall into the life of a story tinker:

Story Smous

he travels, he tinkers
creaks his wagon
into the marketplace
and drops the flap
to display bottles,
all tints, shapes and hues.

roll up. try this patent.
pops the cork
and a whiff of story
breathes from the neck.

Route 77

> stories for sleeping
> for the knocking of the heart,
> rogue-romp adventures.
> tales to raise the veil,
> the rainbow and the shades between.
>
> this one tastes
> like licorice on the lip,
> sambuca black.
> but look how the light
> breaks in on the dark liquid.

For some seven years before I leave Namibia, I moonlight to bridge university as salary and living out on a limb. The city Windhoek is abuzz with foreign embassies. Our children at school with theirs. I teach English at the French Embassy. At the American Embassy, U.S. officials and local Namibians are not jiving. So we go off for a weekend, where they draw in crayons a picture of work they did as a child, with their non-dominant hands. Ambassador pairs with caretaker: Caretaker: Here is me looking after my father's cattle in Ovamboland. Ambassador: And here is me looking after my father's horses in Kentucky.

On Monday when Mr Caretaker comes to work he is no longer merely in a caretaker role. He is a person with a shared story. A year later they tell me how this impacted positively on their relationships.

Dan McAdams – *Stories We Live By:* 'If you want to know me then you must know my story, for my story defines who I am. And if I want to know myself, to gain insight into the meaning of my own life, then I too must come to know my story.' This echoes William Stafford's *A Ritual to Read to each Other:*

Vocare

> If you don't know the kind of person I am
> and I don't know the kind of person you are
> a pattern that others made may prevail in the world
> and following the wrong god home we may miss our star.

And SIDA – Swedish Aid Agency. Five years on after Independence 1995. Where has all the kroner gone, long time passing? What has been done with the cultural support? I travel throughout Namibia meeting the groups/organisations who received the money. I base my report on the parable of the sower = donor: "Some seed fell along the path, and the birds came and devoured it. Other seed fell on rocky ground… other seeds fell into good soil and produced grain…" (Mark's Gospel). Behold (surprise surprise) government birds devoured it. Small focused enterprise seeds produced harvest. The battle between accountability and entitlement.

The time comes to leap. Will the parachute billow open? The stories in this section touch on the varieties of blissful work. Tortoises all the way down.

Route 77

COSMIC LAND AND OCEAN: LOGO

The waters; the moon; the Earth Mother;
the beginning of creation; time;
immortality; fecundity; regeneration….
In China it is possessed with oracular powers.
The Cosmic Tree grows out of the back of the tortoise.
(J. Cooper, An Illustrated Encyclopaedia of Traditional Symbols*)*

Creative Wordshops

Dorian Haarhoff

082 873 6802

dorianhaa@gmail.com
www.dorianhaarhoff.com

storyteller facilitator speaker writing-coach poet

Enter the tortoise

Tortoise appears as logo on books and card, courtesy of Annie, Bob and Dominic. I am often asked why the tortoise. A corporate designer tells me they won't take you seriously. My inner response – then they are somebody else's client.

The tortoise/turtle swims in the cosmic ocean of stories. There's no culture nor country without a tortoise / turtle myth. Here is one:

The Tortoise who saw the World

One morning Tortoise rested at a waterhole. Eagle landed next to him. Tortoise said to Eagle, "Look at this huge waterhole and these reeds. This is all there is."

Vocare

Eagle flapped his wings and ascended, bearing Tortoise in his claws. Tortoise saw the pond slipping away, becoming smaller and smaller. He saw the other animals running across the plain. Eagle flew so high that Tortoise saw the curve of the earth.

Eagle set Tortoise down back at the waterhole. Tortoise travelled as fast as he could go to tell his tribe the world he'd seen when he ascended on Eagle's wings. The other tortoises said, "Nonsense, you were dreaming. The waterhole and the reeds – that is all there is."

But one tortoise asked, "Where can I find that eagle?"

This creature has many symbols inscribed in its shell. In China the cosmic tree grows from the back of a tortoise. Some say the shell was used for divination. Precursor of the I Ching?

> In the beginning
> there was a great tortoise
> who supported the world.
> Upon him
> all ultimately rests....
> He is all wise
> and can outrun the hare.
> in the night his eyes carry him
> to unknown places.
> (William Carlos Williams)

I too travel with my house on my back. And since I indulge in word play, there is the Alice in Wonderland remark, "We called him tortoise because he taught us".

Once around 2004, the tortoise logo ended up on a bag of a narrative family therapy conference in Durban. I shared this story there:

Route 77

How Tortoise Cracked his Shell

> There was great feast in the sky and the sky gods invited all the birds. Tortoise wanted to go along too so the birds carried him. On the way tortoise explained that when you dine with gods, the custom is to give yourself another name. "My name will be 'Everyone'" he said.
>
> When they got to the feast and saw the spread, the birds asked, "Who is this food for?" The gods responded, "Everyone."
>
> Tortoise gobbled it all up. All the birds went hungry. On the way back the birds dropped the heavy tortoise and he fell to the earth and cracked his shell. His wife helped him put it together.

A psychologist at the University of Nairobi came to up me. "Our logo in our Department is a tortoise because of this story. Tortoise cracked his shell when he was out of community." My Namibian friends, Petro and Matti Kimberg, have a sixty-year-old tortoise, Megan, as a pet. Call her she comes. Scratch her back, she wriggles. Ah yes, the creature recalls Namibia:

Tortoise Land

the back of this land is tortoise shell,
its case cast by ancient waves,
its plates taken from ancestral fish.

rivulets run dry round
outcrops and hills
scorched to a sea rim.

Vocare

> the head, soft belly
> and ring of lungs
> hide from a predator sun.
>
> it shifts on scaled legs
> in the shade of rocks
> that once were sea bed.
>
> and led by an amphibian chin,
> in folk-tale steadiness,
> it crawls ever towards water.

A professor and an old peasant woman are discussing how it is that the world is held up in space and does not fall down.
"Well you see," says the old woman, "the world rests on a giant plate."
"Interesting. And what does the plate rest on?"
"On the back of a giant tortoise."
"And what does that tortoise rest on?"
"On the back of another tortoise …"
"And what does …"
"Don't bother your head, professor. It's tortoises all the way down."

And it is stories all the way down.

Route 77

A WORLD OF STORIES

> *Sad is the man who is asked for a story*
> *and can't come up with one…*
> *The man rubs his chin, scratches his ear.*
> *In a room full of books in a world*
> *of stories, he can recall. not one…..*
> (Li-Young Lee)

We are surrounded by stories. What we offer our attention to shapes our reality. Offer us alternative responses to the changing and the challenging. As we work in a story heaven, undiscovered planets swirl into our ken.

So how do we know which story to cherish? Clarissa Pinkola Estés in *Women Who Run With the Wolves: Myths and Stories of the Wild Woman Archetype* writes:

> Asking the proper question is the central action of transformation – in fairy tales, in analysis, and in individuation. The key question causes germination of consciousness. The properly shaped question always emanates from an essential curiosity about what stands behind. Questions are the keys that cause the secret doors of the psyche to swing open.

Choosing the right story is much like asking the right question. Estes speaks of how stories can be medicine. A different story for a different ailment. "The story is not told to lift you up, to make you feel better, or to entertain you, although all those things can be true. The story is meant to take the spirit into a descent to find something that is lost or missing and to bring it back to consciousness again."

I often tell the "Norman the Barking Pig" story. In a wordshop a participant high up on the insurance scale of earning approached me,

"The entire day has been worth it just for that one story." I do not know what was happening in his personal or professional life or in what way the story spoke to him. The story found something missing and raised it to consciousness. I heard that shortly after the storyshop he had left the company and sought pastures new.

Choosing the right story arises out of paying attention to our inter and intrapersonal skills. Stories invoke a triple listening. I listen to myself, I listen to the story that arrives asking to be told. I listen to the audience – their eyes the bodies. Here is more of the Rumi poem:

> There is a moon inside every human being
> Learn to be companions with it.
> Give more of your life to this listening.
> As brightness is to time,
> So you are to the one who talks
> to the deep ear in your chest.
> I should sell my tongue
> and buy a thousand ears
> when that one steps near
> and begins to speak.

Acquired story literacy develops our intuition. Once, facilitating a workshop at a Buddhist Retreat Centre a little voice prompted me to tell an Irish pub joke. Incongruous as it seemed, I listened. One of the participants, Warren, came up, "I needed to hear that story as my battle is with alcohol." If you trust your intuition and read the atmosphere, you can be pretty sure that there is someone who needs the story that rises to your tongue.

A couple of years later Warren asked me to tell stories at their wedding at Madikwa where the names on the map – Derdepoort Abjaterskop

– feature in the Oom Schalk stories. Saturday night was Bosman for the guests. That morning waiting for the bride, the priest, groom, and storyteller under the canopy. After an Ovid story about couples growing old together, the Irish joke gets another airing:

> Paddy, on a Friday in the pub orders three pints of Guinness and sips them simultaneously. The publican advises, "Let me pour you one at a time as the others are going flat." Paddy explains "You don't understand. Two of my friends have left Ireland so I keep our friendship alive this way." This becomes a ritual, "Same again?" Three pints. Until one day Paddy responds, "No, only two pints." 'There is a hush in the pub as the publican approaches Paddy, "I'm terribly sorry about your friend." "What do you mean?' "Well, I assume that one of your companions has died." Paddy responds. "Oh they are both perfectly well. It's just that I have given up drinking."

While telling a story look into the eyes of the listeners. You will find clues there. For storytelling is an opportunity to lay down our story next to the one being told so that they can talk to each other. We can take Li-Young Lee's admonition seriously and invert it. Happy is the woman or man who when asked for a story, knows which story will speak to the moment.

Chimamanda Adichie talks about the dangers of a single story, "We can so easily get stuck in one version." Salmon Rushdie says that every story is an act of censorship. If we are telling it one way we're blocking out other ways of telling.

I often ask writers who believe they can't write, to find the name and address of the story-teller inside them. It is as if this is another person. Writing helps us find this companion self or selves. That part of me that

Vocare

accompanies all I do, the part that Carl Jung called the twin. But who are the other me's? And how do I find them?

In 2012 Jo Viljoen, friend and narrative therapist at Clearview Clinic near Pretoria, invited me to facilitate a wordshop. I chose as my title *Climbing Out of the Dark Hole: Stories, Spirituality and Substance Abuse.* This poem, based on a Nasruddin story, emerged:

Climbing out of a Dark Hole

in the story the man rides his donkey
down a dirt road. a bray of donkey riders
trot towards him. trembling at these robbers
he slips from his mount, climbs a stone wall,
drops into a graveyard and tumbles
into an empty grave. lies on his back
gazing at blue sky. his heart a flutter.

the men slide off their mounts, jump the wall,
creep through the burial ground and
circle the open grave. their heads appear
as black clouds in the rectangle of sky.
they are fellow villagers not thieves and ask
Nasruddin, what are you doing in this grave?

gazing up, the trickster speaks.
it's a long story. let's say that I am here
because of you and you are here
because of me. the story ends here.

but today in a wordshop bearing
the title of this poem, at a rehab centre,
once a wedding venue, in the chapel

> where two stained glass doves ascend,
> I add another ending. the villagers,
> who could be his other selves,
> wrist locked to wrist, raise him
> Lazarus like, from the black hole.
>
> for they each have a story as valid and as current.
> so they mount their donkeys and he-haw he-haw
> bray their way together down the rural road.
> clods of earth slide off his clothes and head.

Since we are fiction, our minds do not distinguish between imagination and experience. In imagining a story lies the possibility of healing and finding new ways of responding. Working creatively with symbols helps us select what we need from a story. Look at our lives and ring the changes. Stories are about remembering as opposed to dismembering so they help us reconstruct our lives.

In his book *The Uses of Enchantment*, child psychiatrist Bruno Bettelheim, documents how fairy stories, so rich in symbols, bring healing to traumatised children. In *The Healing Art of Storytelling, a Sacred Journey of Personal Discovery*. Sam Keen, author of *Your Mythic journey: Finding meaning in your life through writing and storytelling*, believes that communities provide us with our 'single best hope for healing because it requires something of us and gives us something back'.

'Freud's greatest discovery was not of the unconscious but... that a person receives simply in the act of telling her story to an attentive listener' writes Alan Parry. Our healing lies in this. The skilled listener might come up with questions that open up other insights and strengthen other aspects of the hidden story. I often find myself in the merry company of narrative therapists, working alongside them. I am a closet one of them.

TWO SISTERS: UNICEF AND SLED

Once there was a Storywell Project (UNICEF) – Creative Ways of providing Psychosocial Support to Caregivers who work with Orphans and Vulnerable Children.

A UNICEF story begins. 2006 – 2008. At Vermaaklikheid, a retreat on the way to Hemel en Aarde. We're there for a weekend. In the apartment above us, a family. A pediatrician shows an interest in story work. Soon his daughter Karin Leoning who works for UNICEF and I walk to the waterfall, talking story. There we set in motion training rural caregivers who look after vulnerable children in the art and craft of story. A team of four. I recruit El an environmentalist, Toto from an NGO, and Phillipa, a Ugandan storyteller. Off to Upington and beyond Nelspuit for a series of storyshops.

Here is part of our submission: Stories offer powerful ways of dealing with loss, grief and social adjustment – as well as creating a sense of hope. The Storywell methodology involves a play on words. We work in a way that enables participants to:

- story-well – tell stories that engage listeners. Listen attentively to stories as they are told, so as to both honour the storyteller and to learn from the story
- use story to get well – we believe that telling your story and being heard, that listening to others tell their stories, and honouring them brings healing
- a story well – develop a reservoir of stories

A story is like a well. Individual wells feed from communal streams. Teller and hearer drink the waters. These waters nourish body and soul and bring healing.
(The Storywell Team)

Route 77

I have learnt that stories are powerful. You can hide the positive in your heart and take it out when you are scared or broken-hearted. Stories give you a way of talking about your problems
(Caregiver 2006).

I'm not able to go on a UNICEF follow-up trip into Africa with Karin as I'm busy with her sister Carla over an October 2009 weekend. Carla works for SLED (Sign Language Education Development). We're at Eagle's Nest, Franschhoek where I offer 'Hearing-Impaired' teachers an understanding of how stories work and how to transfer the skills of storytelling and listening to develop stories for the sign language curriculum. The teachers prepared stories for filming. All this via an interpreter.

We found ways of invoking ritual. We lit a candle to help us focus on the simplicity of stories. In linking us to ancestral traditions, the candle evokes the energy of the story. Candles, like stories are portable. The wick like a story line, keeps the flame steady. Candles also allow in shadows for there is no story without a shadow. Given hearing challenges, some participants struggled to grasp symbolic thinking – essential to understanding the metaphors that stories evoke.

More education for Dori – telling stories with no one looking at his body telling or hearing his pauses, intonation, voice, and a delayed responses, all eyes on the interpreter.

In a 1 January collage (I create them every year to invoke intention). I had included an ear, not knowing why. On observation it was made of silicone. In October the image revealed itself in this work. For the collage surfaces the unconscious, which I believe is ahead of us. 'Now the ears of my ears awake. And now the eyes of my eyes are opened' (ee Cummings).

PLEASE SIR, MAY I HAVE SOME MORE? NAMIBIA

Namibia. Out of the desert sands, a call, responding to an article on my storytelling in *Flamingo* the Air Namibia in-flight magazine. "You taught me at the training college in 1979. I'm now work in Gondwana. We are keen on stories." Manni Goldbeck. Manni also taught my son Damian geography way back when.

So I go storyshopping at showcase events and train storytellers in the fourteen lodges from the Fish River Canyon in the south to the river lodges in the north. Themed lodges these. One as a shebeen at Etosha, another a vintage car theme. A 1940 Mercedes ambulance next to your restaurant table.

An imaginative company. It began buying derelict karakul farms in the south, taking down fences and reintroducing game. How to finance this? Finding lodges next to 'travel go-to' sites. As one lodge employee says in response to hearing the Tortoise and Eagle story, "That's what Manni the eagle did. He took the tortoise Gondwana into the air and looked at tourist attractions and built or bought nearby lodges."

Training storytellers in the art of night fire Saturday entertainment. Helping some 600 employees to be proud of the larger story. Whether washing dishes in the scullery or digging in the garden, they belong to the formative conservation story. At a Windhoek promotion training, two Gondwana tellers join me as we enact a myth I'd reworked. The telling is in Nama and English:

The Generous Elephant

When the Earth was young, and the breath of creation had not yet cooled, before Africa and Australia split at the hip, a great Gondwana super continent covered half the globe. The ways of the world were not yet shaped.

The animals of Gondwana ate each other, devouring the flesh and scattering the bones. One morning, after a night of hunting, they gathered. How could they stop eating each other?

Big Elephant, gazing over the hills into the far valleys, came up with a plan, "When I am dead I will be a mighty spirit. I will no longer need to eat or drink, and I will look after you."

"How will you do that?" asked the other animals. "My legs and trunk will become trees, my tail the branches, my tusks the roots. My ears and tendons will become plants that will spread across the earth to grow juicy melons and wild cucumbers. My hide will become grass to cover the ground."

All the animals cheered and accepted Big Elephant's offer. But how long does an elephant live and how long would they have to wait? Then Shiny Snake hissed, "I can kill Big Elephant with my poison." So she bit Big Elephant on the foot. Big Elephant's body and spirit changed into trees, plants and shrubs. Grass provided food for the animals. Seeds promised there would be food tomorrow.

Water-snake remembered her promise, "I'll bring forth underground waters." She slithered beneath the ground and fashioned the bubbling springs, and the grass and trees flourished. But the water didn't reach the plants on the mountains. They asked Moon and Stars for help but Stars and Moon had no water to spare. The plants at the springs wept for their thirsty siblings. Moon and Stars cried with them. Their teardrops fell at night onto the leaves. In the morning they were wet with dew.

Brawny Buffalo could never find enough grass to eat. He snorted, "I will make rain so more grass can grow." He galloped from spring to spring, flinging water up into the air with his head, tail, and shoulders. The sparkling water collected in the sky, forming clouds that made animal shapes. Winds blew them until they rained down on the grateful land.

Thereafter, all animals had water and food, except in drought years when the spirit of the Buffalo was called on once again. Hippo, Rhino, Giraffe, Antelope, and new Elephant ate the fruit, leaves and grass. But Lion, Falcon, and Owl said, "We will still prey on other animals." Vulture and Hyena said, "We will clean up the fields."

And so our world was shaped. Each living thing depended on the other and co-existed in harmony and balance (based on *Versamelde Boesmanstories 1* by GR von Wielligh, 1922.)

I sometimes stay at The Delight Lodge, Swakopmund when I do outreach work. Oysters for breakfast. A delight it is. Some story work with staff thrown in. And recently working with a Gondwana team to look at how we can use stories when interviewing potential employees, telling, say the Eagle and Tortoise story, and discussing how the story applies to working for Gondwana.

MENTORING: YOU ONE FOOT, ME THE OTHER

I have worked one-on-one across genres with many a client. I've never been sure what the difference between coaching and mentoring is though many have tried to explain. It's a whatever works. Matching approach to needs whether it's a novel for self-publication, poetry for friends, letters to an unborn great-grandchild, personal odyssey, spiritual quests, research, business ideas, motivation, depression, healing, a book on dying, life coaching, a film script, sea foraging, tales of a human rights lawyer, an encounter with the wild. Often the book team has included Annie and Dominic (proofing, lay out, cover design, liaison with printer, specs, getting publication onto Amazon et al).

Here's part of the mentoring flyer.

Need a Writing /Storytelling/Journey Mentor?

You make me sound like myself (numerous clients)

I'm interested in the joy of creating and crafting, and hold a deep belief in your potential. I can't teach you how to write/tell stories but will encourage you to teach yourself. How to invoke your skills, creativity and imagination and be at home with words. How to enter a space where the writing 'arrives.' How to be present. How to celebrate the five senses. A key question: how can the writing involve the reader as a creative participant? We can also use the writing process as a way of exploring new possibilities and potential or deal with personal/professional issues. I don one shoe, you the other and we walk through the territory you wish to explore, I another pair of eyes and ears.

Word of mouth passes me on. Though I prefer mentoring, sometimes the ghost writer request comes my way. Friendships born in many of these encounters.

CAN YOU SPEAK COW TALK?

Now and then a conference keynote request arrives. Once, taking on something that my heart was reluctant to take me to (a bank merger where clients needed ten million to be clients) my voice went on strike. Unhappy clients cancelled a second session. Corporates. Often the least favourite engagements.

Here is a part of the talk of one that was fun – a Dairy Conference in Port Elizabeth (2015) – *Can you speak cow talk*, with some bio built in.

Vocare

Ride 'em Cowboy

As a child I sometimes stayed on a dairy farm along the Vaal River. The dairy farmer, Boet Smith, was my father's friend, and his son John Smith junior was mine. I remember the milk room, holding a mug beneath the pouring spout as the milk cascaded down the corrugated wall. The milk fell into those heavy cans with the peculiar lids.

Then as a boy watching those cowboy films. Gene Autry, the singing cowboy, Roy Rogers and Trigger, The Lone Ranger, Tonto, and hi ho Silver. Hopalong Cassidy. Later wondering why they were called cowboys. These men were not bound to a cattle ranch or moving herds across the plains. They were lone heroes busting the badmen. The movie, seldom had anything to do with cows. At school I recall poems about cows. Gray's Elegy, *'The curfew tolls the knell of parting day. The lowing herd wind slowly o'er the lea.'*

Cow Bells

In 2014 I walked one the many Pilgrim Paths that criss-cross Europe and greeted many Norwegian cows announcing their presence via a cow bell. Apart from the obvious help in looking for strayed cattle, I wonder if the tinkling of a bell helps in milk production? Cow Bells go back a long way. Archaeological evidence dates back to 5000 years ago, in Neolithic China. Pottery cowbells then later metal ones tracked cattle, goats, and sheep. In Switzerland the Trychel, or large cow bell, was a rare and much-coveted item. In Swiss folklore, the Simmental legend tells of a young cowherd who strays inside a mountain. A fairy offers him three choices – herself, a treasure of gold coins, or a golden Trychel. Guess what? He chooses the Trychel. And as I discovered Simmental is also the name of a breed.

Then the call came in December last year to address you, the dairymen and women – farmers and folk connected to the dairy industry through passion and practical and technical know-how. When friends asked, "What will you talk about?" my response was a single word – "bull". Then my subject found me.

Synchronicity, meaningful co-incidence. In February 2015, I was storytelling in Windhoek, working with teachers and parents who encounter children along the autism spectrum. Stories can reach parts of the brain that other modalities don't seem to do. This is because stories work in sequence – one thing at a time then the next. They connect one thing to another showing how things belong. Stories connect the emotional to the rational brain. Stories are in line with how autistic brains fire – through association, repetition and through pictures and can help socialise and develop empathy – attributes that for an autistic child do not arrive naturally through observation but need to be taught.

An email arrived from the organiser asking for a photograph. ASAP. That day I was with Petra Dillmann who founded the Autism Association of Namibia. She had a camera slung around her neck so I asked, "Please take a photo." While she was snapping away I told her about the conference. She promptly showed me three books by an autistic woman, Temple Grandin. One title was: *Animals in Translation: Using the Mysteries of Autism to Decode Animal Behavior.* She was a revelation. I had found the theme for my conference talk."

Temple Grandin (1947) is an American professor of animal science at Colorado State, a best-selling author, an autistic activist, and a consultant to the livestock industry on animal behaviour. She also invented the 'hug box', a device to calm those on the autism spectrum. Like many children with autism, human touch creates anxiety. This has to do with over-sensitivity to sensory stimulation often making it difficult for such children to turn to other human beings for comfort.

The hug box consists of two hinged side-boards, with padding, which form a V-shape, with a control box at one end and tubes leading to an air compressor. A person lies or squats, between the boards and controls how much pressure he or she needs. Cattle squeeze chutes were Grandin's inspiration for her hug machine. On a visit to her aunt's Arizona cattle ranch, she noted that when cattle were confined in a squeeze chute for inoculation and pressure was applied they calmed down.

The subject of an award-winning, 2010 biographical film, *Temple Grandin*, she was listed in the TIME 100 list of the one hundred most influential people in the world in the 'Heroes' category. She is the subject of the Horizon documentary, "The Woman Who Thinks Like a Cow,'" (BBC 2006)

It seems that with the help of Grandin and others like her, we are moving away from the way some humans have regarded animals. God said, "Let us make man in our image, after our likeness: and let them have dominion over the fish of the sea, and over the fowl of the air, and over the cattle, and over all the earth, and over every creeping thing that creepeth upon the earth." (Genesis)

I'm reminded of Andy Merrifield's *The Wisdom of Donkeys: Finding Tranquility in a Chaotic World*: "The demon of speed is often associated with forgetting, with avoidance… and slowness with memory and confronting, (Milan Kundera's *Slowness*.) Andy Merrifield sets out on a journey of the soul with a friend's donkey, Gribouille, to walk amid the ruins and vistas of southern France's Haute-Auvergne. As Merrifield contemplates literature, science, truth, and beauty amid the French countryside, Gribouille surprises him with his subtle wisdom." (Google books)

In South Africa in 2005, Jurg Olsen, a policeman turned conservationist, and Karen Olsen started Jakani, a wildlife park near Plettenberg Bay for wild animals that had been mistreated. There was a viscous black leopard Diabolo there, and all he did was snarl. Jurg did not believe that humans and animals could communicate. Then came Anna Breytenbach the animal communicator. Anna has dedicated her life to interspecies communication on both personal and spiritual levels. She sends detailed messages to animals through pictures and thoughts (Grandin would concur). Anna transformed this snarling black leopard into a relaxed cat. Diablo became Spirit.

Here's a man–dog story. A man who dies on the same day as his dog. Man and dog walking along the road of death come to a high, white stone wall. A pearly gate in the arch leads to a street made from gold. They walk up to the gatekeeper. The gatekeeper tells them, "This is Heaven." The traveller asks for water for himself and his dog but the gatekeeper shakes his head, "You can enter and drink but we don't allow pets here."

> The man turns away and with his dog and takes to the road. They come to a farm gate at the end of a dirt road. The gate looks as if it has never been shut and there is no fence. A man leans against a tree. The traveller asks for water for himself and his dog.
>
> "Yes, sure, come through. There's a tap over there, and a bowl for your dog." They slake their thirst. "What do you call this place?" the traveller asks. "Heaven." "I'm confused," the traveller says. "The man down the road said that was Heaven." "The place with the gold street and pearly gates? Nope. That's Hell." "Doesn't it make you mad for them to use your name like that?" "No. They do our screening for us."

What about cows? What possibilities are there for this kind of interaction? In preparing this talk I came across *Milking to Music* The blurb reads: "The timing of milk production in bovines is a carefully balanced biological ballet. Stress can inhibit the release of oxytocin – a hormone key to the milk-releasing process. So the happiness of cows is very much on the minds of farmers.... Some farmers swear by playing relaxing tunes for maximum milk results" (Anna O'Brien).

So much to digest, to ruminate over, to turn over in our second stomachs. I'll leave you with an adaptation of the poem quoted at the beginning of this talk:

> The cowbell tolls the knell of conference end,
> The lowing herd wind slowly o'er the lea,
> The dairy farmers homeward plod their weary way,
> Thinking how to leave the cow world more stress free.

REFLICKOLOGY, YOUR LIFE, YOUR MOVIE

As an Athenium Fellow at University Colorado in Boulder way back when, I taught a Jungian approach to Story and Script. Jim Palmer who brought me to Colorado was an inspired Jungian. Here's blurb from the seminar: Life is a tragedy viewed close up and a comedy in the long shot (Charlie Chaplain)

Imagine scripting and directing your life as a movie. Let's apply the metaphor and techniques of cinema to scripting a life story. How would you work out the story board line? How do you include the many selves? How would you start it – with what dramatic sequence? Who would some of the other characters/antagonists be? What symbols and metaphors carry the energy? And technical skills? What angles, lighting? What close-ups? Zoom? Where would you cut certain scenes? What songs and theme music? And the ending... and rolling credits? What of dramatic sequence, moment, intent? What Archetypes and Myths, Metaphors,

Route 77

Alchemy and Symbols will theme your story? And techniques – angles, lighting, close ups, zoom?

Recently I watched *Heaven Can Wait* (1943), thinking about how it might apply to my life movie – Playboy Henry dies and arrives at the entrance to Hell, a final destination he is sure he deserves after living a life of profligacy. The devil isn't so sure. Henry recounts his life's deeds. *Route 77* is a similar recounting.

The movies we love offer clues to our stories. I often tell people to, "Write cinematically as if directing a movie." And so I share this poem:

Cinematic Speed

I love the generation film
that spans the forehead
of a family line.
the wheel spins hair
on a ninety minute reel,
forming fluff, now blond
then grey, now silver shade
sewn on a wintry head.
seasons stitch the hands
that scatter seeds, with moles.
baby skin toughens in the sun,
stretches then flakes to brittle bone.
the flower of a face buds,
blossoms and withers
in a cinematic speed up.
before my flickering eyes,
as a life flashes by in strips,
I see my stills in cycle.

LIVING THE MYTH

(partly adapted from The Writer's Voice)

My calling is themed by the size of the myth we live by. Earlier I wrote of Jung's question about the myth he was living. Authorities dictate to people what their stories are. At a time of transition, of personal and communal pain, there is a need for what the Jungian, James Hillman, refers to as 'restorying'. We unconsciously live out myths (mythos = story) that influence behaviour. The age into which we are born, the culture we live in, parents, teachers, tell us who we are, and we live the stories they have prescribed. Many of these providers of our myths have never explored or made conscious their own myths inherited from previous generations.

The word, 'myth' is problematic. We use the same term for two concepts. I'd like to distinguish them by introducing the idea of a minor and a major myth.

A minor myth is a prejudiced belief, a superstition, a group lie. It operates through inclusion and exclusion. In the name of race, gender, class, and religion. It draws a boundary around my group at the expense of another group. It declares we are the chosen people. Minor myths depend on defensive strategies and on guarding cultural boundaries. Control is key. This myth consolidates the tribe, whatever the tribe thinks itself to be.

Minor myths tend towards making things literal. The in-group believes the lie. The assumption is treated as a literal fact. Its truth is always simple and absolute. Humour, if there is any (this kind of mythology is serious business) is at the expense of an out-group. Minor myths distrust any form of make believe. As Chinua Achebe suggests, 'malignant fictions never say, Let's pretend.'

In minor mythology there is no room for alternative paths to divine grace. No room for the unknown, for minor myths presume that everything is knowable. In this sense minor myths constitute an ideology. It deals with answers not with questions and uncertainty. Terry Eaglelton argues that 'Ideology is a kind of contemporary mythology, a realm that has purged itself of ambiguity and alternative possibility'. Ken Wilber in *No Boundary: Eastern and Western Approaches to Personal Growth* suggests that wherever we create a boundary between us and other, be it humans in and animals out, we create a potential battle zone.

The mythologist Joseph Campbell writes, 'Every religion is true one way or another. It is true when understood metaphorically. But when it gets stuck in its own metaphors, interpreting them as facts, then you are in trouble'. Religious persecution and the denigration of traditional African religion by colonial Christianity are examples of this kind of trouble. The death sentence on the writer Salman Rushdie originates in a minor myth mindset. A good life story tolerates ambiguity. As James Hillman says, "literalism is sickness".

Major myths speak of our human commonality. Creation myths are major myths. In an Owambo myth (Namibia) people originated out of a tree stump. Australian aborigines believe the ancestors created themselves from clay and climbed out of the earth. Other cultures cherish beliefs about the ancestors and the afterlife. A Zulu myth tells how death came into the world. God sent the chameleon with a message, "Tell people they can live forever." But the chameleon was so slow. God in anger, sent snake with another message, "Tell people they have to die." The snake got to us first.

Greek myths deal with the lives of the gods. Some of them (Demeter and Persephone) explain how it is that we have spring and winter. Plato in his *Symposium* tells a story of how the sexes came to be. In its simplified form, once there was a creature with both sets of genitals. The gods feared this creature so one suggested that it be split in two. The two halves would be so busy finding each other they would no longer be a threat to the gods.

Major myths deal with the cosmic questions that surround the human journey – questions about origins and endings. In admitting so much is unknowable, these myths stress our common heritage as human beings who all suffer, deal with evil (our own and other people's) and death. Through them I discover how my own story flows into communal lands. How my story connects to other stories.

Major myths seek to understand the mystery of existence through story. They accept their fictionality. And in doing so they release their truths. Major myths also help us make connection to the earth, our home. Campbell comments on the way people anoint the land and are empowered by its energy. "The sanctification of the local landscape is a fundamental function of mythology."

Here is just one source that led me into this dimension of my calling – ex James Hollis, *On this Journey we call our Life, Living the questions*:

> Nikos Kazantzakis's novel, *The Last Temptation of Christ*, is a powerful rendering of this dilemma. The greatest temptation of Jesus the carpenter is to have an ordinary life, untroubled, comfortable, married. How do we find our vocation? In the end, it is through the capacity of the ego to forego its need for security and comfort in service to some deeper force. Usually, the choices we face require us to leave some familiar stance and move into the unknown. Usually, they require the acceptance of a greater level of anxiety, ambivalence and ambiguity than we find comfortable. They require us to grow, often painfully...

> In the end, the choice of vocation is also an acknowledgment that something is in fact choosing us. It may have little regard for what we, the ego, wishes. It is what the gods wish that determines vocation. If we can bear that truth, and serve it, then the gods and our vocation serve us, however perilous the path.

I am daily grateful for such a path and those such as Hollis and Wilber who have gone ahead to show the way.

WORDS ON A MIRROR: REMEMBERING OUR STORIES

> *Now I am a lake. A woman bends over me,*
> *Searching my reaches for what she really is*
> (Sylvia Plath, *Mirror*)

Another aspect to my calling. I have facilitated five courses in which participants contributed a life story, sharing space in a collection which we self-published. The process of wordshops and group plus one-on-one mentorship culminated in a grand launch where each writer received eight copies of the book. Each of the volumes dedicated to the writers who graced these with presence, courage and voice. Dominic designed the covers: *Words on a Mirror, The Door is Always Open, The Stone Road*.

In *Words on a Mirror*, the writers reflected on the process:

> When we arrived, we shared a common commitment – to write. When we left, we shared so much more. Having discovered a home space that offered enrichment and blessings, a magic maestro to keep us inspired and safe, and kindred writers for support, encouragement and laughter, we looked deep inside, opened our

hearts connected to our grief, dropped our masks, celebrated the child in us then looked in the mirror to see…ourselves.

Here is part of the Foreword to *Words on a Mirror:*

> An Empress approaches the sage, "You speak of interconnectivity. Can you explain this?" The sage escorts the Empress into a hall entirely covered with mirrors – walls and ceilings, doors and windows. The Empress sees their reflections disappearing into infinity in all directions. Then the sage suspends a crystal ball in the centre and lights a candle next to it. The Empress sees the candle reflected in the crystal, reflected in the mirrors travelling to infinity. Turning to her, the sage whispers, "That, Empress, is a mere hint of interconnectivity."

The title of *Words on a Mirror* connects to this story and speaks to the life stories in this volume. Words written on mirrors seem to be written on our bodies as we catch our reflections in the looking glass. The letters lie between ourselves and our image, perhaps to hint at the differences between living our lives and writing about them. And that we work in symbols to create the life we choose to write about. Mirrors too are slippery surfaces for 'words strain, crack and sometimes break… slip, slide…will not stay in place… will not stay still' (TS Eliot).

One of the pre-reading passages given to the group of participating writers (for our first writing teachers are the books we read) included Judy Cannato's *Fields of Compassion*. She writes of wider circles that too are mirrored, for we, 'view our lives as a composite of stories – of the archetypal, universal…that we experience collectively, and the individual and unique stories that… come with our personal lives. Like mirrors, spoken or unspoken, stories are powerful containers for the energy of our lives.'

In this collection, the writers share aspects of their days while the silent stories ghost behind them where the silver thins. For the act of writing arises from what we say and what the reader intuits through silence.

Writing is an organic process. These writers have grown and cultivated these stories from the first spontaneous outpouring in a creative writing workshop to the distillation of form in a crafting one. Then the necessary toiling, teasing the text into its aliveness. Finding resonance and echo as one part of the story opens a conversation with another part. Searching for the metaphors that place our experience in a larger world.

George Lakoff and Mark Johnson, in *Metaphors We Live By*, link metaphor to the life of the senses, 'It is as though the ability to comprehend experience through metaphor were a sense, like seeing or touching or hearing, with metaphors providing the only ways to perceive and experience much of the world.'

In these stories of ecstasy and grief, of courage and resilience, metaphors become a sixth sense. *Words on a Mirror* invokes ancestors, childhood, children, tribe, celebrating lives lived, landscapes evoked, suffering endured, the new grass of courage and hope springing forth green in season. These writers talk of power, of word *muti* and the shifts within themselves as each writer in her own voice, attends to the mirror, the crystal and the candle.

I marvel at this mystery of words on a mirror – how these writers shape a literary reality through creativity and imagination. When we attend to these twins, healing arrives as a silent third. We discover a fictional reality that like Don Quixote, searches for the *pan de trastrigo*, the bread that is made from more than wheat. And we invite readers to share in this feast.

5

WRITING LETTERS

The conversations in this section are adapted from eleven monthly blog letters from the last seven years – lifted out of some 280 letters (see doriahhaarhoffblog.co.za) These record the flares in my reading path, guiding me as I land the plane with its cargo of words.

NO, NO IT HAPPENED LIKE THIS: MEMORY AND IMAGINATION, MARCH 2016

Every time we speak, write or act,
we sacrifice completeness
(Deena Metzger)

Often we find ourselves arguing about past events – about who did what to whom and in what order. We disagree, not only over content but tone and emphasis – the way the other person loaded the words. This so easily degenerates into an endless tennis volley, "Yes, you did." "No, I didn't."

A couple go for marriage counselling. The therapist listens to the wife and husband's version separately and then says to each of them, "You are right." A trainee, present at both sessions, queries this response, "How can you say to both the wife and the husband that they are both right? The therapist turns to the apprentice and says, "You know, you are right."

Route 77

Years ago while facilitating a wordshop with teachers in Tanzania, I asked them to share a career breakthrough moment. Here is one response:

> One night I was sitting in a bar when a man approached. "You taught me twenty-five years ago."
>
> He was vaguely familiar. "You taught us Macbeth."
>
> "Yes, I loved that play."
>
> "I will never forget the moment when you put on a purple cloak, came down the spiral staircase and gave one of Lady Macbeth's speeches."
>
> I chose that moment because I never put on a purple cloak and there wasn't a spiral staircase in that school. Yet, I must have taught in such a way that I touched that person's imagination. He created it as his reality. That is my breakthrough moment.

There is a saying "Never let what happened get in the way of a good story." We are fictional human beings. We love stories because we are stories. Enter the imagination. Writer Patrick Harpur's *The Philosopher's Secret Fire* offers a history of the imagination: "The art of memory reminds us that memory is a dynamic place, a theatre, where the images stored take on their own life, interacting like the gods and myths of which they are composed. They create new connections and new imaginative configurations that we do not merely remember but recollect."

In a novel, *The Horizontal Instrument* by Christopher Wilkins, a watchmaker whose wife has died prematurely from Alzheimers, makes a watch as a way of grieving. He contemplates the illusory nature of time and memory. The book is divided into four quarters, each section prefaced with a quotation. Here's the quote for the Third Quarter, "I confess to thee, O Lord, that I am as yet ignorant what time is" (St Augustine). And another:

> Imagine the mind as a library where the books are memories arranged on the shelves, not according to subject matter or any alphabetical system but simply in the order in which they were acquired… suppose the rules of the library dictated that every time a book were taken from a shelf it had to be replaced not in its original position but right at the end with the newest volumes because it would now be a new edition of a previous one. Every time we retrieve a memory do we remember the remembering? And what becomes of the old memory – is there now a gap in the shelf?

The watchmaker concludes that the memory book is rewritten every time we take it out and replace it. Each multiple version has its own place in the time-line library. So before and after get confused. Each is a new version of that past. We are not just the repositories of our memories we are their authors… there is no detectable difference between memory and imagination.

The Chilean-American writer Isabel Allende talking about meeting her husband says, "I have several versions of how we met… at least twenty. And I'm sure they're all true. He has one. And I'm positive that it's not true."

Here is the Chinese American poet, Li-Young Lee on memory. His father, A man who devised complex systems of numbers and rhymes, taught his children Mnemonics (a memory strategy via association):

Route 77

> Slender memory, stay with me...
> I was cold once. So my father took off his blue sweater.
> He wrapped me in it, and I never gave it back...
> ....there is no order
> to my memory, a heap
> of details, uncatalogued, illogical.

We are, when we remember, making meaning and myth from memory. In a sense reinventing our lives, painting like Tagore, our past. To allow others to hold their artistic version of the shared or separate past and not impose our truth.

So happy reinventing.

TAKING WORDS FOR A WALK: NOVEMBER 2016

This month I read *An Altar in the World* (Barbara Brown Taylor). Her book celebrates the body. She writes, "What is saving my life now is the conviction that there is no spiritual treasure to be found apart from the body experiences of human life on earth. My life depends on engaging the most ordinary physical activities with the most exquisite attention." One of her chapters is entitled, Practice of Walking on the Earth – groundedness.

She quotes the late Thich Nhat Hahn, the Vietnamese Buddhist monk: 'the miracle is not to walk on water but on the earth.' She tells a story set in Plum Village, a community in Southern France where he resided and taught many forms of attention, one being walking meditation. What happens when Thich Nhat Hahn asks somebody in a wheelchair to watch carefully and practise breathing? I was moved by this story and responded with this poem:

Wheelchair Walk

*to watch a monk's walking meditation
is like watching a lunar eclipse*
(Barbara Brown Taylor)

at Plum village a monk walks
in slow motion, bare foot,
the way only humans walk.
heel first touches the earth.

then the arch curves down
as in the lowering of a bridge.
the ball follows in a slow step
dance, with foot two, in tow.

five toes arrive one by one
to land on the grass,
a royal flush laid on a green cloth,
ace big toe the last to fall.

a woman in a wheelchair attends
to the monk's amble as she
inhales each subtle shift
in angle, posture, skin stretch.

in his arrest and mid stride gait
entrained in a moon glide,
her breath begins to walk
among the stillness of the stars.

and the monk's step instep
enters her lame limbs, and

Route 77

> passes through ankles, pores
> down to her quiet feet.
>
> like the child who walked once
> upon her father's feet, moonlighting,
> she no longer knows whose footfall
> caresses air or touches ground.

When I shared this poem with somebody at a poetry festival in McGregor, she responded that she had recently been to Plum Village and the sage himself, aged around ninety, was in a wheelchair.

I have long been inspired by the act of walking and its affinity to writing. The poet William Wordsworth, who "wandered lonely as a cloud" had walked over 300,000 kilometres by the time he reached midlife. Deena Metzger writes "When I was young, determined to learn to be a writer, I decided that there was an affinity between walking and writing... I practised walking like a writer, imagining what a writer might observe and think about. As I grew older the walk became longer."

No other creature walks as we do. Bruce Chatwin's *Songlines*, about Australian aboriginal creation myths, refers to how people walk along ancestral paths where the world was sung into existence. Ralph Waldo Emerson observed, "When my creative energy flowed most freely, my muscular activity was always greatest." In walking we can focus attention on what is happening to our bodies as we move. How do our limbs shift? Ankles? Feel thigh muscles contracting and expanding, our skeletons flexing. Listen to breathing and blood pulse beating.

So how about walking your first draft? If you don't have a dog, try what Dorothy Brande suggests – "take that rough draft of a story for a walk with you." You will stumble upon metaphors that line your path.

MAPS AND SCAPE IN STORYLAND: APRIL 2017

Do stories take place in space and time or are space and time stories?
(David Loy)

I love encountering mythic landscape in books, sometimes the map drawn in the frontispiece (*Harry Potter, Treasure Island, Lord of the Rings*). While aboriginal dreamtime places are stories... song lines, story lines, from horizon to horizon, to the Irish 'the literal representation of the country was less important than its poetic dimension. In traditional Bardic culture... every place had its legend and its own identity... what endured was the mythic landscape. Providing escape and inspiration' (R F Foster).

Numinous settings – island, forest, cave, undersea, mountain, desert – echo the tales set on/in them. They become story and aspects of story – character, atmosphere, and context. David Loy in *The World is Made of Stories* writes, 'Landscape is the palimpsest: a manuscript on which more than one text has been written, with the earlier writing incompletely erased.' Here's the redrawing of an emotional map:

Palimpsest Poem
palim, again, psestos, rubbed smooth

every poem is a palimpsest
where words hide words
in a layered manuscript.

it's a child's delight, inscribing
in orange juice ink, squinting
and raising the dim page to the flame.

Route 77

    take for instance, a merry widow's first version.
    anger lines the letters. yet how to hide relief
    for a hundred happy's at the patriarch's demise?

    so in literal vein and hidden metaphor
    she overwrites on parchment
    a story through a new-born season.

    now she steps into a garden of images
    where migrant birds return to perch
    among blossoms, the sun thawing their wings.

    she prunes and plants, plucks up weeds,
    light of foot. her words fall as compost,
    the spring is in her skip among sprigs.

    she plays Vivaldi's Seasons in the dawn
    and Rites of Spring in the dusk hours
    composing again another cover.

    she raids his cellar, now hers,
    dusts off and uncorks the shiraz-a-tazz
    bottled when she was an endless fifty-nine.

    so her layered landscape texts
    with buried ghosts and skeletons, soothe
    her widow's brow and keep her secrets.

Written beneath our modern obsession with land ownership stories, rising through like hidden orange juice (remember this secret childhood writing?) are the First Nations stories, Chief Seattle's oft quoted response to ownership, for example: "If we do not own the freshness of the air and the sparkle of the water, how can you buy them? Every part of the earth is sacred to my people. Every shining pine needle, every sandy shore, every mist in the dark woods, every meadow, every humming insect."

Here's Irish writer, Frank Delaney in his novel *Ireland*:

> I liken Ireland to whiskey in a glass – a cone of amber, a self-contained passage of time, a place apart, reaching out to the world with sometimes an acrid taste, a definite excess of personality, telling her story to all who would listen, hauling them forward by the lapels of their coats until they hear, whether they want to or not. But always, always – the story is the teller and the teller is the story.

Tales breathe at the margins of these storyscapes. Here is the beginning of one from my children's stories *The Guano Girl:*

> One misty morning Gaila left her grandmother's cottage and walked down to the harbour. "Aaai aai aai." She heard the cormorants calling along the shore-line. They swooped down to eat scraps of fish. Their droppings stained the quay like splashes of whitewash.
>
> Gaila lived in a fishing village on the coast of Africa. Here the Namib Desert met the sea. On one side the fog washed the Atlantic Ocean. On the other, high sand dunes reached from the coast back into the great land. It seldom rained here. The desert wind blew and sand covered the track that led to the outside world. When this happened Gaila sighed for she longed to see the world outside the village.

Route 77

And here's Anne Michaels, novelist and poet from her collection, *Skin Divers*:

> There is no city that does not dream
> from its foundations. The lost lake
> crumbling in the hands of the brickmakers,
> the floor of the ravine where light lies broken
> with the memory of rivers. All the winters
> stored in that geologic
> garden....

Maps unfold their own stories within stories. In pre-Google days I wrote:

To Scale

driving a country road,
we enter a farm stall
on the edge
of new terrain.
a local sells me
a one-to-four legend.
on the car bonnet
we unfold a region
that suddenly exists.

roads measure in quarter kilometers.
old man wind puffs his cheeks
above a pine grove that rises 3D,
towards the scudding clouds.
B and Bs, quaint-named craft markets
and a goblin geography

Writing Letters

> expand before our sight.
> the river passes a park, runs to a lake.
> fish jump through rainbows scales
> fine-fin defined, laughing.
> a hiker with a staff huffs and
> ascends a spiral mountain.
>
> we tread amid new lines
> and latitudes, through
> a village of signs,
> with fields and forests,
> fish and lake.
> we tumble wonderland
> to wander in scale,
> in a map unfolding.

When next you encounter a map, literary or geographic, rural or urban, may it transport you to these mythic scapes and infuse you with story.

In 2022 I based our writing theme for the Magic Carpet group on *Maps of the Imagination, the writer as cartographer* by Peter Turchi. Over the months we drew a writer's island, inhabited and worded it.

Route 77

POSTCARDS FROM THE EDGE, AUGUST 2017

My mother is a great artist, but she always treated her paintings like minor postcards.
(Isabel Allende)

Once we sent or received postcards – the image on one side and on the reverse the vertical line dividing message and address. *Slapstick seaside, Sufi temple, Parthenon. Wish you were here.*

Postcards from the Edge, a semi-autobiographical novel (Carrie Fisher), adapted into a motion picture, revolves around movie actress Suzanne Vale as she tries to reassemble her life. The prologue contains postcards written to her brother, friend, and grandmother. What of poetry? Here's a verse from Margaret Atwood's Postcards:

> I'm thinking about you. What else can I say?
> The palm trees on the reverse
> are a delusion; so is the pink sand.
> What we have are the usual
> fractured coke bottles and the smell
> of backed-up drains, too sweet,
> like a mango on the verge
> of rot, which we have also.

Postcards feature in the lives of musicians and writers. *Manuel de Falla* sent *Debussy* a postcard that depicted the Alhambra Gateway in Granada. This inspired the prelude *La Puerta del Vino* (The Gate of Wine.) Postcard lyrics abound. *James Blunt*: "I'm sending postcards from my heart." The golden age of postcards? From the late 1800s. Nowadays a popular collectors' craze – deltiology. Ancestor of pictogram? There are many writer postcards. Kafka, Kerouac, Hemingway. *Scott Fitzgerald* send a quirky one to himself. One of the exhibitions in the Synagogue at a Hermanus FynArts Festival, included fibre/fabric art Gina Niederhumer's work. It depicted 366 embroidered postcards for 2016. These were displayed in months.

A postcard can teach us to how to fill an ocean with a trickle of words. How metaphors expand space and meaning. This fabric idea inspired me to commit to writing post card size journal entries with a text of around seventy-seven words plus an image. As a daily practice this creates a ritual of intention and reflection. Quotes, stories, synchronicities, poems, insights, edge experiences find a home here.

Here is one sample: Today in a special needs school in Swakopmund, staff commented on a magazine picture of a vintage truck loaded with implements parked in Gondwana's Roadhouse Lodge restaurant where I story-worked in 2013. I asked, "What does the picture say about teaching?" A teacher responded, "Some children are empty trucks. I will help them load the truck with values, attitudes and skills and so they can go on their life's journey." (seventy words)

How about you writing a dozen postcards? Cut out a magic picture for each one.

Route 77

GAGA, JANUARY 2018

> *An aged man is but a paltry thing,*
> *A tattered coat upon a stick, unless*
> *Soul clap its hands and sing, and louder sing*
> *For every tatter in its mortal dress.*
> (Yeats)

Gaga (not talking of Lady) offers two dictionary meanings – no longer in possession of mental faculties, and enthusiasm, going gaga over something.

In 2018 I facilitated GAGA wordshops (Gracious Ageing, Grateful Ageing). These covered various themes – old bones, young ideas, new wine in old bottles, rituals, intimacy with self and others, cultivating the funny bone, exercise and energy, nourishment, the loveliness of slow, inner ear-inner eye, bodyfullness, life is a cabaret, 'in my end is my beginning", keeping the child alive, living your myth.

This interest arrives from way back. My mother, matron of a geriatric home introduced me to many aged beings. I'm blessed with friends splendid, vibrant in their mid eighties and beyond. Like a child I count the birthday in-betweens – halves, thirds and quarters. Joseph Campbell, mythologist, often quoted Browning's Rabbi Ben Ezra:

> Grow old along with me
> The best is yet to be,
> The last of life, for which the first was made…

Again I turn to Jacob Needleman 'Faith cannot be shaken. It is the result of being shaken'. Years ago I came across a dozen copies of his booklet *On Love* in Bikini Beach Books Gordon's Bay and filtered them to folk important to me. "The act of conscious attending to another person – when one once discovers the taste of it and its significance – can become the center of gravity of the work of love." It's rich in Rumi and Rilke quotes. Here's Needleman in another of his books, *Time and the Soul*:

> The exercise is simply this….Try sometime to treat your life like a script that has already been written, as a play in which you are only an actor rehearsing a part. Try to regard the immediate future as already existing.
>
> You are like a tiny insect crawling up a tree. The tree exists already, the roots, trunk, branches and leaves are all already there. What you call time is only your movement from the roots to the branches… The insect imagines that the branches and the leaves are appearing out of nonexistence, but it is not so. The branches and leaves are there, waiting.

In a letter included in *Take My Advice: Letters to the Next Generation from People Who Know a Thing or Two*, philosopher and writer Martha Nussbaum writes a recipe for GAGA ageing:

> What is the remedy of these ills? A kind of self-love that does not shrink from the needy and incomplete parts of the self, but accepts those with interest and curiosity, and tries to develop a language …to talk about needs and feelings.
>
> Storytelling plays a big role in the process… As we tell stories… we learn how to imagine what another creature might feel… we identify… and learn something about ourselves. As we grow older, we encounter more and more complex stories – in literature, film, visual art, music – that give us a richer and more subtle grasp of

Route 77

human emotions and of our own inner world. You will not be alone with an empty self; you will have a newly rich life with yourself, and enhanced possibilities of real communication with others.

Here is one of my 2017 poems for Annemarie:

Shape Shifting

you tell me you were
once upon a seventeen
in skin, slim-figured,
a bikini beach girl.

hour glass sea sand
drifted through you,
shoulder to hip to thigh.
well breasted. hair spiced
a shade of ginger pepper
running fire down your
waterfall of a back.

now past mid seventy your
maiden form has rounded,
concave to convex.
wrinkles show the road
your face has furrowed.
yet I sense still the
seventeen sparkle inside.

she's shape shifted
into your voice, gestures, timbre
and in your eye twinkle

> young as after ever.
> now a grain in seasoned wood,
> in laughter, mischief, your yes
> to the power of seven.

May Mary Oliver's words ring in our inner ears:

> When it's over, I want to say: all my life
> I was a bride married to amazement.
> I was the bridegroom, taking the world into my arms.

May we all, three score and ten plus plus give birth to such a self.

THE END OF STORY? JUNE 2018

Death closes all: but something ere the end. Some work of noble note, may yet be done, Not unbecoming men that strove with Gods.
(Tennyson)

Do you believe in an afterlife? Our myths reach back to our beginnings as thinking beings. Some people believe there is such an abode, some like Ulysses say, "death closes all" while for others who are convinced that we reincarnate, death opens an in-between-lives space. Given the mystery, we create an imagined reality, an extension of the life we know in time, distance, place and space. A bodily existence.

Pharaohs were buried with the artifacts precious in this life, needed in the next. Many cultures offer images of a geographic afterlife – an underworld or skyworld. The Mesopotamians thought the dead lived on in the Dark Earth. Caves or ponds could be an entrance to that place. Pacific islanders imagine a mirror image of the upper world. Divers in

Route 77

New Guinea claim to see the souls of the dead working in undersea gardens. In Navajo mythology, the dead also descend into a watery underworld. For the Ibo (Nigeria) the goddess Ala receives the dead into her womb. The Pueblo believe we become clouds.

While physical details differ, the themes in mythology and religion echo each other. The Persians gave us the word 'paradise' (a walled garden). In Zoroastrianism on the fourth day after death, we cross the Bridge of the Separator, which widens when the righteous approach. A maiden, the feminine embodiment of good works on earth, escorts you into the House of Song to await the Last Day.

The Ashanti people of Africa tell of Kwasi Benefo, whose four wives die. He travels to Asamando, land of the dead, to seek his lost loves, passing through a trackless forest. On the far side of a river, Amokye, the old woman who greets dead women's souls, allows Kwasi to cross the river where he finds the invisible spirits of his wives. Other African myths invoke an upside-down mirror image of a mountain. People sleep during the day and are active at night. Chinese myths tell of 'China ploughed under.'

Whatever our faith or non-faith, we project a story into the unknown. It features the familiar objects of this earth – doorways, gates, rivers, harps, flames.

In Judaism some rabbis use the term *Olam Ha-Ba* to refer to a heaven-like afterlife. The Talmud often interchanges this term with *Gan Eden* (the Garden of Eden). In Islam, Heaven is a garden where the faithful lie upon couches surrounded by 'bashful, dark-eyed virgins, chaste as the sheltered eggs of ostriches'. They drink from crystal goblets and silver vessels as 'immortal youths' hover about.

For C S Lewis, life after death involves a bus ride from a 'grey town'. A man waits at a stop till an angel bus driver arrives. The bus flies through the rain into a clear, pre-dawn sky. As it rises the bodies of passengers, it become transparent and vapour-like. Per contrast the landscape remains solid. Shining figures, known on earth, meet them and promise that as the ghosts travel onward and upward, they will become more solid. In the New Testament *Book of Revelation*, New Jerusalem has a wall with twelve gates, inscribed with the names of the tribes of Israel along with an angel. There are also twelve foundations, one for each apostle. A river of 'the water of life' flows from God's throne, and trees of life line the banks. The Buddha taught that desire is a flame that burns us, causes suffering, and keeps us tied to the cycle of death and rebirth for the flame continues burning into the next life. Nirvana is the extinguishing of that flame, which is also the end of suffering.

Yet in no time, no place (Utopos) no sequence, no motion, living in an after-death internal now, a story is not a possibility. This is the paradox. In this life we make meaning through sequence, motion, narrative. Beyond lies mystery. There is a Rabbinical saying that God created human beings because God loves stories.

This makes it all the more urgent to create and share stories of the living and of the dead. When we tell, like Lazarus, the dead resurrect in the telling.

Here's my poem on story as a gift to this side of life:

Once Ever After

fling your story
over your shoulder
as you walk into
the after-this-time mist,
crossing bodiless into

Route 77

eternity, Eden revisited
where no tooth and claw abide.

where oneness reigns
in storyless realms,
Nirvana, the source,
floating in the Bardo,
the arms of the promised virgins,
Utopia, no place no time.
no this-then-that sequencing.

be the bride facing away
who throws her garter and posy
for those still this side
of the veil, entangled
in the mystery of their narrative,
to catch it and hold it aloft.

for those who still plod in plot
shape, place, seeking pattern,
who live in the geography,
in history with invented calendars
thick with birth-death dates,
who entertain the drama,
the antagonist, the denouement.

who still try to reconcile opposites
through metaphor and conceits
mapping a route, a sea journey,
encountering the three muses
Paradox Ambiguity Irony
that you leave behind in your departing.

Writing Letters

> you who have once upon
> happily after, crafted
> experience and imagination into art,
> leave your tale as gift for those
> who carry theirs in a backpack
> like the allegorical character
> in Pilgrim's Progress, journeying
> though the slough of despond,
> the hill of glory to the eternal city,
> shifting the weight of ever
> into whatever happens next.

As in Tennyson's *Ulysses*, we dip our oars and row into the unknown:

> Life piled on life
> Were all too little, and of the one to me
> Little remains: but every hour is saved
> From that eternal silence, something more
> A bringer of new things…

And what of new stories?

Route 77

THE PHANTOM IN THE WORD: WRITER'S BLOCK, APRIL 2019

Delay is natural to a writer… like a surfer – he bides time, waits for the perfect wave… Delay is instinctive.
(E B White)

When I face the desolate impossibility of writing 500 pages a sick sense of failure falls on me… then I gradually write one page and then another. One day's work is all I can permit myself to contemplate.
(John Steinbeck)

You hear of writers talking about 'writers block'. What is this panic/emptiness/despair/loss we feel when confronted by a blank page/screen? We have run out of ideas and writing energy. Here are two approaches to this challenge.

We can either run around the block… tease the fruit off the tree or wait until the ripe apple drops into our hands, meanwhile engaging in something else that offers us awakeness, presence and vitality.

In my wordshop 'tricks kit' I carry a block of a book, called *Writer's Block* with prompts (what I call 'lit matches') galore. These help shift from the target text to a playful process and lateral creativity. Putting aside the text and playing a word game or drawing or responding to a picture to produce the next sentence of the story I'm struggling to write. A teacher Donald Murray catalogues *Twenty-Six ways to Defeat Writer's Block*. Here are a merry seven of them (with added applications):

- Make believe you are writing a letter to a friend who inspires you (Start the piece with "Dear… ")

Writing Letters

- Switch pen to pencil or to laptop… write on cardboard or change the size of the notebook… the shape of the page
- Switch the time of day or the place where you write. Try crack of dawn stumbling out of a dream… a corner in a cafe
- Call the draft an experiment (a friend calls his poems meditations to release the pressure)
- Stop mid word… mid sentence
- Be what the culture considers silly (write backwards, write in code)
- Put a ridiculous made-up name on the piece. It's not you writing this stuff but Hethelberta

Perhaps it is that I'm trying to impress (myself, some future reader) and have forgotten that writing is about expressing… that first words are only first draft. Curiosity not judgement nor comparison = the blessed beginner's mind. It's a 'for my eyes only' first draft. Any words are better than no words for I can rub them out or morph them into a specific image that sings along the spine.

Then sometimes I need to separate from the text when I'm stuck; a question of timing. Respect the Block. I need space. Therapists such as Thomas Moore and Clarissa Pinkola Estes talk of the downside to creativity, the necessary bareness when nothing in our garden will grow. So we go with the season.

Henriette Klauser offers a sign in her *Writing on Both Sides of the Brain*, 'Resistance always has Meaning'. When we can't think of anything to write perhaps our unconscious has a different agenda. Perhaps there is something calling that is more urgent. Driving through a 'Under Construction' sign and a road barrier can end up in a ditch. Dorothy Brande, (*Becoming a Writer*) writes of amusing yourself in wordless ways. She also suggests that a blocked writer can read an obscure text or a

Route 77

dull report and get so frustrated that she starts writing again. Sometimes sex therapy for a couple involves no sex for a prescribed period. Some prisoners locked away without pen and paper for a long period will write with anything on anything.

William Stafford argues, "On a particular day we can't write because we feel we're not meeting a certain standard we have set ourselves. It's easy to write. You just shouldn't have standards that inhibit you." If we relax and give ourselves permission to write out of our poverty today, tomorrow might bring riches.

Here are two Writer's Block 'lit match' exercises. Begin a piece with the words, 'I can't write today because…' and rapid write for 600 seconds. Begin another one, 'If only I had, talent \ time etc. I could write…'

We are never stuck – only a part of us. Other selves can gallop in to assist us. Here is the opening poem in *ZenPenYen*:

A Swamp, a Poet and a Rope

some swamps suck you in.
you sink in slow mud
grips you like a people-eating plant
knee chest and neck deep, the bog
squeezes your last breath, smothers
and buries you in one slurp.

as sludge oozes over throat
you long for solid ground,
long for a passing cowboy
with stetson, boots and stallion
to drag you out of the slime
nostrils above mud, against gravity.

Writing Letters

> no matter how deep the quagmire
> may that poet in you arrive here
> with lasso to fling a word circle
> around and under your arms, drag it tight
> as this horse, snorting tugs you up
> from the muddy grave.

ANANSI THE SPIDER, AUGUST 2019

A little freezing Spider rags and arms gathered in her chest…I saw old Granny at Harare market… a torn little blanket was her web.
(Bonus Zimunya)

In Ghana and the Caribbean, Anansi, the trickster, is the keeper of the Skygod's stories. Anansi tales abound. In one he buys the stories off the Skygod when in consultation with his wife, Also, he meets the Skygod's price – catching the python, a live fairy and forty-seven hornets. There are many retellings of this creature's escapades. Here is one:

> Anansi has six children, each named after a special gift. One day, off on an adventure, he falls into a river and a fish swallows him. The first child, See Trouble, detects the danger. Then Road Builder leads his siblings to their father. River Drinker sucks up the river, while Game Skinner splits open the fish. Just then Falcon swoops down and takes Anansi into the sky. Stone Thrower hurls a stone that knocks his father out of the falcon's claws. The last child, Cushion, provides his father with a soft fall. That night Anansi finds a globe of light shining through the trees. In consultation with the God of All Things, he rewards his six children with the gift of the moon. None will possess it, but they all will enjoy it.

Route 77

A corporate group I facilitated in Accra were delighted that they could apply one of their folk tales to sound business principles. One observed, "We often have to rescue our CEO." Often in storyshops I ask participants what they know about spiders. People offer: eight legs… some are poisonous… spin a web from their abdomens to catch prey… the toughness of silk… parachutes… arachnids… bullet-proof vests… etc.

No wonder the spider is a mythical and symbolic creature. In Greek mythology, Arachne, a talented mortal weaver challenges Athena, goddess of wisdom and crafts, to a weaving contest; this hubris results in her being transformed into a spider. The same cuneiform symbol used to write the name of Uttu, a Sumerian goddess associated with weaving, was used for the Sumerian word 'spider'. An Islamic oral tradition tells of Muhammad, pursued while en route from Mecca, hiding in a cave. Allah commanded a spider to weave a web across the opening. When King Saul was hunting David he also hid in a cave and a spider spun a web over the cave mouth.

And what of Spiderman/women myths and rugby teams who wear spider jerseys? And the movies… a recent one *Spider-Man: Far From Home?* And with all light arrives the shadow – the dark side – trapping prey, poison, and metaphoric intrigue. The stuff of stories.

Mondesa Youth Outreach (MYO) in Swakopmund offers after-school tuition and a place of safety for children from broken, poverty-stricken and/or abusive homes. Storytelling at MYO in the library surrounded by books. In one of the classrooms there is a book, pages suspended on thread from the ceiling, pages open, flapping in the breeze like a bird's wings. I created this next story via puppets in response to a request to encourage the children to read. I had already shared with them how Anansi, keeper of the stories, trapped the python.

Bird outwits Dinosaur

Bird flits happily in the forest, tree to tree, until Dinosaur arrives and wants to eat her. Twice she narrowly escapes. Then she flies to a higher branch where she meets Anansi spinning his web between branches. He tells her, "Books are the answer to your problem."
Bird finds books in the MYO library and builds a fence with them. But Dinosaur pushes down the fence. So Bird takes more books and builds a house. As Dinosaur is about to push down the house, one of the books flaps open and Bird reads how Anansi caught the Python by tying him up with a rope made of branches.
Bird flies off and makes a rope from saplings. She gets Dinosaur to chase her, keeping just out of reach of his snapping jaws until he is exhausted. When Dinosaur falls over, Bird winds the rope round the creature's jaws. When he comes to before she releases him, Bird extracts two promises. He will leave her alone. And he will read a book out of the MYO library about how to eat roots and plants instead of birds.

So many poets have embraced the spider. Here is part of Rabindranath Tagore's *The Journey*:

> We sat beside them to rest in some brushwood,
> And I leaned down to rinse the dust from my face.
> I found the spider web there, whose hinges
> Reeled heavily and crazily with the dust,
> Whole mounds and cemeteries of it, sagging
> And scattering shadows among shells and wings.

May you, through writing and telling, experience the web of tension and interconnection.

Route 77

WORLD CONCERN, SOCIAL DISTANCING AND SPACE, APRIL 2020

> *The One Who Is at Play Everywhere says,*
> *There is a space in the heart where everything meets…*
> *Enter the bowl of vastness that is the heart.*
> *Listen to the song that is always resonating.*
> *Give yourself to it with total abandon.*
> (Radiance Sutras +-800 A.D)

This month I've been thinking about how the current time asks me to look anew with awareness at Lockdown and the space it opens up. Social distancing can bring self-nearing, self-nurturing while placing us in an inclusive cosmos. There are hidden Alibaba doorways into such treasure space. *Open sesame* insights through writing, journaling, storytelling, fairy tales, photography and and…And sitting quietly in our breath and bloodbeat.

Alice Walker *(The Color Purple)* at eight lost the sight of one eye in a shooting accident. Her three-year old daughter, Rebecca, enjoyed a TV programme *Big Blue Marble*. "It begins with a picture of the earth as it appears from the moon. It is bluish… battered-looking, but full of light, with whitish clouds swirling around." One day she observed "Mommy, there's a world in your eye." How do we gaze into space and take the world into our eye? Here's Alice Walker on meditation: "To my surprise…I felt myself drop into…internal space…filled with the purest quiet, the most radiant peacefulness. I started to giggle and then to laugh. Meditation took me right back to…childhood: gazing out into the landscape, merging with it and disappearing."

At a recent retreat, participants chose pictures. One person, in response to her picture of a narrow steeple stretching into a blue sky, mentioned how focusing on blue sky was her way of meditating. The steeple then could symbolise the person sitting upright in this space. My friend Igno writes how photography gifted him with new eyes, taught him another presence – a reality parallel to the one we inhabit in space-time. Marguerite (Osler) van der Merwe *(Eve-olution The Art of Walking)* reminds us, 'You are always in relationship with something greater than yourself'. The Alexander Technique she practices teaches silence… stillness…space.

All this resonates with an article, *Noticing Space*, by Ajahn Sumedho, a Buddhist abbot:

> We (bring) into awareness the way it is, noticing space and form, emptiness and form; the unconditioned and the conditioned. We notice the space in this room…Most people would notice the people, the walls, the floor, the shrine, the furniture. But to notice the space…you withdraw your attention from the things and bring your attention just to the space…When one has a spacious mind, then there is room for everything. We say, "the space in this room", but actually the room is *in the space*; When the building has gone the space will still be here. And the space stretches out through the walls into the vast echoing beyond.

Sumedho considers how we can become aware of the space between thoughts and words. This is a way of bringing background (space) forward and placing foreground (people and objects) in relation to that space. It is there though we cannot see it. As you write, notice the gaps between letters and words.

In such a space, we can imagine, then experience, how solid forms take on a subatomic, quantum reality. We and the objects in the room are largely empty space, molecules vibrating, in constant motion. 'The rock solid physical world', writes the neurosurgeon, Eben Alexander, in *Proof of Heaven* is 'an infinitesimally...dense configuration of strings of energy.'

Our skins are permeable. We become see-through in the nothingness and everythingness. Like Wordsworth 'we see into the life of things'. Lao Tzu writes of the womb that creates this emptiness and fullness.

Adrienne Rich writes: 'The theater of any poem is a collection of decisions about space and time – how are these words to lie on the page, with what pauses, what headlong motion, what phrasing, how can they meet the breath of the someone who comes along to read them?'

Russian-Swedish poet, Edith Sodergran offers us these words:

>On foot
>I had to cross the solar system
>before I found the first thread of my red dress.
>I sense myself already.
>Somewhere in space hangs my heart,
>shaking in the void, from it stream sparks
>into other intemperate hearts.

So then, after sitting in this space for say, thirty minutes, we can return to the other twenty-three and a half hours of day-night as creatures of time, to people and objects. I suggest, after being in such a space, write in your journal. Hold the unfolding loss, social media panic, stats and necessary distancing in such a space, such a paradox. Let us be creatures of more than one world. Dual citizens.

Writing Letters

WE ARE HERE, JUNE 2020

*Looking at your image in a clear stream, you
answer the question by your very presence.*

Living midst the uncertainties of the age, this month's theme centres on ZenPen writing – being and meditation.

I saw a cat on a Covid dawn walk. Perhaps cats are natural meditators. This one seen amid a tangle of branches – (a tangle of non-thoughts?). A dog nearby. I wonder what somatic (being in the body) cats and dogs can teach us about meditation and being? They live and move in and through the life force of the five senses.

And what happens to our writing when we slow down, look, listen, engage in the miracle of the body and write from the stillness, 'the still point of the turning world' as Eliot says? When we enter this slow-down silence? You might recall Eliot's Macavity the Mystery Cat who 'when he's half asleep is really wide awake'. Observing this cat and dog led me to Yeats, 'We can make our minds so like still water that beings gather about us to see their own images, and so live for a moment with a clearer, perhaps even with a fiercer life because of our silence'. And to Blake: 'He ever will perceive a lie who looks at truth with not through the eye'.

I imagined the two teacher creatures encountering each other:

Dog and Cat Seen on a Dawn Walk

the sun sets the edges
of the husky's fur on fire
as he contemplates,
still as a novice monk,

Route 77

> a few feet away
> the saffron robed cat.
>
> beneath the mountain path
> she has placed her presence
> at the centre of a tree.
> her paws arranged in lotus.
> a cat's cradle of boughs
> encircles her silence.
>
> she becomes a cameo
> set in an oval frame,
> quiet as a nun amid
> a rosary of dune berries.
> branches spider out, trapping thought
> in a random cat family tree.
>
> bowing to a feline of reincarnated
> sages, dog yawns a sort of Aum,
> the universe sound of creation.
> then he pads on past guru cat,
> the caress of awareness
> still glows beneath his fur.

I have mentioned engaging with Gondwana staff in Namibia around storytelling – a significant element of their branding. In the foyer at the Delight, Swakop, neon words are superimposed on a map of Namibia. How do we inscribe these words lit on the map of our reality? "We are here."

In Garth Stein's novel, *The Art of Racing in the Rain*, Enzo, the dog narrator, reminds us, 'In racing, they say that your car goes where your

Writing Letters

eyes go. The driver who cannot tear his eyes away from the wall as he spins out of control will meet that wall… Simply another way of saying that which you manifest is before you.' So yes, energy in our texts also follows attention.

In the Zoom age I offer mini retreats. One on the radar connected writing, being and meditation. These states of grace slow us down, increase our awareness and wake us up. We write and meditate on the many changes and transformations as we journey along the river of our lives. We consider how creativity steadies the boat and how writing helps us dip the oars into dark water so we may navigate the river safely.

Remember Rumi? He too talks into this troubled time, "The breezes of dawn have secrets to tell you. Don't go back to sleep. People are moving through the doorway where two worlds meet."

Cat and dog seem to invite us to move through that doorway, that liminal space. And as we step back into this current reality, we bring the gifts of meditation, being and writing. *Muchas gracias* teacher cat and dog. May we be present at the point of a pen and fingertips as they caress the keyboard.

LOSING AND FINDING WORDS, JANUARY 2021

A word is dead when it is said, some say.
I say it just begins to live that day.
(Emily Dickinson)

Words. What are all these slippery symbols? Strung together with gaps between them to create meaning and nuance? To elevate and deprecate? Inspire and insult? Soothe and disturb? Enough words have been written about words to encircle the galaxies. This letter offers a minuscule reflection on losing and finding words in one language of the many tongues – English with its vast vocabulary.

What happens when we begin to lose a world of words? Lose a language with its nuanced imagination? Through ageing, shifts in the culture, stripping significance as we rush into a future?

Thomas Moore, the therapist, says somewhere we have lost words that carry nuances around feelings. Instead, we cover the loss with a summary word such as 'depression' whereas in medieval times there were various words for its different faces. Such as melancholy, gloom, woe. In losing specific words we blunt the sharp tool that can dig out our emotions and hold them to the light.

In *Lost Words: A Spell Book* Robert Macfarlane (incantation, poetry) and Jackie Morris (illustration) bring us words our screen-bound children are losing. They create a poetic manifesto of word spells to reclaim lost words from the realm of nature, wren, willow, magpie. The English philosopher, AJ Ayer felt that 'unless we have a word for something, we are unable to conceive of it, and that there is a direct relationship between our imagination, our ability to have ideas about things, and our vocabulary…. The acrostic spell-poems are designed to be read out loud. The spells carry the spirit of their subject in their structure. Take the brilliant Magpie Manifesto: / Argue Every Toss! / Gossip, Bicker, Yak and Snicker All Day Long!' Not only are the word and the bird restored and celebrated, but the spirit and nature and the clatter of the magpie are conserved within its lines'.

In Judaism, the alphabet and the words they form are holy, with layered meaning from the literal to the mystical. A story: A Rabbi prays in the synagogue with eloquence, clarity, intonation and rhythm. That night he asks God, "Was my prayer well received?" God says, 'Yes." The Rabbi then asks, "Was that not the best prayer that reached your ears this day?" God says, "No." The Rabbi demands, "No? So who prayed more eloquently than I?" God responds, "Kefi." "Kefi? He's the janitor of the synagogue. What does he know? What did he say?" God responds, "Kefi stood up and said. "You know that I am a simple man and that I love you. In order that I do not offend you, I will recite the alphabet and you arrange the words according to what pleases you."

John's gospel evokes different symbolic nuances of 'word'. 'In the beginning was the Word, and the Word was with God, and the Word was God…. The Word was made flesh and dwelt amongst us.' In the annunciation story Mary responds to the angel Gabriel, "Be it unto me according to the thy word." And as the centurion said to Jesus, "Lord, say the word only, and my servant will be healed." And the metaphysical priest-poet John Donne: "To know and feel all this and not have the words to express it makes a human a grave of his own thoughts."

So how do we resurrect words? Like Lazarus raise them up? How can we find lost words? Call them back? One way might be to put on the robe of amateur etymologist, rediscovering roots, usage, cousins. In *Hunger for Ecstasy, Fulfilling the Soul's Need for Passion and Intimacy*, Jalaja Bonheim recalls one such word:

> We inherited the word 'ecstasy' from the ancient Greeks…to them ecstasy was far more than just a state of heightened pleasure…it was a sacred portal into the realm of the gods. Ordinary consciousness could not sustain itself when the majesty, beauty and sheer force of the divine struck the fragile human ego like lightning. One had to step out of one's ordinary small sense of self into a cosmic awareness. They called this process of temporary ego death *ekstasis*, literally 'to cause to stand outside.'

Route 77

Another way might be to follow Emily Dickinson (her quote prefaces this section). Try and taste a word on the tongue. We could also browse a thesaurus (Greek, 'treasury, storehouse') and dictionary – two tomes that ground a writer's word-work.

In 1919/1920, at the start of his career, Tolkien worked on the *Oxford English Dictionary*, later saying he, "learnt more in those two years than in any other equal period of my life." Tolkien worked on words near the beginning of the letter W. His first entry was the noun and verb *waggle* – 'to move (anything held or fixed at one end) to and fro with short quick motions, or with a rapid undulation; esp. to shake (any movable part of the body)'. Slips of paper of his entries in Tolkien's distinctive handwriting survive in the *OED* archives.

We acknowledge that words create our reality. We need to remind ourselves both of philosopher Wittgenstein's, 'the word is not the thing', while celebrating a definitive moment in Helen Keller's life. Anne Sullivan, her teacher took Helen to an old pump house and put Helen's hand under the stream:

> As the cool stream gushed over one hand she spelled into the other the word water, first slowly, then rapidly. I stood still, my whole attention fixed upon the motions of her fingers. Suddenly, I felt a misty consciousness as of something forgotten – a thrill of returning thought; and somehow the mystery of language was revealed…. I knew then that 'w-a-t-e-r' meant the wonderful cool something that was flowing over my hand. That living word awakened my soul, gave it light, hope, joy, set it free!

Here are two of my attempts to recover, celebrate and coin simple words:

Writing Letters

Word Clew

our clew being well-nigh
wound out, let's be cheerful. (Byron)

several strings hide
inside the packed parachute
of a word. meanings and feelings

free-fall out of an alphabet sky.
then you jerk the rip cord and
the canopy opens in a silk flutter.

take the word clew. noun and verb,
it's the first cousin of clue
in its tangled cluster.

here's the winding thread
that Ariadne handed Theseus
to lead him from the maze.

it names the cords of a
hammock that breeze-swings,
slung in summer twixt trees.

yachtsmen evoke it
in the lower aft corner
of a fore-and-aft sail.

the rare rufous necked
wood rail in evergreen forests
in Peru cries crew crew crew.

Route 77

the word that fell
from Byron's silk sky sail
now parachutes in mine.

the chosen shape floats down,
lands, steadies and writes itself
on the grounds of a page.

Azaza – Minting a Word

imagine such a word.
a new note arriving
into currency,
stamped fresh.
azaza. short long long
like Za Za, the film star.
a verb transitive and a noun.
a palindrome. origin?
what could it mean...evoke?

the loop of the alphabet
lies in its arms.
bookends holding the books.
the word contains the cycle
of the twenty-six as they hook,
float, ride inside one another –
the o round mouth surprise,
the round bellied b, kicking k,
genital p and v. t junction, y fork.
geometric shapes with crosses,
diagonals, dots.
this Phonetian-Romance inheritance
all contained here in a word,

Writing Letters

vowel and consonant at play.
at the end of the line. last letter,
it turns round like a swimmer in a lane,
in a fish squiggle z
and splashes back to a.

perhaps its origin is medieval.
no wonder the monks
had such fun keeping learning alive
finding light in letters
and the nib curl
to create the alphabet
growing gospel words
in the scriptorium
above the spiral staircase
above the vinelands.
from strokes, s bends, angles,
following in Zen-like plumb line
they shaped these 26 signs and spaces
to build the monastery of knowing
and not knowing, unknowing,
spiraling through an azaza paradise
filling the word to the overflowing.

6

ACHILLES HEAL – IN POETIC PRAISE OF HEALING

Here are eleven entries from an unpublished manuscript. Not sure if that is a not yet. Bob Commin and I thought of writing it together but somehow…

THE MYTH OF ACHILLES

When Achilles was born, his mother Thetis, the sea goddess (his father Peleus, was a mortal) held him by the ankles and dipped him in the river Styx, the river people crossed en route to the underworld. Thetis wished to make her son immortal. No arrow or sword seemed to harm Achilles who became a mighty warrior. But the immortal waters had not covered his ankles where his mother had held him. Achilles fought in the war when the Greeks fought the Trojans over the abduction of Helen – the 'face that launched a thousand ships'. Paris, killed Achilles, the God Apollo guiding the arrow to pierce Achilles' heel.

The expression 'Achilles heel' has come to mean our point of weakness, the place where we are physically or emotionally vulnerable or the fault we carry (in Achilles' case pride and uncontrollable anger.) The play on words, the Achilles 'Heal', suggests that our vulnerability can be the source of our healing. Engaging in the reading and writing of poetry invokes this process. A poem can distil our rage, depression and grief and work its magic.

I'm interested in the way poetry enters, moves and transforms us rather than cold analysis. Sets us yearning. It's about unlearning the left-brained, rational way many of us were taught at school. Gets us out of the hole we have self-dug. This guide offers a conversation around mytho-poetic ways of knowing and healing and a practical guide to writing. Perhaps *The Achilles Heal* will inspire you to read, learn by heart, absorb and write your own poetry.

> to take what we love inside,
> to carry within us an orchard, to eat
> not only the skin, but the shade
> not only the sugar but the days...
> (Li-Young Lee)

ALPHA TO OMEGA: LETTERS, BREATH, MUSIC, WORDS AND MEANING

Words as things, tangible as the fibery paper and the liquid ink, almost like small objects, rocks or gems. Words as stones, as stars, as seed, tracks, doors, words as mountains, words as skins. Words as colours...
(J Ruth Gendler)

We work with words. Is there something in the material a poet uses that might contribute to healing? Is it the attitude of poet towards this material that opens to this mystery? How do choices or the respect for the material activate such a process?

Achilles Heal – In Poetic Praise of Healing

We begin with the letter. What are these twenty-six signs in an English alphabet? In the rabbinical tradition the alphabet is holy. The five open vowels as we move our mouths through their shapes become a prayer, a mantra. To the echoing, awaking universe. The consonants hissed, popped or exploded tickle the inside of our lips, teeth, palate, tongue. They become the stops we block to make the music. So that the alphabet rides on the breath. The rising and falling, the interruption and sudden release.

Nefesh Haya, a Jewish meditation website, explains, 'The original Yoga and Internal Energy Exercises of Israel based on fundamental teachings of the Hebrew alphabet, (unify) body-breath-mind-soul through embodiment of the sacred signs'. We can develop a prayerful attitude to this alphabet, a 'Prayer of the Body' which opens to mindfulness in the poet, linking word and breath that connect inner and outer worlds. In meditating on the alphabet, known as *Tikun Hanefesh*, we focus on this alphabet that leads up and down Jacob's ladder.

As language arrives in our mouth, we begin mouthing the sounds. A is for apple and then we learn names often in a rhyme. A is for Advent. Then we enter school and write those letters over and over again. Sometimes someone disrupting our education insists that these letters must touch the line above and the line below. The alphabet becomes an agony, an anxiety, a performance and we are taken out of our joy. The accent is on neatness not on flow, breath or creation. For left-handed me, graphite or ink smudges followed by my sweeping hand. Then sixty years on I shared a calligraphy and writing with wordshop Anne-Marie Moore. As we played with the alphabet, curling it over lines, I wrote:

Route 77

Road Rules

writing is weak and untidy
the first report
on my left-hand drive,
carried this sentence.

my pencil infringed blue lines.
letters swerved across the road.
an ink spill and a red pen
left skid marks in my tracks.

I scrawled through cities
of letters, books and degrees,
navigating twenty-six traffic signs.
feared the graphologist cop.

then, my calligrapher friend,
you fixed an L-plate on my pad.
in the passenger seat, took me
a-z through alphabet streets.

through red robots, no left-turn,
one-ways, no overtaking,
we squiggled outside those lines.
you healed zig-zag, my ABC.

Think of the time taken by a medieval monk adorning a letter of the alphabet turning it into art. For there is something illuminating in a letter. For poetry is light rising from a page.

Enter sound. In the beginning was the sound. Dylan Thomas recalls how as a child be fell in love with sounds, 'What the words stood for, symbolised or meant, was of secondary importance; what mattered was the sound as I heard them for the first time on the lips of the remote and incomprehensible grown-ups who seemed, for some reason, to be living in my world.' When asked how he came to write poetry, Thomas referred to loving 'the shape and shade and size and noise of words as they hummed, strummed, jiggered and galloped along'. If words bring not only meanings but sounds, then poetry has the potential to be music therapy as sound works subliminally. A lyrical chant.

> Some sixty years ago the monks in a monastery in France had grown lethargic. They found it difficult to work in the vineyards. The new Abbot called in a physician who checked out the men. Nothing wrong with them. Then the abbot called in a dietician. He said, "Perhaps the monks need a meat diet." On meat and they became more lethargic. These were Benedictines who had been vegetarians for hundreds of years.
> Then the Abbot called in a therapist who worked in a special way. The therapist sat down with the Abbot and asked, "You are new around here. What changes have you introduced?" "Well," said the Abbot, "The monks used to chant three hours a day. In order to make them more productive in the vineyards, I removed chanting from their daily calendar." The sound therapist, Dr Thomatis, urged, "Put back the chanting. The Abbot did. In a short time the monks had regained their level of energy.

Chanting energises the brain. The word 'enchantment' comes from the same root. So does 'canto/cantare,' meaning 'song', in Latin. As children, many of us chanted nursery and skipping rhymes, caught up in music, rhyme and rhythm. We entered the beat, gesture and sway, playing with sound. We used our bodies as drums and made simple musical instruments – sticks, stones in bottles. Chanted poems depend on change and repetition and so evoke our daily rhythms. They draw upon poetry's ancient roots in spiritual rituals and ceremonies. Tibetan Buddhists chant the mantra (prayer), *Om Mani Padme Hum*, to invoke compassion. Monks often carve the mantra onto stones or around a *Mani* (prayer wheel). Our bodies are brains, our cells are intelligent and poetry combines brain-heart intelligence.

In some cultures rap is a way of expressing orally that which gives us life. In an article *Poetry as Power*, Andrea Shen writes about Steve Caton, Professor of Contemporary Arab Studies at Harvard. As a child, Steven Caton saw the film *Lawrence of Arabia*. 'On top of these cliffs, women in black are ululating and on the bottom you have these men (Bedouins) riding through the wadi, chanting poetry… That kind of beauty made me really want to go to the Middle East.' Caton moved to Yemen where 'the mountains rose, arrow-like, thousands of feet into the sky to research oral tribal poetry. He had become fluent in Arabic. Yemeni tribal poetry has regular metre, dazzling alliterations, and intense use of metaphor. Caton studied the central role that poetry plays in Yemeni daily life at weddings. He also witnessed 'poetry-mediated negotiations between warring tribes' who chant poetry to try to deal with possible violence.

Many poets have written about their love affair with words, their nature, capacity and possibility. From the title poem in Naomi Shihab Nye's collection, *The Words under the Words:*

> Answer, if you hear the words under the words –
> otherwise it is just a world
> with a lot of rough edges,
> difficult to get through, and our pockets
> full of stones.

Achilles Heal – In Poetic Praise of Healing

Words carry denotative or dictionary meanings and connotative or emotive associations that ghost around the poem and echo in the silence. When we use words their ancestors (original meanings) arrive. Words such as 'ecstasy.' From the Greek, *ek-stasis,* 'to call to stand outside'. Standing outside the ego? In Sanskrit ecstasy is *ananda,* one of the names of the Divine.

You might have heard the saying, "Words don't mean. People mean." The axe can chop wood for the night fire or can slice our lives in two. There is a dark myth of a tyrant who has built a hollow clay cow with reeds in its mouth. He places human beings inside the cow and lights a fire under the beast. The reed converts their screams into music.

Yet there is something in contemplating our words that can be linked to healing. We work in a powerful medium. In the story shared elsewhere, the praying rabbi uses words to draw attention to his powers. The janitor allows the words to come through him. So this *prima materia* of all writers opens to choice. And after the word choice for writers arrives the choice of how to combine words.

Poems evoke meanings hidden in and around them. We enter a tradition, joining other people who have used these words. Like Hopkins the poet, we can coin words, acknowledging that language moves and evolves, borrows, takes on shades. Like the crust of the earth we rest on shifting plates of the language that we write, trying to capture it before it flies. William Blake reminds us:

> He who binds himself to a joy Does the winged life destroy.
> But he who kisses the joy as it flies Lives in eternity's sunrise.

The challenge is how to live lightly with words for the poet is dealing in transience, in change. Words don't only represent what we construe as reality. They create and transform reality. Here is part of an Inuit poem about the time when humans and animals spoke same language:

>That was the time when words were like magic.
>The human mind had mysterious powers.
>A word spoken by chance
>might have strange consequences.
>It would suddenly come alive
>and what people wanted to happen could happen –
>all you had to do was say it.
>(Magic Words, David Guss (ed), *The Language of the Birds*)

Here is an exercise around words. This involves the creation of an alphabet of metaphors for a poet. We name what a poet is by referring to a related activity. e.g. P for painter or producer…M or magician or medicine man… L for lover of words or lighthouse keeper….B for builder or brewer. The idea is to enlarge our concept of what a poet is or does by breaking any stereotypes that constrict our thinking. Draw three columns and write you alphabet.

LETTER (A-Z)	METAPHOR	REASON (NOUN)
A	architect	designs a structure, plans space.
S	singer	makes word music

If you can't think of a noun for a particular letter you can make one up. e.g. question-maker for Q.

Achilles Heal – In Poetic Praise of Healing

OUR BEGINNINGS – GROWING SOUL THROUGH POETRY

The parent helps the child discover what may be done with its lips and limbs. This is the first poetry.
(James Fenton)

How does poetry find us? How does it enter our lives? Perhaps in moments of lostness as in David Wagoner's poem, *Lost*, we hear a voice saying, "Stand still. The forest knows where you are. You must let it find you." Pablo Neruda, the Chilean novel prize-winner poet, records how:

> I didn't know what to say
> my mouth could not speak
> my eyes could not see
> then something ignited in my soul
> fever or unremembered wings?
> and I went my own way
> deciphering that burning fire
> and I wrote my first bare line
> pure wisdom, pure folly
> of one who knows nothing
> and suddenly I say the heavens
> unfastened and open.

There is a story about Nasruddin who is searching for a lost key outside his house. Abdul, a friend, comes by and helps him look. After an hour of trailing their fingers though the dirt, Abdul sits up on his haunches and asks, "Nasruddin, are you sure you lost the key here?" "No" responds Nasruddin," I lost the key inside the house." "Then why are we looking here?" asks the frustrated friend. "Nasruddin replies, "Because it is too dark inside the house."

In 2007 a therapist organising a wordshop approached her group and asked, "Would you like a wordshop on Poetry and Therapy?" She was met with audible silence. So she asked, "Would you like a wordshop on Metaphor and Therapy?" They all raised their hands enthusiastically, then chucked at their response.

We are intimidated by the word poetry. We need to search for the key where we lost it. Mark Twain says, "If we were taught to speak the way we are taught to write we would all stutter." Many people talk of turning away from poetry in childhood. For many of us it became inaccessible and reminded us of how limited we were. In a left-brained Newtonian world we were asked to decode the intention and meaning, to analyse it, and never asked whether we enjoyed it or if an image or line moved us. How do we recall poetry into our lives so we can receive the gifts it offers? We can begin listening to poets talking of their beginnings. A Rita Dove poem begins, 'When I was young the moon spoke in riddles and skies rhymed'. It ends, 'the world was already old and I was older than I am today'.

Harold Bloom, a life-long student of comparative religion, writes of his awakening to his potential at the age of around nine and ten. He was reading poets William Blake and Hart Crane. 'The self came to its belated birth (or second birth) by reading visionary poetry'. Poets such as these, 'have the power to awaken their readers to an implicit answering power'. Bloom quotes William Wordsworth who called this sensation 'something evermore about to be' and Hart Crane who writes 'and so it was I entered the broken world to trace the visionary company of love its voice an instant in the wind'.

Achilles Heal – In Poetic Praise of Healing

Bloom links this experience to the feeling children often have that their parents are not really their parents. Freud called this the changeling fantasy. Adoptive parents have plucked us away from fairy land and pass themselves off as our mother and father. Reading the poets gave him this feeling where the language 'gave the pleasure of excited thought, of a thinking that changed one's outer nature, while opening up an inner identity, a self within a self'.

Earlier I shared a poem about revisiting my childhood home. On that visit I walked into the room where I had written my first poem in May of 1956:

> The day our Saviour went back home
> My daddy went there too.
> He saw God seated on his throne
> And worshiped him for me and you.
>
> Safe in the arms of the King
> My daddy in peace their lies.
> Hope and joy the angels bring
> To all in heaven in the skies.

For much of my poetic life I have hidden this beginning. Embarrassment perhaps? The monotony of the sing-song rhythm? In terms of my belief I have moved from the literal to the symbolic. Yet as I write out this first effort learnt by heart, I understand why this poem offered comfort. Much of this was unconscious. This in itself suggests that when we enter the language of poetry, we move to what is yet to be born.

It is a rhyming ballad in iambic tetrameter – appropriately the beat of the heart – *da dum* to the power of four – to commemorate death by the heart. It could also be sung to many of the hymn tunes or love lyrics. Or chanted. Many children's rhymes ride on the same metre. So it is part of a greater body of work. It belongs.

Linking my father's death to Ascension Day, places the event within a Christian calendar and introduces a sense of ritual, which lifts the event into a different time-space continuum. I have entered cyclic time, the time of the seasons. I am no longer in 'tick-tock' time but in the time of epiphany, the time of the moment, the event that creates time. Entering poetry time we enter the great present. As TS Eliot suggests, 'Only through time is time conquered.' Linking a personal and a symbolic event – the death of a man and the ascension of a god, constitutes an image – the beginnings of a metaphor. And a metaphor is about relationship, in this case of the part to the whole. It points towards living the symbolic life.

In evoking the angels, I was also tapping into a great tradition – that we are surrounded by beings of light – intermediaries who can affect and effect the quality of our life on earth. So the poem points towards life beyond the visible and experience beyond the senses. The line about resting in peace, evokes my mother's words over the open grave, the words she had inscribed on her husband's tombstone. "Rest eternal grant him Lord and may light perpetual shine upon him."

The ending moves the poem down the well grief to that communal place where our suffering, our shared humanity connects us to other people. The 'all' in the last line becomes ambiguous. While at that time I believed what I was told, namely that only your brand of religion gets you to heaven, the nascent poet is also saying that all persuasions can lead to heaven – once again speaking beyond conscious limitations. And that heaven is also within.

Here is the beginning of my developing eclectic self. And the well of images that I draw from. While I am open to many spiritual beliefs, the main source of imagery began as Judaic-Christian – the stories that resonated from that tradition. In this poem I evoke from the Old Testament the throne alluded to in texts such as the vision of Isaiah, "In the year that king Uzziah died I saw also the LORD sitting upon a throne, high and lifted up, and his train filled the temple." (Isaiah 6:1)

I have come to understand that as a poet I can entertain a belief and play 'what if' and 'let's pretend' with and around it. To try out the belief on 'appro' as it were (taking a garment home before deciding on buying). If the fruits of the new belief bring a greater quality of aliveness then I allow them in. I am also linking a personal event to the mythological and creating a resonance between that personal experience and an evolving mythology. Long before I encountered Hopkins' assonance I was using it – the internal vowel rhyming – 'day – saviour' … 'back – Daddy.' For in a limited range of sounds in a given language, it is inevitable that we will rhyme.

The poem also attempts to supply a geography – a sense of place – the where of the story – in this case the skies. While this image suggests separation, it is part of a search to name that geography. Years later when I encountered Meister Eckhart, the medieval mystic, and his 'God is an underground river that nobody can stop and nobody can dam'. I responded:

The Grounding of God

in answer to my 'where is..?
the priest intoned that
God resides somewhere
above the bright blue.
winds of heaven blow gently.

Route 77

> but where? where was this place,
> sans geography and address?
>
> the mystics must have been
> in search of landscape
> for they embedded God
> as an underground river
> that no one can dam.
>
> this river flows its tides
> through climate change, rain
> air bubble and turning earth,
> under-breath, under-skin,
> bringing God home.

This first poem is placed in a personal canon, suggesting that our lives can be read backwards as well as forwards. As I revisit the old home, so the poem can be revisited, reminding me of the boy who bashed those typewriter keys. Through his words I at seventy-seven plus have direct first-hand access to him at eleven. In a sense I father him now from the experience of being a father and a poet. And in the subject the young poet faces death. Poetry teaches us about little and great deaths. Each poem is a greeting and a goodbye.

While the gendering of God as male is a beginning belief I have outworn, in this poem there is something appropriate in a father lost going to a Father. It is the severing of the male line grieved here. In those days when I prayed the *Our Father*, it was to both heavenly residents, the genetic father and the Divine one.

In *Our Fathers Well's* Peter Pitzele reminds us:

The poet John Keats described the world as a 'vale of soul making'. The Bible calls this vale 'the valley of the shadow'. Soul is formed, like clay, in those depressions where death and suffering shade human life. Those vales are places of excess and extremity, places beyond the settlements to which one is brought by a summons, by circumstance, and only in part by one's own will.

Soul solitary and soaring may be exhilarated on the peaks but the soul does not only fly. It plods along the dark road of linear time. It struggles in its house of clay to know and to be known; it wrestles with itself. Much of its knowledge comes when the heart is broken. In those rending experiences we see what shaped us, changed us, and opened us more deeply to the mystery. The vales of soul making are those experiences that in their psychic intensity bring us a knowledge of who we really are.

I believe that poetry is a primal impulse within us all.
I believe we are all capable of it and …
that a small, often ignored corner of us yearns to try it.
(Stephen Fry)

ECOLOGY: TREES, POETRY AND BELONGING

A man is a bundle of relations, a knot of roots,
whose flower and fruitage is the world.
(Ralph W. Emerson)

Trees, like all of nature, are ecosystems – like the story *The house that Jack built*. These are the leaves that draw the rain that feed the roots that grow the stem that nourish the branches that create the leaves. A cycle. As a

Route 77

Malay proverb asserts, 'Though a tree grows so high, the falling leaves return to the root'.

No wonder trees, as beings, feature in world mythology. The drama of Genesis begins around a tree with the knowledge of good and evil. In Norse mythology the world tree, Yggdrasil, binds heaven and earth. It is the giant ash that links and shelters all the worlds. Three wells lie at its base: the Well of Wisdom, the Well of Fate, and the source of many rivers.

In the shamanic journey through the three worlds – underworld, middle world and upper world, we often find the tree as the symbol for those worlds and their interconnection. Take the baobab for example. According to mythology the gods planted this tree upside down. This poem celebrates a particular baobab in Namibia:

Baobab Myths

the tree, dumped from heaven
whole and upside down,
raises its trunk
above flats sands.
a millennium of lovers, shamans,
travelers, vandals,
warriors and ivory tusks
have carved her cross-road bark.

a kingdom of creatures seeks
its succulent gravity,
its rope stems and healing leaf.
at night, fruit bats suck
luminous white blossoms
from palms and fingers.

Achilles Heal – In Poetic Praise of Healing

> by day, animals crack pods
> in search of monkey bread
> while buffalo birds weave nests
> and web the sticks in song.
>
> if, in the beginning,
> people came forth
> leaping to life from a stump,
> then this is Eve of trees,
> lending shade to cryptic myths.
>
> a village replete with cattle
> hid with grain in its hollow
> from spears and burning sticks.
> letters wedged in crevices
> telling of deaths and ceremonies
> passed this postal route.
>
> casspirs in low-lying Africa
> smoking in a border war,
> cooled in its knotted shade.
> the bowl now serves as chapel
> with arches, wooden pews
> and the cross of a mother's loss.
> girthed like a Goddess
> with a sub-Saharan womb,
> the baobab roots the fertile sky.

Buffalo birds offer travellers the four directions too for they build their nests in the west wing of the tree. This in addition to the other two directions on the vertical plane – up and down. Locals stored water in its in natural hollows. David Livingstone treated sores with poultices of powdered baobab leaf.

A poem too is an ecosystem, parts working towards one whole with the whole greater than the sum of the parts. The roots lie in the earth of our experience and tap deep underground into the unconscious – our dreams, memories and forgotten moments. This is not only the personal unconscious of an individual life journey. It is also the ground that we share with all living creatures – with our poetry ancestors.

The roots ferret in the soil, binding (in the sense of belonging) us to certain traditions and ways of thinking. Searching for the living water that feeds our poetry. We are in the underground kingdom of the archetypes, those giants, where myths and spirits dwell. The trunk could be the body of the poem, the way it shapes itself on a page, spreads out, stands in the forest of other poems. Our own corpse, plantation and those groves of other poets. And there is movement within as sap rises and falls. So the rings in the trunk could be layers of meaning. The way a poem ages as we grow and live with it.

The leaves cluster as words on the stem of a line offering us their seasonal shades. On the dark side, mixtures can be used to poison tips of arrows. And perhaps each branch is a verse bearing its fruits and offering them to the sky, to the air of ideas, giving off oxygen. Dropping the poem ripe in the reader's hands. Feeding the bird intellect. Attracting moisture in the rain cycle. The moisture at the tip of the leaf is reabsorbed into the roots in the way the end and the beginning of a poem speak to each other, are in conversation with other parts.

Baker poet's apron

So many poets have trees standing in the middle of their poetic works or their reflections. In *Song of the Open Road*, Walt Whitman muses, 'Why are there trees I never walk under but large and melodious thoughts descend upon me?' Then there are the oft-quoted lines, 'I think that I shall never see A poem lovely as a tree'. (Joyce Kilmer). The mythologist, Joseph Campbell, reminds us, 'God is the experience of looking at a tree and saying, "Ah!"' In Celtic mythology the green man lives in harmony with nature. He is wild and natural. In medieval times his face was often carved on church walls:

Route 77

The Green Man

only your eyes and mouth show,
bright birds in a tree
that is all foliage.
companion to the woman
who tends the well,
your cheeks, chin and brow
are wreathed in spears
sharp with summer's
stalk, blade and vein.
ancient man, Celtic man,
cast in church stone,
you call us to restore
our water source,
drawn from deep earth,
man in a leaf mask.

Matsuo Basho, the great 17th century Japanese Haiku master, writes:

> Go to the pine if you want to learn about the pine, or to the bamboo if you want to learn about the bamboo. And in doing so you must let go of your subjective preoccupation with yourself. Otherwise you impose yourself on the object and you don't learn. Your poetry arises by itself when you and the object have become one, when you have plunged deep enough into the object to see something like a hidden light glimmering there. However well-phrased your poetry might be, if your feeling isn't natural – if you and the object are separate – then your poetry isn't true poetry but merely your subjective counterfeit.

A poem is about belonging. It is alive and interactive as the tree and is in conversation with great mythical trees. And if we are part of an ecology of poets, we belong. The poet Stanley Kunitz reminds us, 'Solitary as you are in writing the poem, you are in touch with the whole chain of being'. When lonely we can lean against the bark of the poem that you or another poet has grown. Communicate as one living form to another. Draw in your time of dryness, from the moisture and rhythm that was poured into the poem at the time of its writing and that is available to you in your current crisis.

Offering you shelter from the burning sun, fruits to sustain you, rope from bark and roots to bind what needs to be bound and medicinal roots to heal us. The fibre from the inner bark can string your musical instrument. You can shelter inside a hollow trunk of a poem in the same way as you can in a baobab. The wood pulp can be used for writing paper.

Ecology involves balance. As a tree is balanced by roots and branches, so is a poem. It stands on it own and does not need external support. We don't need the writer to stand next to it and explain it. Anne Sexton's poem, "*The Balance Wheel,*" shows this balance in its structure, theme and content. Here are a few lines:

> I saw birds swinging in, watched them multiply
> Into a tree, weaving on a branch, cradling a keep
> In the arms of April sprung from the south to occupy
> This slow lap of land, like cogs of some balance wheel.
> I saw them build the air, with that motion birds feel.

When you write a tree poem, you are tapping into an ancient tradition. There is a Chinese proverb, 'Keep a green tree in your heart and perhaps

Route 77

a singing bird will come'. I wrote this poem after this visualisation as part of a group, Leslie Kenton's book our guide:

Inside a Tree

I approach a tree in a grove.
touch its hem. finger the bark.
press my body against it.
align palm line and ear lobe
spread out arms
to soak in shades.
await osmosis.

I am absorbed as mist
through the bark.
tree life shifts round
fluid in the womb.
sap passes through
greening, graining me.
shrinks me to tree cell
I abide a while in the nub.

then it expands my shape
to fill the inner skin.
solar plexis sits in the bowl,
legs extend underground
tapping the root path.
arms trail the branch curve
tongue a caterpillar
licks along inner leaf
finger nails are pips

inside fruit pulp.
head rises to tree crown.

slowly as breath
returns me to human shape.
I huddle there, then
after seasons, travel
through rings to the wall.
to emerge where I entered
first pressed to the tree.
walk away. enter
loss as I leave.

in rustle wind
I hear tree speak
now I carry human shape
while you bear tree figure
inside the pith of us.

Perhaps we carry each other in this way when we love them. And we can carry the poems we love inside us and let them shape us. At one retreat many participants arrived burdened – a bipolar husband, a death of a child, cancer returning – so I asked them to find a tree and pour out their hurt and longing in the presence of the tree, listen to the response and then write. Many came back light of step.

ACORN TO OAK LEAVES

I facilitate a zoom retreat entitled *Acorn to Oak Leaves* based partly on James Hillman's acorn theory in *The Soul's Code: In Search of Character and Calling*. Our potential for growth is encoded inside us. In the exercise people take a line, image or verse and expand it into a poem via story or memory. The lit matchstick blazes into a fire.

For example, Kunitz's 'how shall the heart be reconciled to its feast of losses?' or 'I have walked through many lives some of them my own' are acorns.

This exercise is also based on listening, as in the Rumi poem in this book. When resonating with the prompt, especially if we read aloud, we hear the voice of poet perhaps from a different time and place. A past vibration echoes in the present. We tune in to the music which booms in the cavity of the body, in the resonating chambers of the head. The fire of the words now warms us from inside. We belong to the ancients who first intoned in oral cultures. To monks who chant. The bards of the mead hall who recited *Beowulf*. We're listening to silences too. As our eye shifts from the end of a line to the beginning of the next one. To the great silence around the subject, to what is not being said. We're listening to the conversation recorded in these acorns.

Here's another acorn to inspire your oak leaves poem. In *The Writer*, Richard Wilbur listens to his daughter writing a story. He can hear the typewriter clattering in her room:

> A stillness greatens in which
> The whole house seems to be thinking,
> And then she is at it again with a bunched clamour
> Of strokes, and again is silent.

Apart from lines by other poets, we can open our eyes to signs everywhere. This poem was inspired by a craft beer bottle label:

Achilles Heal – In Poetic Praise of Healing

Beer Bottle Story

in the brewery at Stanford
wheat hops malt ferment
with honey hived from fynbos flowers.
on the honey blonde label
the image of a whale fin
rises from the foam, telling
the tale of a wreck (early1852)
from days when Melville's Moby Dick (late 1851)
was captain of the hunt and whale watchers
along Walker Bay were yet to be.

the iron hull HMS Birkenhead, troopship,
bound for Algoa Bay and the 8th Xhosa war,
643 aboard, docked in Simonstown, loading
cavalry horses, bales of hay and tons of coal.
rounded the Cape hugging the coast
two miles off shore. paddle wheels
churning a steady eight knot speed.

at 02.00, 26 Feb, the ship asleep,
the leadman sounded safe fathoms
then a sudden submarine rock, unchartered,
mined the vessel, ripping its rib cage.
water stormed into the hold,
buckling the plates of the bilge,
tearing open the bulkheads,
flooding engine rooms.
a hundred soldiers submerged in their berths.
horses gymkhana'd the railings
to thrash the two mile swim, eight making it.

> a survivor wrote of those lost
> in shark fest waters
> before the age of cage diving.
> a scattering survived the suction.
> twelve hours later, hanging on
> to wreckage, making the beach.
> troops under orders stood on deck
> watching the first 'woman and children first' drill.
> they boarded midget boats. only two navigable.
> the ship split with 445 buried in water graves.
>
> artists and poets painted and poem'd this wreck.
> now the Danger Point after-the-event
> lighthouse (1895) with an in memoriam plaque
> plated to its base, beams across Walker Bay.
> at Birkenhead brewery do they pour
> a ship into every bottle
> as the woman and children arrive
> safe on the fynbos shore?

OBSERVING WORLDS: RETRAINING THE EYE

A ruby is not lovelier than a rock.
An angel is not more glorious than a frog.
(Angelus Silesius)

A poet needs a triple LLL sign on the back window of his-her car. Look Listen Learn.

 A monk wishing to climb a sheer mountain, asked his teacher how to accomplish this. The teacher told him, "Fetch a stone from the mountain." The monk scrambled up the lower slopes and returned with one. The teacher locked him in a room for a year with only the stone as companion. When he released him, the monk easily ascended the mountain.

We begin in observation. If you want to improve the quality of your writing, improve the quality of your looking, your observation. Cultivate curiosity. If we have the gift of sight, we are born taking in the world. Then slowly we are told how to observe the world and then we stop seeing what is there. Our culture, parents, teachers, politicians hypnotise us to see the world in their way so we see selectively. William Blake reminds us, 'the fool does not see the same tree as the wise man'.

In retraining the eye, we begin to notice. Once, in a workshop when I asked participants to bring something from nature, one woman brought in the stem of a flower. In surprise as she looked closely, she exclaimed, "This stem is square. I was taught that stems are round." Poets extend their looking. Remember the German mystic, Angelus Silesius, who studied medicine and philosophy (two ways of training observation) and who in the mid 1600s served as a Court Physician? His definition of sin? Not noticing the flower grow.

We are called to observe the world afresh. This creates new worlds beyond worlds. Imagery is born in observation, as in Hopkins comparing the egg to 'little low heavens'. Stafford likening poetry to a faint star. Seeing establishes belonging. At a retreat after meditating in robes, a woman spent time with a flower and wrote, 'the flower is meditating in its saffron robe'.

What of Playing in Scale? As children we played in scale – building a mud house, upturning a table to sail the seven seas, arranging a doll's tea party, bending wire to build a car, turning a shoe box into a railway station. These games were preparing for the writer in us. Perhaps this is what Jung means by serious play, the necessary child-like play of adults. In his adult years he used to construct villages and bridges across streams in his garden. In scale imagination expands our view. William Blake extolled us, "to see a world in a grain of sand."

The Dutch photographer Kees Boeke (1884 – 1966) in *Cosmic View: the Universe in 40 Jumps* presents a series of photographs that show the scale of things, from large scale down to atomic. He photographs a mosquito squatting on a cut in a finger. Focusing on the subject, he moves the camera out ten times till we are in space. Then he zooms to the power of ten into the mosquito and the cut on the hand through decreasing scales of size to the atom's nucleus. The outermost and innermost photographs are identical. 'We need to develop a wider outlook to see ourselves in our relative position in the great and mysterious universe' (Kees Boeke).

Poets look at the world through diverse lenses. Look at a drop of blood under a microscope. At a star through a telescope. When we do we extend our vision. In Any Tan's novel *A Hundred Secret Senses (1996)* Kwan urges her sister to, "Use hundred secret senses." She means, "Same kind of sense as ant feet, elephant trunk, dog nose, cat whisker, whale ear, bat wing, clam shell, snake tongue, little hair on flower." These senses are secret only because we have forgotten them. We have limited our range. Through attention to our instincts we can recover them.

Many insects with compound eyes, such as flies, wasps, and bees, fly at great speed. Images speed across their retinas. Humans can detect light that flickers sixty times per second. A fly can detect a light that flickers 300 times per second. Many nocturnal insects see in the dark. Grasshoppers migrate, dung beetles roll balls in straight lines and moths forage from night-blooming flowers.

The discipline of poetry calls us not to confuse what we see with 'reality' but to open to other ways of seeing the world. William Stafford suggested, 'Poetry is the kind of thing you have to see from the corner of your eye. You can be too well prepared for poetry.... It's like a very faint star. If you look straight at it you can't see it, but if you look a little to one side it is there.'

In perceiving through our senses we extend them. Here is part of Elizabeth Bishop's *The Fish*:

> and then I saw
> that from his lower lip
> — if you could call it a lip —
> grim, wet, and weaponlike,
> hung five old pieces of fish-line….
> Like medals with their ribbons
> frayed and wavering,
> a five-haired beard of wisdom
> trailing from his aching jaw.

Her growing respect for the fish leads her to release the old warrior back into the brine. The poet's observation leads to compassion and kinship. We are reminded of our capacity to endure suffering and respond to each other's suffering.

This poem arose from observing a beach sculpture:

Kelp Elephant Creation

the beast reclines
on the beach today.
the artist offers contour
and big game shape
through patted sand,
and a washed up stump.

Route 77

seaweed, shells and pebbles
embed her body.

instead of washing
at a water hole
in an inland reserve,
she graces the waves
next to the pier
with her bulk.
she's like a land whale,
this beached creature.

the sculptor shapes
her ear flaps
thin as a sting ray.
her tusks are bleached –
driftwood ivory.
he's manicured
her five toenails
in blue bottle bubbles.

despite the sea season,
his tin trumpets
only a few coins.
tonight's tide will take
this sand mandala,
kelp trunk and all,
leaving a grey zen
loose skin of sand.

John Roome: Kelp Elephant Creation

RITUAL, MANTRA AND MEDITATION

Your vision…will become clear only when you look into your heart. Who looks outside, dreams. Who looks inside, awakens.
(Jung)

What about the heart? "Biting my truant pen, beating myself for spite, "Fool", said my Muse to me, "look in thy heart, and write". (Philip Sydney). Books arrive in our lives and say, "read me now." John Selby's *Quiet the Mind* is one of these. I always thought that the journey from head to heart was a long one but Selby offers a route instantaneous. He suggests that we are 'thoughtaholics'. I think therefore I am" As a friend, Nelleke, suggests, this is putting 'Descartes before the horse'.'

Here is Selby's 'finer than rubies' wisdom (www.johnselby.com), when we move into one body sensation, say breathing, we don't cut out thought, stress, judgement, excessive planning. But if we focus on two sensations, say breathing and heartbeat and add listening to rib cage rising or the chirp of a bird, we short-circuit the thinking brain.

Selby says that had he been asked twenty years ago how it is that the heart, a pump, has become associated with emotion, he would have given an esoteric answer. Now he offers a scientific one. For 65% of brain matter is found in the heart. The heart links to the limbic system as a fifth brain. And then the heart begins to do our thinking, intuitively, breaking out of rational mode. We inhabit poetic time. Time beyond linear. This is where our writing sings the rhythm of the heart.

Writers draw ideas from silence. Caitlin Matthews in *Singing the Soul back Home*, reminds us of the Gaelic poets who practised as shamans do under the guidance of a master-poet. This insight inspired a poem:

> The Stone on the Stomach
>
> in the Celtic twilight
> Gaelic poets incubated
> the silhouette of a poem.
> the master offered aspirants
> the subject for composition,
> matched to the movement
> of frequencies and fingerprints.
>
> each bard retired to a place
> womb-dark, moon-dark,
> lay awake alone, with a stone
> pressed to the stomach
> to keep watchful, balanced.
> slowly they divined shapes
> beneath lids and lips.

Achilles Heal – In Poetic Praise of Healing

the pattern, rhyme and rhythm
fell and rose, riding their chests.
images breathed inner into outer.
as the sun touched huts and hearts
they rose and stretched limbs
long as lines, and delivered,
apprentice to the words within.

This next poem emerged at the Buddhist retreat during my first visit in 1993:

Men in Meditation

the winter bells sounds
calling us from dreams
of couplings and celibacy
to a temple meditation.

our crafts drift though fog
to this walled port
where a turmeric light
spices a white wall.

the last stars are dying
as we lock our bones
in a lotus cross
or kneel as if in chapel prayer.
we rest like a menology of saints
on an eastern calendar.

like ancient mariners
navigating ocean poles,

Route 77

> we have fathomed
> the slime of the deep.
> now mendicant all
> we live these three days
> off the alms of brotherhood.
>
> on a black mat anchor
> saffron sailed,
> the mast of my body
> rides amid a male fleet.
> we rise as the sun gongs
> across the ticking sea.

When we are silent, the universe rolls through us.

WAYS WITH WORDS – AMBIGUITY, PARADOX, IRONY AND WORD PLAY

The paradox of faith begins in the nature of God.

When you realise that 'heart' and 'earth' are spelt with the same letters, it starts to make sense.
(sign at the West Coat Fossil Park)

Ambiguity

The title of this sixth section, the *Achilles Heal*, came from a misspelling (what I call a Jungian slip) while writing a poem. The language of poetry? Ambiguity. We work with only a few words – in miniature scale – so the words carry multiple meanings, sometimes contradictory.

Achilles Heal – In Poetic Praise of Healing

So many words open to ambiguity. Take the word such as 'play', for example, which brings with it so many nuances. While context determines the primary meaning, other meanings ghost around. Echoing it in other dimensions. Here are some of the dictionary meanings of the word *play:* Both a noun and a verb. To amuse, caper, take part in a play, act, play music by ear, play the fool, gamble, take part in sport, play up, action. We play games. Play suggests movement and hence also movement in words. Play invokes our curiosity – an antidote to grief.

Around words ghost other words. Their grandparents (ancestry) and cousins (contemporary meanings). Rhyming also allows other meanings to arrive. A child might hear in a priest's words, "let us pray," "let us play." They are forms of each other. Prayer as play?

Word ambiguity can teach us how to live ambiguously. Keats spoke about this concept in his letters – negative capability, how to hold contradictions without the need to resolve them, 'when a man is capable of being in uncertainties, mysteries, doubts, without any irritable reaching after fact and reason'. This is living the 'both and' rather than the 'either or.' In this space that the Spanish poet Antonio Machado writes of, 'between sleeping and dreaming there is a third thing. Guess it'.

William Empson's *Seven Types of Ambiguity* is about the riches of linguistic ambiguity in English poetic literature. Verbal nuances that give rise to alternative responses to the same text. Empson's studies unearth layer upon layer of irony and suggestion through close reading.

Shakespearean drama (extended poems) offers many examples. Macbeth curses the witches who 'palter with a double sense'. Yet, it is rather his inability to read ambiguity and to choose the meaning that he prefers that creates a blind spot. He is trapped in a perception, an appearance. The witches chant, "none of woman born shall harm

Macbeth." So Macbeth believes he bears a charmed life. In the final battle Macduff, born by caesarean birth, beheads him.

Making choices is not easy. The choice is often between a lesser or greater wrong or a lesser or greater right. Take what you want to and pay for it. There is a cost to action and so in action we need to hold the ambivalent consequences. In situational ethics (ethical choices emerging from the situation) we're often faced with decisions that depend on us staying in ambiguity.

Paradox

An apparent contradiction or non-sense statement which hides an understanding or truth. You must lose your life in order to find it. You bind yourself to set yourself free.

Rumi's poetry is rich in paradoxes:

> Birds make great sky-circles
> of their freedom.
> How do they learn it?
> They fall, and falling,
> they're given wings.

Many words open to paradox. The word 'light' because of its multiple meanings is one such word as in this verse from Emily Dickinson's *There's a Certain Slant of Light*:

> There's a certain slant of light,
> On winter afternoons,
> That oppresses, like the weight
> Of cathedral tunes.

We can also coin words that hold ambiguity and paradox, that offer us the bitter-sweet experiences. e.g. 'joyloss'. Shelly wrote, 'our sweetest songs are those that tell of saddest thought' and Shakespeare ends one of his sonnets about growing old:

> This thou perceivist which makes thy love more strong
> To love that well which thou must leave ere long.

Irony

Walt Whitman writes, 'Do I contradict myself? I contradict myself, I contain multitudes'. Irony springs from our complexity as we meet a world where appearances masquerade as reality. We are creatures of not knowing, or knowing partially. We inhabit these tensions. We live in illusion.

The Achilles myth is rich in irony. Achilles, like Macbeth, lives under the illusion that he is immortal. He too will be dragged down to Hades. His dragging of Hector's body by the ankles foreshadows his own way of dying.

The Russian poet Yevgeny Yevtushenko reminds us how irony can be a double-edged sword. Here are a few lines:

> …like any Faust, we've been prejudged.
> With Mephistophelian smile, irony,
> like a shadow, dogs our every step.
>
> In vain we try to dodge the shadow.
> The paths in front, behind, are blocked.
> Irony, to you we've sold our soul,
> receiving no Margaret in return.

A Play on Words

How do we cultivate the poet's playful attitude to words? There are puns and there are puns. Clichés elicit a groan. The punster tries to be clever and the play on words does not advance meaning in any creative way. Yet, some puns can create language in a new way. e.g. the phrase 'hobo sapiens'

In Sanskrit poetry, puns are common techniques to achieve suggestion and create a larger context. In a poem "The Lamp", in which the lamp observes lovers, the Buddhist poet-scholar Vidyakara uses the word 'intercourse' to open to wider meanings.

We have heard much of the healing power of humour. There is a story of a man who watched comedy movies to cure himself from cancer. Playful puns often elicit a smile. Perhaps what is important is that the word play is integrated into the poem, contributes and does not call attention to itself.

So welcome to the four sisters, the muses – Ambiguity, Paradox, Irony and Word Play. They will arrive, invited or not in your poems.

SAVED BY A POEM

> *I have woven*
> *a parachute out of everything broken,*
> *my scars are my shield: and I jump,*
> *daylight or dark into any country.*
> (William Stafford)

John Fox's *Poetic Medicine: The Healing Art of Poem-Making* (1997) includes stories of people from his workshops who exemplify how poetry has aided them to become more whole. Kim Rosen's *Saved by a Poem, The Transformative Power of Words* (2009) comes with

Achilles Heal – In Poetic Praise of Healing

an accompanying CD where a number of prominent poets read their favourite poem – own or by others, and talk of its impact. She holds open poetry's first door: 'the intimate and unobstructed voice. She shows how the practice of saying a poem can be limitless, revealing our fullest capacities of heart and mind, and returning those capacities to us in times when we have forgotten our way. It comes straight from the original fires in which poems are forged.' (Jane Hirshfield, *Nine Gates: Entering the Mind of Poetry*).

Some dozen of us share in a monthly Pringle Bay Poetry Moments circle where we read own and others and allow the words to sift through us, emerging euphoric after touching the hem of the muse. We also write for each other. Here is a poem I wrote for Mary in 2021 (and all other Mary's) whose son Kim, while running, fell sixty metres off Table Mountain to his death:

Lightning Strike

the lightning does not always
strike first, the long-lived tree.
this bolt struck the seeded one,
your sapling, in its prime, sap rising,
trunk sturdy, ripe with berry
and seed for kindred kind.

the spark split it, toppled,
scorched in a whipping wind
that seared the green leaf
and hurled his limbs off balance,
only a charred stump left
to mark his flourishing.

> did you, the elder, with mandala rings,
> left alive on these forest slopes,
> your withering bark gnarled,
> your branches and twigs brittle,
> will that the jagged Z flash
> strike your stem instead?
>
> yet in the ground beneath
> the fury of the firestorm,
> you, the elder, stand beside
> the ghost of the younger,
> still rooted in shared story,
> entwined in this fertile earth.

In *Lament for a Son*, Nicholas Wolterstorff, a Professor of Philosophic Theology, and clinical psychologist, grieves for his son Eric who died falling off a mountain at the age of twenty-five. He had considered sorrow as an island but after this loss sees sorrow as the sea. 'There's a hole in the word now… How can I sing in this desolate land when there is always one too few?'

So we can place grief in a poem that will hold us.

TEMENOS GARDEN OF THE BELOVED

For a decade Temenos has hosted a Poetry Festival. A joyous date for sung and unsung poets. Poetry recitals, music events, art and workshops. Temenos sacred space, McGregor. A Spiritual oasis in a sometimes arid town. A place of pilgrimage inspired though Billy Kennedy's vision and devotion.

Here is a dedicated poetry library. Billy, generous host, creator of the garden with poetry hung in trees. Poet Patricia Schonstein, another generous soul, publishes annually an anthology of participating poets. Bob Commin sometimes offers a Sunday eurcarist in the Little Way (St Teresa of Avila) chapel. Jesus and the Buddha embrace.

Competitions for youth and oldies. The theme for 2019: The Heart of the Moon. Here was my entry:

Lucifer, 1969 and the Moon

Some say Lucifer the devil fell
from the heavenly realm
for he saw himself as the source
of light, not reflecting divine fire.

In a cold war space race
fifty years ago, was it part Lucifer
that landed the Eagle lunar ship
so man could plant the Stars and Stripes?

When the first man, his heart thumping,
giant stepped first on our world's moon,
did his boot scraping the surface
raise a spark of Lucifer light?

As our astronaut thrust a spade
into her crust in search of a sample,
he uncovered a heart made
of moon shadow and mirror light.

For the moon in all four phases and faces,
humble powdery planet that she is,
does not see herself in such a grand way.
She bathes in shades of ambiguity.

Route 77

> She speaks to our planet in a tongue
> that shifts the tides, calls night crops forth,
> breathes to the rhythm of a woman's cycle
> and makes space for lunatics, lovers and poets.

Here is my 2021 entry (Theme Garden of the Beloved):

The Sacred Heart of the Garden

With a turtle dove at rest on a shoulder,
a pilgrim wandered, seeking the garden
heart. Then ambling around the outer ring
he sent the winged one on such a quest.

Bird alighted on the Buddha
who raised a silent flower.
She fluttered to The Well where
bubbling over stones, a Bethesda
angel troubled the story waters.

To the white rose angel of lost children
whose spirits wander ever the paths.
Little Way Chapel intoned Theresa's vision.
Let this presence settle into your bones.
Where oh where? Was the centre within Celtic cross,
icon art – Christ Buddha embracing, or the world
in the lap of a Babushka child in Mary's lap?
In the mystic symbols of a Baraka shrine?

Or somewhere beneath a crescent Mecca moon
intoning the ninety-nine names of the Divine?
In the lit seven cup candle stick, the menorah,

> the cosmos in Krishna's throat, in Brahman's breath?
> A thatched cottage named of Benedict's cave
> where the Saint composed a trellis for faith,
> a copy earthed in the foundation. But where?
>
> Was it Rumi's rustic doorway where worlds meet,
> the labyrinth, the spiral still point, willow or oak?
> Tanden energy, two fingers below the belly,
> the axis in qigong and tai chi? Bell, alcove,
> seed, bud, duckpond, fount, a handful of soil?
> Within the charitable Caritas chorus of books?
> In poems that festival the branches in spring?
>
> After all nightday circling, the turtle dove
> descended with an olive branch in her beak
> to whisper the secret in the pilgrim's inner ear.
> It pulses here as an infinite sphere whose centre
> is everywhere, whose circumference nowhere.

In such a place as Temenos you align with the power inside and amidst ducks and peacocks, poems pour forth from the source. Here I facilitate retreats such as *Hundreds of Ways: Writing your Spiritual Journey:* So here's to annual poetry pilgrimages.

PRAISE POEMS

I have praise-poem'd for many – some commissions, others gifts. A privilege to hear a loved one talk of their loved one and feed me the gifts of their life. Here are three extracts.

For Sybbie there were poems for birthdays, seventies, eighties and the nineties, she departing in her early nineties. Here is part of the nineties one:

Route 77

Dame Sybbie, our Sybbie
(an i-sibbi-bongo praise poem)

what do you call,
a theatre dynamo,
doyen of the stage
tamer of a zillion lines,
all Sybil syllables spoken,
with the *chutzpah*
of a dozen divas?

who sips her whiskey,
watches the tennis stars
bounce on the court?
spots and winks at the folks
stuck behind curtain lace
peering at her buoyant life?

who took off to faraway lands
off the SA map, opening
up worlds behind worlds –
China, Argentina, South Pacific
chewing Rennies for indigestion
when her tourists misbehaved?

wakes to Fine Music Radio
dresses, drives to stats work
those three mornings a week
in the only car with a down-tug
rope looped to the roof of the boot?
who could draw you a blue map
of Jozi on the back grid of her hand?

Achilles Heal – In Poetic Praise of Healing

she who buried a husband, going blind,
saw two of her children laid to rest,
bid farewell to many friends.
calls herself 'the titless wonder'
sage survivor, who revels
in books and movies.

great greatest gran. a nonagenarian?
rather a non age unwearying geranium.
wise as Sophia and Solomon combined
we celebrate you, *mazel tov. l'chaim*
matriarch of moments and marvel,
you, filled with Sybil fizz and ageless age,
waltz through the gateless gate
on the arms of our endless love.

Ray and Lali. Many Killarney stayovers and shabbats, visits to the liberal synagogue, cheffing in their kitchen, recipes stuck on the kitchen fridge. Here's to these Elders (a few selected verses):

Lali the Spider Woman @80

we sing, we sing a song
for a spider woman.
you scuttle across ceilings,
hang upside down
abseil on a single thread
in a ray of sunshine.
you hide in the corner
of granny's cupboard,

Route 77

dancing out of reach
of the feather duster.

pluck your web here
it trembles there.
vibrates and shimmers
in a tai chi breeze.
you display the courage
and chutzpah, dear bubbe,
of a marvel comic maiden
who adheres to many a surface
and directs her serum at the baddies.

mazel tov oh maiden mensch
as you dance along your silk road.
shalom shalom shalom.
(24 October 2015)

Ray of Light

(for Ray at eighty: 20 August 2013)

I sing of a four score man
a Samson of Stories,
man of the sun who finds honey
in the carcass of a lion,
who knows as many tales
as hairs on his head, chest and legs.

these stories breathe close
to his skin. jostle for attention.
tell me they call I'm the one

for this occasion – barmitzvah,
board room, braai or bedside.

he lets the story climb into
his bush brows and jawbone,
curl around his tongue.
delight the pupils in his eyes.
it unfolds to wrap you
like an lion skin, a bear hug,
a shawl, a Shabbat prayer
Barukh atah Adonai....

larger than life one in a thou,
you attend to the graves.
talk to the dead and the quick.
a chant in your chest
a gleam in your eye
a spark in your heart
a flash in your smile
beaming, beaming,
yeah, a ray of eighty lights
lit alongside the eternal flame.

Then one morning, at a Killarney breakfast there's a gift from Lali and Ray in an ancient wicker basket with lid and clip. "Guess Dori." After wild guesses, I wave my hands around in a circle. "Yes," says Ray, "close." "A world globe?" "Warm." I give up, open the wicker. It's a tea basket, black velvet wrap. Unearth a yellowwood stand, and, yes a crystal ball.

The story? 'Some forty years ago a gypsy kind of dressed woman hurried into our Granny's Cupboard in down-town Jozi, our antique store, "Have to sell this… been in family for generations.'" R100 (1960s) exchanges hands. Now it arrives in mine.

In some praise poems for mutual friends, Barbara Kennedy (who also lives in Pringle Bay) has added to the honouring by backing the words with her intuitive cello. She and I offer cello and poetry /story events, sometimes in aid of KidsCan, a local charity that supports two after school care units, offering extra tuition for some 64 children. She the virtuoso, I the ou soandso.

7

Loves Within, Loves Without

Once again, falling in love, even in its most exquisite forms, represents no more than a taste and a promise of a more profound quality of conscious life.
(Jacob Needleman)

A cynic approaches a Rabbi, "If you can recite the Torah, the first five books of the Old Testament, while standing on one leg, then I will believe." The Rabbi balances on one leg and begins. "You shall love the Lord your God with all your heart, with all your soul, and with all your strength. Deuteronomy 6:5. You shall love your neighbour as yourself: Leviticus 19:18." The Rabbi then returns the raised foot to the floor and says, "All the rest is footnote."

Sanskrit has ninety-six words for the nuances of love. CS Lewis was fascinated with the four Greek words.

Storge – An affectionate, familial quality – for parents, siblings, children, pets. To Lewis, *storge* is the most organic form of love.

Philia – The reciprocal quality with a friend. Lewis describes *philia* as having a dispassionate quality. Friendship love – some come and go, some stay.

Eros – Romantic passion, rapture, euphoric. 'You know you're in love when you don't want to fall asleep because reality is finally better than your dreams.' (Dr Seuss). The energy dynamic, fluid, and it can come and go at any time. Love within the pleasure pain wheel.

Agape – Something within you containing all the love you could ever ask for. Its root form, means 'wide open', in a state of wonder, connecting with awareness itself, not clinging onto anything. Constantly letting go. Opening to the divine moment. Observing my being part of the wheel.

So where to enter this morphic field? I choose within. If I attend to the flow of water sprouting from the fountain of the self then the water can nourish those around me.

THE NIGHT NOVEL – DREAMS

Once Chuang-Tzu dreamt he was a butterfly, fluttering around... Suddenly he woke up...But he didn't know if he was Chuang-Tzu who had just dreamt that he was a butterfly, or a butterfly now dreaming that he was Chuang-Tzu. (Chuang-Tzu)

The image that comes to mind when I think of this girl (herself) is the image of a fisherman sunk in dreams on the verge of a deep lake with a rod held over the water. She was letting her imagination sweep unchecked round every rock and cranny of the world that lies submerged in the depth of our unconscious being. (Virginia Woolf)

I keep a dream journal. Once part of a dream group. Our approach, the gestalt – all in the dream represents an aspect of our many selves. The longing, the fascination, the dark, the hidden revealed. In a lifetime we dream-sleep (REM) around 2000 hours. What of these stories? These loves? We conjure images that delight us and make us tremble. John Bath, a writer, who believes that professional storytellers are professional dreamers, feels that 'icons in good fiction... take on that dreamish voltage'

(Eppel, *Writers Dreaming*). In her book twenty-six writers speak of the impact of their dreams on their writing.

The Talmud tells us, "A dream that is not understood is a letter that is not opened." What of the story about Rabbi Ben Isaac of Krakow? In a dream, a messenger told him, "If you go to the city and dig under a tree at the emperor's castle, you will find hidden treasure." The second night he had the same dream, and the third night. So he went to the city. But the castle was heavily guarded and he couldn't get in. Every morning the Rabbi walked around the castle. One day the captain of the guard asked him, "Old man, what are you doing walking round and round the castle?"

The Rabbi told him the story. The captain laughed, shook his head, and said, "Dreams are foolish things. I had a dream about a poor Rabbi who came from a village like yours. He dug up his own hearth and found a treasure hidden there." The Rabbi thanked the captain, walked the long road home, dug beneath his fireplace and found the treasure.

Perhaps it is important to stay with the images from our dreams. This is one face of inner love, sewing our night and day travel into one garment. To move into a poem the moment we awake. John Sanford in *Dreams and Healing* discusses how we all write a novel at night – dreaming and writing are first cousins. We process our dreams as narratives – atmosphere, plot, characters, conflict and form.

I once dreamt of an elderly woman who loved literature and approached, "You must look at your ear." I told her that my ear was too far round the side of my face. Then she took me by the hand and led me round the four corners of the room. I wrote a children's story, *Chameleon Vision*, out of that dream published in a trilogy *Legs, Bones and Eyes*. The story involves a boy with blurred vision who learns to see and hear in a new way. Assisted by his pet chameleon, Camo, he saves his schoolmates when the dam above the school breaks.

Here is one 2021 night travel tale. (Dear psychologist friends, enjoy yourselves.) A flight is delayed. We are to be ushered off to a game reserve at our own cost, at R3300 per night. We find ourselves in an elderly couple's home. He asks, "How does the delay affect the presentation you are to give?" My response. "It gives me time to spend with you two before the event." He hands me a long-published book relevant to my story topic. The woman asks, "What do you plan to achieve in the lesson?" I draw a parallel line (a literal line of how the students might see the world) and next to it an expanding cone (student world view after contemplating the mythical, the metaphoric.) She nods in approval. I respond, "It's the quality of your question that brings forth the insight."

Here's to loving this inner night travelling and to how it opens to understanding of how love moves within our world. By day we are white light, by night a dream prism separates us into rainbow shades in the drama of story. How to love all of us in me?

DREAM CHEF

Poems and, yes, Recipes

> *There is no such thing as an enlightened person.*
> *There is only an enlightened activity.*
>   (Zen Master, Suzuki Roshi)

In my poetry or olives apron, I chef in 'taste as you go mode' – sprinkle or this… that …

A lawyer and a chef are in a hospital, lying side by side. They become friends. The chef is dying.

L: have you left a Will?
C: I have nothing and no one to leave it to.

L: That is irrelevant. By making a Will you are saying "I was here. I existed." So the chef asks for a scrap of paper and scribbles away. After he dies the lawyer retrieves the paper from under his friend's pillow and unfolds it. It is the chef's favourite recipe with all the secret ingredients. The lawyer's name is on it.

So here be three recipes.

Meditation on Fasolia

Sometimes during a writing wordshop, I cook for participants. Don an apron. Invoke the Dream Chef (I dreamt this poem, whole as an almond) and raise the pan for blessing:

> Dream Chef
>
> he travels by sea, by land
> with the taste of Asia,
> this night conjurer
> who comes to cook for me.
> loose top, loose shoes.
> recipes in cursive
> scribble his pants.
>
> skillet in hand,
> wok on the flame,
> he fills the kitchen
> with seeds, greens, bulbs,
> roots and oils.
> he serves a dish
> so rich in East
> my mouth's an aroma cave.

Route 77

> I lick fingers
> and hug this giant
> who feeds me such cuisine.
> I rest my cheek
> against his ribs, his heart.
> my arms embrace
> this dream god's roundedness.
> I hear food music from within.

The meditation begins, the recipe text inside my head. I think of the *Kitchen Mystic* who writes, 'I see God in onions… I hold up the slice to the sunlight pouring in through the kitchen window and it glows like a fine piece of antique glass. Cool watery white with layers delicately edged in imperial purple' (Mary Hayes Grieco).

Perhaps I might add green peppers and potatoes, depending on mood. And with Rumi, Persian Sufi, I say to the onion, peppers and potatoes as I steer them though olive oil with a spatula oar:

> Don't you try to jump out.
> You think I'm torturing you.
> I'm giving you flavour
> So you can mix of spices and rice
> and be the lovely vitality of the human being.

And all the while, the white beans – that as children we put in a bottle and guessed how many, or grew them damp and dark under cotton wool, waiting for the green sprout – are steaming their minutes in the sauna.

The raisins join the pan party and swell buoyant in red wine. And the beans arrive chewsoft… while olives tinkle their notes. And it rains cumin and sesame seeds. And garlic breathes on the waters. And all the while I'm tasting… tasting… a touch of marmalade… of lemon juice. I

Loves Within, Loves Without

think of my children and how they remind me of the day I sprinkled in the Horlicks… Taste guides quantities.

Now I hear the voice of a chef friend, Leon (his prawns take me to where angels sing.) "You have the texture… what about the colour? Be guided by this and the dish will arrive home on the palate as sacrament." And so the feta slips down an olive oil slide, splashing into the sap. White as a Greek church. And sprigs of dill green as a Christmas tree. May the ancestors – and Zorba and Kazantzakis dance in this pot.

A Meal for Writers

in a Cretan taverna,
a tin of oil butting the door
high as a goat,
an olive grove dusting the road,
I tasted fasolia.

I bring you peasant days:
beans fat as fish, cumin,
feta white as sea light,
citrus groves with orange suns,
onions, orthodox as churches,
vine stock, raisin rich,
and potatoes from another island,
rich as Croesus in its own poets.

may you lose yourself
in a maze of tastes,
find the labyrinth to
your black-cat stomach.
may gods and goddesses
Kazantzakis and Zorba

Route 77

> dance on the rim of your bowl,
> arms akimbo, eyes ablaze
> in the blue haze
> of a siesta afternoon.

Dori's Bread of Leaven

In a mamma of speaking, it's not the exact measurement but the instinctive guess that designs a quality bread.
(sauce unknown, possibly attributed to Sir Herb Baker)

- Fine grind 1.87ish cups of mixed seeds: sunflower (61.3%ish), pumpkin (18.8%) linseed, sesame, poppy, chia, (da rest %)
- A snow fall of fine coconut flakes
- add a triple fat pinch of Italian or Mix-ican herbs, a thimble of cinnamon
- a two-year-old's handful of fine chopped pecans/almonds and cranberries
- large desert spoon bran to die gest for
- four fifths t-spoon chili salt or him-or-her-malayan salt
- a sneeze of black pepper
- t-spoon xylitol
- 2.23ish heaped t-spoons baking powder
- 1 desert spoon psyllium husks
- Mix de lot in a bowl, whisk, whisk, then add and stir in 249 grams plain double cream yoghurt
- 4/6ths coffee scoop-spoon apple cider vinegar
- beat in 3 large eggs (hen not ostrich)
- sprinkle with 'here comes the sunflower' seeds
- pour into butter greased container

- bake in pre-heated oven @ 182 degrees C for 48.3ish mins
- enjoy enjoy enjoy

(copywrong: Dori the Baker 2020)

Feeesch el Dorilaliray

(adorned Ray and Lali's fridge)

- Chopped onions/leeks and fennel bulb fried in olive oil/coconut oil
- with garlic ginger chili cumin curry turmeric cinnamon (sprinkles of)
- chopped tomatoes with skins
- a little lemon rind
- apple or pear slices
- dill seeds
- add lemon juice und white wine for merry simmer
- enter the feeesch gently bubbling
- simmer simmer simmer
- what else is in the fridge?
- green honeybush rooibos mint tea
- keep tasting keep tasting
- yoghurt or coconut cream
- garnish mit fine chopped fennel fronds or dill

I chef for all who wish to 'feast on their lives' (Derek Walcott).

CROSSING ORANGE – RIVER SEA MOUNTAIN FOREST

December 1997. Midnight. Full moon, I'm swimming in the Orange River, near the border crossing. I look north, farewell Namibia. I

Route 77

turn south, hello South Africa. Leaving behind university, shifting to entrepreneurial wordshop facilitator and mentor. I'll cross this border many times.

Moments such as this, at one with the natural world. The porous skin does not know any distinction between what's without and what's within. Many such experiences filter elsewhere through this book as I hike mountain trails, plunge rock pools, tidal ones, immerse in river and ocean. Gather mussels off low tide rocks. With the boy who grew up in inland thorn-tree country, flatlands, with the occasional hill. With poet Hopkins, 'let them be left, oh let them be left / long live the weeds and the wilderness yet'.

Such places call me to wake up and love the wild wide-angle moment for itself:

Beach Light

back pressed again a dune,
a woman dangles her arms
on raised knees, head slumped.
a beached whale, who sees
no way to heave her weight
back into water.

she does not see
her silhouette shine
as i do, walking
the sea-edge sunset.

the sky halos her hair,
the arch of elbows,
the letter A of her legs,

Loves Within, Loves Without

the Z of her ending.
Golden, she hunches
in a womb of light.

Bird Hide – Langebaan

this hide, with its bench
and window ledge
where you kneel,
to rest your elbows
and cup your hands
to the twilight,
serves as communion rail
in this cathedral of lagoon and sea.
the setting sun is choir master
to the fluttering of a thousand wings.
a flamingo in priest's robes
blesses the wine-water
and the bread mulch in the reeds.
I ingest in silence
the bird's cry and the sea roar
and taste the salt marsh on my tongue.

Tsitsikamma trail in the rain, slip-sliding, drying hiking boots at the fire's edge. Swimming in Baltic, Mediterranean, Gulf of Mexico, Sunshine coast Australia, off the Mozambique coast. And of late, close to daily swimming among reed-thronged nests with saffron finch and cormorant wings hung out to dry in Buffels lagoon at Pringle. Learning to love the natural world. Here's part of a fynbos poem:

Route 77

In Praise of Fynbos

evergreen, it reaches into soil,
drought-dry, nutrient-thin,
this kind of West Cape heather
so fine, so fine, rooted here,
only here, in this strip of earth.

restios reeds thatch the veld,
the honeybush invites the bee.
on rock ledge heights
steep as mountain goats,
in kloof and crevice,
plants shake off water
like a beach dog
to drop tannin
into a goldflow stream.

here flowers in season
bloom in subtle shades,
in primary blue yellow red,
disa erika protea blushing bride.
the beetroot shoot shapes
a candle-tipped mandala
that will tumble in a ball of air.

As in Hopkins' *Inversnaid*, the beginning of the poem:

> This darksome burn, horseback brown,
> His rollrock highroad roaring down,
> In coop and in comb the fleece of his foam
> Flutes and low to the lake falls home.

Nature animate, all infused with spirit.

ELEVEN JUST MEN

> *...My mariners,*
> *Souls that have toil'd, and wrought, and thought with me–*
> *That ever with a frolic welcome took*
> *The thunder and the sunshine, and opposed*
> *Free hearts, free foreheads–you and I are old;*
> *Old age hath yet his honour and his toil.*
> (Tennyson, Ulysses)

I have been much blessed with men friends, these helping angels who support and challenge me. Tolerant of my foibles. Sharers in 'laughter holding both its sides'. Bonded we are in mutual love, in *philios*. There are many more than eleven, the cricket team number. To include these is to exclude all those to whom I apologise. To run off an alphabet of names might not mean much to you, the reader. I celebrate them in poetry, hoping to touch the hem of their essence. Some here, others in other sections, scattered like the good seed that produces the crop from the rich ground. They wander through other pages as poem assisters, hiking companions, colleagues, elders, youngers. Some 'mentorees' turned into friends. Igno and I driving though the eastern Free State en route to Dargal to join the horses who teach leadership. Bob and Peter in our play date sleep overs in Somerset West cottage.

Route 77

Immersed in Water Words

three men friends
take to the pool
in the early evening
catching up, splashing
in the ripple of their
seventy plus lives.

then toweled and settled
on the sofa, they share
red wine, pizza and tiramisu.
while they unpack recent reading.
each surfs a wave of books
washing over the coffee table.

trailing their hands in the great waters,
they let each other's voice
spill the text through their hands.
each intones quotes that float past
the whorls and lines of fingers and palms.

each chosen passage
stirs words so holy
they walk on water
and in the same moment
snorkel us into the each other's
underwater world.

Jim, woodturner for our conversations around the restaurants of the Cape, around your enquiry into secular spirituality and the wine route.

Loves Within, Loves Without

Here's to your book *Conjectures*. Aha learning Bruce, player of many instruments. Bruce ex Westerford colleague.

And extracts from poems (many written for birthdays) Barbara Kennedy backed this one with her cello on the banks of the Modder River):

Igno Photoman, Highfive Ou

enthusiastic admiration is the first principle
of knowledge and the last
(Blake)

of Igno we sing we sing, highfive ou,
Bethlehem boy, boeremark bookbuyer,
believing is seeing man, broker bringer of
us to each other and home to ourselves.
in your presence our eyes wide angle open.
we focus hocus pocus, swap lenses, filters
adjust and shift our shutter speed.

the eternal child dances and prances
twinkle toes in your eyes and on your lips.
something of an impno trickster in that grin.
you're Tigger in Winnie the Poo
we can't ignore your bounce and zip
you star in Circus McGurkus
and in a Cat in the Hat too.
funnyman, teacherman, leaderman,
noble not ignoble, no ignoramus here.....

Route 77

family man, finefather, friend of friends,
your generosity, velocity, Ignocity,
your passion rubs off on us.
in Igno presence we inflate,
like an air balloon over Bloem,
fly in wider circles, brave the winds. soar....

we sing, we sing, dear man
of igno photoman, highfive ou.
you igspire us, you ignite our lives.

The Story Priest
(for Bob Commin)

when you, the playful priest,
ring the cathedral in tales
of rabbits, giants and lions,
you baptise us in a river of images.

stained-glass saints tilt halos to listen,
pew cushions leap off hooks,
the isle carpet prickles, candles flicker,
lilies in Our Lady's Chapel bloom.

hymnals clap hallelujah hands
the font splashes, bells peel
the rafters hum and buzz.
the organ pipes the everafter.

the divine story-teller sifts through you,
the hour glass, our hunger for the Christ,

Loves Within, Loves Without

who gathers narratives and children,
through your outstretched arms.

Ferryman
(for Peter Fox)

light fades in rose blaze
clouds mask the evening star.
the moon dies three days in its tomb.
I wait at water's edge
black as the mineshaft
I dived as a boy.
the current tugs memories
from under my feet…

and you appear at the prow
a lamp hangs, splutters.
you guide me into your boat.
wrap a cloak around my shoulders.
sit me at rowlock and oar.
together we spade
into the night crossing.

our voices carry songs
up and down river –
stones that skim across water.
the last page of the story flutters open.
you, the final presence,
ferry me fullstop to the other bank.
to the morning star beyond this mist.

Route 77

Hand in the Sky
(for John Roome)

as we walk the morning beach
my animated artist friend offers
an image for this overcast day.

the stratus clouds form a hand
with fingers stretched above us
in longitude over earth and ocean.

is it the chapel ringed blue
right hand of a multi fingered god,
palm hovering over creation to bless,

whose index finger stokes the globe?
he reaches down to touch many Adams
drawing us, tip to tip, into animation.

Loves Within, Loves Without

John Roome sketch in ZenPenYen

I seem to collect renegade alternative priests, perhaps to hedge my bets? Here's another part poem for Pringle Bay friend, priest, versed in the mystics, seeking salvation through poetry. Part of our local Poetry Moments group:

Birthright Day

for Gerald Steward at 27 029 days

on this your birthright day –
I see you as a kind of Jacob.
the Biblical one who scored years 147.
you're only a tad over half-way there.

Route 77

> he's our man as he's fallible like us,
> diddling a twin, born a heel ahead of him....
>
> you're a travelling Jacob.
> fleeing priestburnout,
> you lay down here to rest
> finding a rock sharp
> as your wit, pithy as your spirit,
> to lay your spinning head.
> in the dream rising rising
> the ladder stretches its rungs
> into the cloud of unknowing....

Pat Grayson the Ozzie writer who published *The Halo and The Noose* prefaced by the quotation, 'A halo only has to slip a few inches to become a noose.' Now of Heartspace Publications. We share the long roads of writing and relationship, publishing this tome. 1001 thanks.

Gert van der Westhuizen, ex academic, fascinated by childrens' conversations, and Matti Kimberg, gynae and poet with Estonia in his blood. I mentored his first poetry volume. *Viewed through my Lapraroscope*. Clive Goodchilde Brown, accountant by day, crime writer by night. Late into fatherhood. Werner Schmidt, musician maverick, with a lightning brain. Spending time with Brian Thorn in the Waterberg, Namibia and in his high hut on the mountain above Piketberg. He the ex-smous of the Camelthorn Windhoek antique shop.

A common denominator? In their eyes a boy still alive. 'Give me back the soul I had as a boy matured in fairy tales'. (Garcia Lorca) And Rumi:

> Has anyone seen the boy who used to come here?
> Round-faced trouble-maker, quick to find a joke,
> slow to be serious, red shirt, perfect coordination,

sly, strong muscled, with things always in his pocket:
reed flute, worn pick, polished and ready for his Talent.
You know that one. Have you heard stories about him?
Pharaoh and the whole Egyptian world collapsed for such a Joseph.
I'd gladly spend years getting word of him, even third or fourth hand.

ELEVEN JUST WOMEN

Taking its motif from ancient Greek literature, the Three Graces depicts the three daughters of Zeus, each of
whom bestows a particular gift on humanity: Euphrosyne (mirth), Aglaia (elegance) and Thalia
(youth and beauty).

On the sea route map of *Route 77* this is where you find open seas, smooth sailing, siren songs and also the sign "Here be Dragons."

I'm not strong on absorbing other languages. Yet, not sure how or why, I have learnt smatterings of Womanish. Was it daughter Martine who coached me? Platonic and unplatonic, crones, age mates? Friendship born in writing wordshops? Many of these women who in fifties and sixties come after a life of service to husband, child, home, now released, rocket into writing retreats, offering openness, teachings, companionship. Seeking the mythic life. These women are 77 % of wordshopper clientelle. They say male elephants have six ways of communicating, female ellis over forty.

Poets, some. Psychologists, trauma counsellors, and narrative therapists a plenty, who tell me they too hear stories as alive, fraught and fine as those I hear but they are bound to vows of silence whereas I can

Route 77

sing those I hear alive in books. Retreat set-uppers, others. Beach walker coffee sharers. A thousand thanks to these graces and amused muses.

Once I dreamt of a crone who told me, "If you look from a distance, only some women are beautiful. But if you look so close that your eye lashes touch a woman's cheek then all women are beautiful." Aye aye.

Once more a dilemma. Many of these muses grace other pages. So, once more eleven… the women's cricket team. And not in batting order. I follow clever Neruda – his love poems not attributed though you might recognise your generous selves.

Head Massage

your hands explore
equator, tropics and poles.
you gallop your fingers
over skull dongas, deserts,
bone valleys, forests, craters.
thumb traces from temple,
from ears to nape.
index travels the sinus line.
your web spiders
my forehead span.
you affect the weather
as you raise an almond breeze
a mustard sun, coconut clouds.

so your words massage this globe.
scan my brow, length and breadth.
raise the blood through roots and stems,
set me a-tingle, fontanel to nape.
you anoint my head in image oil.

Loves Within, Loves Without

Healing Winds

she sat with her client,
whispering so as to wake him
from day sleep, dreamless and drugged.
she breathed mouth to mouth,
the cosmology of myths
to launch his yacht
from dry dock
and shallow basin.

they took to the doldrum sea.
she puffed her cheeks
to unfurl the sails.
heaving wave and change
cycled beneath their feet.

so he shifted from his known map
to a storied crossing.
she spiraled away on wind
into her own narration,
leaving her image
carved as figurehead.

Soup Spoon in a Restaurant

the spoon gathers,
in its outer rim,
autumn-leaf curtains,
a Cape-scape,
St Joseph lilies,
a candelabra of stars.

Route 77

in the inner ring,
two wine glasses link
red-silver lovers, upside down.
in the concave mirror,
Mercury curves and ghosts
flying from lip to lip.

Photographic Father

after his shots
for the local press,
her father snapped her
to finish the spool.

he built the sets –
she at a cottage cake
with candle chimneys,
posing in a grotto,
mouth wide for a tooth pull,
gap grin on a sun stoep.

before his camera stilled
in shuttered silence

on grey pages
in his click tongue,
he wrote her alive in ligh

Loves Within, Loves Without

Advent

in early December, Sunday
I climb inside a carol,
come let us adore,
and find you there,
candlelit, aglow.
your lungs and limbs
trumpet and organ
holynight, starfollow
through ribcage rafters.
descant trills your cells,
bass ascends belly and spine.
the choir sings your blood,
skin-tingles your breasts,
your heart tolls a birth bell.
stablebare, Maryjoseph, shepherds,
Magi, heraldangels, cattle lowing
and Christchild advent in you.
born once more, you incarnate
a love larger than a cathedral.
the divine arrives in your eyes.

Goddess Authority

my friend, deep-dyed purple,
church school et al,
baits the bishop
and befriends his rebel priests.
she has taken to the tarot
and plays cards with the devil.

Route 77

places the manger
beneath the bodhi tree,
raises the Christ child
onto a Hindu elephant.
copies texts in Zen calligraphy
and mixes mural women
in last supper shades.
she lays out the Gnostic pack,
turns up the fool
who hop-hips off the church steps,
and with the sisters, ordained,
leaps into the abyss.

Translating your Poem

how intimate this
touching of tongues.
lips enfold as I probe
your teeth and soft palate,
searching for the way
you say your words.

these labials, aspirants, explosives
within your breath, beneath your breast.
I taste their dart, thrust and roundness,
their edges and silences
right inside this mouth.

finger prints move to pulse points
in wrist, neck, ankle, elbow, groin.
my ear follows the rhythm
in the rise and fall of a line.

Loves Within, Loves Without

run my tongue over and over
the nipple of a nuance,
its areola glow in an image,
then circle your belly edge
where the knot leads to
the origin and ancestor
of each word in your mother tongue.

so in words for play,
I rub my chin in your
syntax stubble and curl,
kiss all the hidden genitals
that alliterate with
c for consonant and v for vowel.

in pauses, in caesura,
we shift position, then
we rhyme in gender endings,
in little deaths,
and in cadence, climax.

now we lie close
after the lick of flame
on opposite sides of the sheet,
linking these fingers that held
our pens and caressed them.

Route 77

The Greatest Show On Earth

loving you is like
going to the circus.
the clowns tumble skills
in rubber clumsiness.
a star sparkle woman
barebacks on flashing steeds.
acrobats spin saucers.
a tamer dips his beard
in a roaring mouth.
a couple trapeze across the ceiling,
timing ticking in their wrists
and the high-wire man
balances a cycle
above a safety-net.

and we are audience,
caught in the oohs and aahs
in the clapping beat,
dangling on the edge
of a breathless next.
and we are the cast
where ringmaster and lion lady,
elephant and juggler,
clown and fire-swallower,
light the cannon fuse.
we arch across
this big tent love.

Loves Within, Loves Without

Good Luck Charm

don't want a silver dollar
rabbit's foot on a string
the happiness in your warm caress
no rabbit's foot can bring (Elvis)

it's a both way happiness,
charmer, Elvis, croons of,
that offers the lucky touch
beyond traditional charms.

four leaf clover, horseshoe, key ring.
in Africa the mojo bag of magic.
in China cat with raised paw.
In India a one-tusk Ganesh.

elsewhere the tortoise shell,
a round of Buddha rubbed tums.
or those tokens, soldiers
carry hidden into battle.

as I age I'd like to turn
into a good luck charm.
rub me anywhere
cheek, pate, elbow, there...

and the your wish genie
will arise in my eyes.
I'll morph instant into your
special childhood charm.

or into a chameleon
which some luck seekers fear.

Route 77

> lifted off an autumnal leaf,
> I'll perch on your finger.
>
> smuggle me up your sleeve,
> snuggle me between your breasts
> close to your four leaf chamber,
> that other ticking lucky charm.

Aneta my friend, takes me to yoga where we meet Gerda who will become a fab friend and fabric artist. The three of us often walked the Strand beach ending at Timeless Café which became the venue for book launches. Me? Yoga?

Falling in love in a Yoga Class

> the only hamstrung
> male in the class,
> an old creaking oak
> among willows,
> I have fallen among
> a troupe of acrobats.
>
> looselimbed loslyf
> the women raise a hand
> north past ear island
> in line with shoulder
> to salute sun
> while they slide the other
> down south to shinland.

Loves Within, Loves Without

I, tendon tense,
point my palm
towards the door.
its companion reaches
just below kneeland kopje
before it runs out of stretch.
their angles are acute,
mine obtuse.

six hundred and something
muscles rise Atlantis like
from the forgotten deep.
mine are drum skin,
lactic acid, theirs spandex.
they are like the dolls with
elastic threaded limbs
so you can turn the
legs and arms backwards.

our teacher is a reincarnated
rubber tree snake, swimming
through the S bend in a river
flowing though Himalayaland.

body lithe in line
she raises her heel
to salute the moon,
names the asanas
evoking India with its
levitation, lotus pose
tucked toe yogis
incense air
and snake charmers.

Route 77

    Eve's dance with
   snake energy dazzles
  this Adam, gritting teeth
 in a rib stretch locust pose,
  trying to prevent the fall,
   in awe of the double
  jointedness of these women
and their pelvic and wrist swivel.

 after another – what sounds
    like trickyasana –
   we come to stillness
  hands together. bow.
  this pose comes easy.
    body tingles.
   glands suffuse,
   hormones grin.

  I fall over in love
   with the grace
 of women's joints and
  my limb limitation.
 in supple Namaste
we enter Nirvanadise.

Was it a man who designated the three fates as women?

The Fates appear within three days of someone's birth to decide fate. The three Moirai represented the cycle of life, standing for Birth, Life, and Death. They spin (Clotho), draw out (Lachesis) and cut (Atropos) the thread.

So here's to our origins and as doulas, to those women present at our origins, journey and passing.

Loves Within, Loves Without

CHILD TRIBE

Blessed am I with four children – Damian, Martine, Dominic and Adam. Resilient beings. Yes, Kahlil Gibran, I hear you, "your children are not your children". I have poem'd them across the years so here are a few to their younger selves.

To a Three-Year-Old Son
(for Damian)

your clown face ringed with tea
we find the sign of a stickman
stuck on the toilet door
top hat and cane
ringmaster at our private circus.
stand in the public place
legs astride, companions
at this urinal,
frown in unison
and listen to the applause of aluminium,
ease features, shake,
grin and zip
then walk back
secret with achievement
to the waiting women.

Route 77

Burying Love
(for Damian)

St Valentine's day has come
and gone three weeks ago.
in the middle of a vlei
with a mountain ring
and a dry-flecked dam wall,
he drives the spade.
he digs, he digs
the measure of a man
down to the centre of the earth.

the hole rises like slow tide.
he steps on the shovel, till head
and a shock of blond fall
below land level.
then, in the tradition of diggers
he steps on the shoulder of the blade
thrust sideways into the earth
and stands beside the sure grave.

two boys on bikes, out for bird's eggs,
stop and watch. the mosquitoes cycle them away.

alone again, he raises a cardboard box
that once held wine. red wine.
echoing the accents in her name
he drops the carton in the hollow
then heaps in spade on spade,
shovelling, stomping, shouting.
knots of love and frustration

Loves Within, Loves Without

ripple from biceps to wrists
then slip from his fingers.

a woman walking her dog,
struck to see a young man
mad as Hamlet astride a pile of earth,
calls Are you OK?
raising the spade in a freedom salute
he shouts back, I'm burying love.
shame. she understands.

as digger, mourner, priest
he buries love by rite,
laying grief to rest.
shouldering the spade,
he swings from the site.
sweat and dust map
his chest and back with fine clay.
blisters rise like funeral mounds.

Mining her Diamond
(for Martine)

and that immortal diamond
 is immortal diamond (Hopkins)

androgynous God of earth
and underground,
as supplicant born in a city built
on kimberlite and diamond,
I pray for my daughter.

Route 77

guide her with your miner's lamp,
as a third eye focussed
on the face before her.
dig with her deep the tunnel
down the shaft of days.

seek with her the jewel
impacted in sand,
embedded in pipes.
buried in alluvial rivers.
cycle through her life.

equip her in patience to raise
her stone to the earth's surface.
then to shake and sift the rubble
crumbled on the belt of years.
apprentice her to divide
the dull gem from the ground.

so sit her, fingers cutting, polishing,
at a spinning wheel, dusk to dawn,
until she lights with sure hand
on the hidden prism
refracted in her eyes.

let the facets dance fire
in the spectrum of joy.
so set the crystal, centrepiece
priceless in her queen's crown.

Loves Within, Loves Without

To a Seven Day Son
(for Dominic)

you lie on your back
under a pump that bleeps
like a video machine.
disco lights purple
this city world
where you pin-prick shape
gyrates a blood beat.

umbilical cords dandle,
terminals to a heart,
air to windsock lungs,
plaster goggles fastened
on forehead.
controls to cockpit
for permission to land.

your eyes hide inside
a slipped sweat band.
in a fist tight
as a joystick,
you clutch a love
expressed in a little finger.
and now you've kicked a week.

Route 77

Bone Growth
(for Dominic)

you walk the long corridor,
you leg fresh baked
in a plaster crust.
the hospital drape
hangs blueloose
on your body.

you swing on crutches
to pace my step,
your teen legs
thin as the candle
I lit when you lay
those incubator days
in your first home.

tonight, visiting time past,
death ambles with us,
past the other wards
a silent third who listens
to breathing and bleeping.

we hug and you rock back
down the number road
hung with signs
of living and dying.
and like a baker
watching bread rise,
I fill with the leaven
of fatherhood.

Loves Within, Loves Without

Matching Faces
(for Adam)

in the Sciencentre
like gods we make faces.
we peer at each other
through a glass and mirror frame,
a slatted venetian blind.

my eyes arrive between
teen head and chin.
while I acquire cowlick,
mouth and jawbone jut,
he gets forehead, lips and stubble.

so this is bald, he calls
so those were pimples, I think.

we shift. his eyes ring
the equator my face.
mine shine between
his cancer and capricorn.

in early years
we matched card faces:
baker, farmer, robber, cop.
now father and son, in mixing ages,
hint at and hold a line
that genes in chingrin, mapcrack
and seadeep eyes.

Route 77

Name Changes
(for Adam)

What ever dies, was not mixed equally;
If our two loves be one, or, thou and I
Love so alike, that none do slacken, none can die.
(John Donne)

father and son walk in a park
sweet smelling of that
first spring garden.
you share a sensitive something
around family names
(none given in Eden).
you're engaged
to your first love,
made of her own clay,
not drawn from any rib.
she holds your heart.

no cumbersome double barrel
long-signing surname for you.
she's about to lose hers
so you'll forfeit yours.
your shared logic leads you
to resurrect another line –
your maternal grandpa's name
which burrowed underground
with your mother and her sisters.
and I already am patriarch
of a male line tribe.

Loves Within, Loves Without

> the spirits of my reading join our walk.
> Anais Nin's in search of a sensitive man.
> Juliet's rose by any other name
> smelling as sweet. what's in a name?
> and John Donne balanced hemispheres.
>
> twenty-one years ago
> we named you Adam,
> though not first born.
> was it some instinct
> for an earthy child?
> as I hug, I hold in my arms
> Adam original,
> quintessential you.

These four people teach me about love in all four shades. And they have brought into my life a dozen tribe of grandchildren. I have exported my two oldest children across the waters – Damian (Conroe, near Houston) and Martine (Brisbane). I wonder, when we have no choice, what happens when we pretend that we do? What story emerges? Dominic, is the kind of man who might end up meditating on a mountain top in Tibet in a wet sheet and drying it through raising his body temperature.

Boy and Bone

> as his skeleton stretches
> from sapling to fine stem
> and his rib-cage branches
> round lungs that cried
> before their time,
> this child, like a shaman,

Route 77

>throws the bones
>in a rush of saying.
>
>his journey has not yet descended
>through Ezekiel's dry bone valley
>to see Homo bones, Sapiens,
>stripped of flesh.
>nor has he sung 'dem bones'
>with a longing for liberation.
>
>he does not know the chapel,
>its Roman vault adorned
>with skulls of many monks –
>fibulas, femurs, jaw and hip,
>carpal, crown and socket –
>laid rococo on the curved ceiling.
>
>he holds no conscious knowledge
>of cosmic huts ribbed with bone
>and grassed with holes
>to let in the African stars.
>
>yet, told of God internal,
>he houses HimHer in these genes.
>and then, one morning
>fresh from dream,
>this boy, bearing the vision
>of medieval saint,
>bursts forth to prophecy.
>
>when you and mom die I'll take your bones
>and build a house for my children.
>your skull can be the chimney, your hand the latch.

so our bone child, our vertebrate
who left early his pelvic home,
with tongue drumming his palate, annunciate archetype
and sucks the marrows of this metaphor.

And Adam. Maths, Physics, Astrophysics and Applied Maths. Four cum laudes. They bring blessings like spring blossoms. I am blessed.

Damian and family

Route 77

Off to camp at a Texas State Park

Duncan, Mia, Martine

Loves Within, Loves Without

Dominic

Adam and Sophie

Route 77

STORIES WITHIN STORIES

> *Ever since I heard my first love story*
> *I have been looking for you (Rumi)*
> *I have told so many stories that I have become fiction.*
> (Rumi)

The gifts of story in my life? A never-ending story. Gifts abound. Multitudes of insights that open to agape. 'We spend our years as a tale that is told'. (Psalm 90: 9) Learning to live lightly and with humour. Stories are a great antidote to taking myself too seriously. The trickster archetype tugs at us. Suspending judgement for stories invite curiosity and movement. Here are seven narrative poems:

The Storyteller's Art

the Great Storyteller knows when
to tap his pipe on the boot of creation,
to roll the drama down the mountain,
flood the plain, trumpet down walls,
arrest a man with a burning bush,
fly chariots across the sky.

bring in the who of story,
a snake, he, she, the apple core.
fireword prophets, lusty Kings,
queens and pomegranate lovers,
brother-betrayers, fishermen
a whale who coughs up a man.

knows how to arrange the tale,
choreograph the where,

Loves Within, Loves Without

three crosses on a hill,
a leading star lighting a stable,
a broken-open tomb,
a ghostwalk with a stranger.

so the story mounts on eagle wings.
spits sight, eye to eye
in the lightening flash, the love look.
in the once upon a miracle play.
the divine teller entices us
to his art, to apprentice us.

How Long should a Story be?

it's a how long
is a piece of string?
kind of question.
plus a sort of tug of war
between teller and listener
matched equally
holding the tension
in the line.

for a story to thread a theme
that entangles and enchants,
a string the width of a hand
is too short to tie,
all thumb and forefinger,
the loop of a plot.
too tight a tale
leaves the listener

Route 77

brow furrowed, grasping
at some cryptic code.

this story is too short

a ball of twine unrolled
in full, stretching
door to door
lies too tangled in length,
slack as a skipping rope.
the one receiving the tale
smothers a yaaaawn,
glances at wristwatch and door
while teller rambles on
oblivious of the eye shift
in a nodding audience.

this story is too long

so let the story be
a thrice braided twist of twine
enough to tangle tie
Goldilocks, three bears,
porridge bowls, chairs and beds
and the eyes, ears and heart beat
of a teller-listener duet
in the same knot.

this story is just right.

Loves Within, Loves Without

The Story Chair

it's a first class flight of fantasy.
our plane booked and boarded
we lift off, rise in this recliner
with matching footrest.
our seat cover is scribbled
in linen words
in various fonts sizes tongues
cursive capitals scrawled
everywhichway.

it's the same space where
your mother midnight sings to you
and croons till demons flap wings,
retract claws and depart in haste.

with bear sitting aware
on the headrest, propped
against the nursery wall,
we soar into tale after tale
with the writer pilot
and hostess illustrator.

they serve us a cocktail of characters,
a cuisine of zany escapades,
plots as thick as clotted cream
that channel the imagination
flickering in our hearts and heads.

Hairy McClary's doggy body
unravels in threads and tatters
as he skids across the page.
there's Richard Scary and his village tribe.

Route 77

Poo Bear's honeyed favourite days.
Cats in Hats that Seusssly scratch
a patch and tingle our skins.

we 'chaise' a tale
mayhem madness without
miracles whatevernext within.
like your mom and I did
in another land, time, and room
when she was also
thirty months young.
we circle once again
and again this wonder world.

sky-high we cloud-drift
through knowing, unknowing
glide between earth
and its turbulence
down down there and
life pulsing we land
in this story chair.

Chess Board Sculpture

Tis all a Chequer-board of nights and days
Where Destiny with men for Pieces plays
(Rubaiyat of Omar Khayyám)

he stood behind her in her studio loft,
her husband of twenty five years,
he a quarter century older than she.
she sculpted while he watched.

Loves Within, Loves Without

she shaped a figure of a naked nymph
tracing with her moving finger,
head bent, arms folded to embrace herself.
she kneaded in oxide white, the clay.

he stood behind her close as breath.
no longer could he recall
even her name. yet recited, flawless,
verse after verse of old Khayyam.

she scratched the words as backdrop
shrine-shaped, for the figure to lean on
and adopted as signature a chequer board
remoulded to her heart's desire.

How to stay the Sultan's Sword

how did she stay that morning sword?
night after night in the king's chambers
as the moon rolled through its crescents
full to gibbous to three days gone.

after the sex, sleep and wakefulness
the wise, the witty, the well-read and bred,
Scheherazade, her hair lustrous
and trussed with ribbons and snakes of tales,
beguiled Shahryar with jeweled words set in gold.

he who beheaded each night's virgin wife.
as dawn broke its fast she paused
the tale. cliff edged, mid-sentence.
left him lusting for and then?

Route 77

in daylight hours did she absorb stories,
learn poems by heart, carrying in her belly
the seed of the climax and denouement?
knotting a kilim in her consciousness and cortex?

or did she in the moment
allow plots to arise as a self-surprise,
spontaneous as a nightingale
glittering as a scimitar suddenly unsheathed
as she in skill and craft breathed and
awaited the light of each new day?

perhaps a touch of both modes,
rehearsed magic and moment,
pace and pause, timing and tension,
taking her cue from his eyebrow twitch,
seeking amazement in his open mouth.

Scheherazade in slow moon mode seduced,
civilized the Sultan, till he, tale entranced
by the time of the 1001st once there was,
crowned her his Allah-given story queen.

Weighing Words

in the Palace of the Inquisition,
in the Caribbean town, Cartagena,
they weighed women
on a platform
hung on chains
with a metal balance
hooked to the ceiling.

Loves Within, Loves Without

if you were too thin a woman,
were you so because you flew?
catch questions line the walls.
do you use the devil's name
in your incantations?
who is your master?
who taught you to fly?

the authorities squirted
liquid into your eyes.
if you did not cry
you were witch.

tonight in this Palace, on a platform,
three poets pitch words into the space
where the ash of 800 women
floated through the air.
I read of Osiris who weighed
your heart against a feather.
of Aquinas who imaged hate as ice
and love as a melting.

my fellow poets, women,
raise questions, author images,
cast spells, smoulder words
that melt my tears
and set the hall burning.

Route 77

In the Balance

this woman loops sticks
in a ring of wire
and bundles them into one load.
she steps out of the desert
bearing wood for one fire.

this pile will flicker away
part of the night in a
dry quick burn. this snap
of kindling raised
on head and arms.

she moves as one
on high wire, the pole
extending outstretched arms
to hold the see-saw centre
sprung across shoulders.

above the hushed ancestor crowd
who will her not to fall
off the dust-line into hunger,
she balances for a moment
her family in these branches.

As they say in Turkey 'the mouth of the person who last told this story is still warm'.

MUSIC OF THE SPHERES

> *In shamanic societies, if you came to a medicine person, disheartened, dispirited, or depressed, they would ask four questions: "When did you stop dancing? When did you stop singing? When did you stop being enchanted by stories? When did you stop being comforted by the sweet territory of silence?*
> (Gabrielle Roth)

The love of music, vocal, choir, instrument, in cathedral, concert hall and chambers. Growing up with the radiogram and the long-playing 78 records. Then the church organ, and Charles Wesley hymns with mass choir trumpet and organ, the Strauss waltzes as a youngster. Then LM radio backwards hit parade. Giving up, alas, on the piano lessons (Mom did try). Playing the mouth organ. One of the regrets not pursuing with singing lessons in later life.

Writing songs. Several Namibian school anthems. And hymns. This one (stipulation 4 line rhyming ballad with chorus) won a national competition in the 90s. R3000. (That's R18.98 per word):

The Rain Carol

In Africa, our cradle home,
A land that breathes with grace and pain,
The cycle of the season turns.
The long drought softens into rain.

And in a land of stone and earth
We trace the rain of our rebirth.

Route 77

> The game that treks through burning bush
> And grazes on the bone-dry range,
> Stirs the dust round water holes
> And sniffs the air for signs of change.
>
> And in a land of stone and earth
> We trace the rain of our rebirth.
>
> The wise ones from the mountain side
> And herders from the cattle belt,
> Plot their way by Southern Cross
> As thunder rumbles on the veld.
>
> And in a land of stone and earth
> We trace the rain of our rebirth.
>
> Below a swollen summer cloud
> Beneath a twisted camel thorn
> A lonely lowveld cloud reveals
> The miracle of Christ reborn.
>
> And in a land of stone and earth
> We trace the rain of our rebirth.

In my passing, may a doula sing me into the next world. And at my one-day dawn to dusk wake, part of a Mozart Coronation mass please, plus *The Rose* that Dominic sings on his CD *Seasons of Love*.

OTHERWORLDS

*It is a landscape filled with allegories, where the imagination is law, and storytellers can spend entire
days resuscitating mysteries...
The door is always open; we wait inside and also outside it,
fitting all possible tales into chronicles of our making.*
(Roy-Bhattacharya)

In Irish mythology *Tír na nóg* is one of the names for the Celtic Otherworld. What openings lead us there? In what state of grace are we in when we find the doorless door that suddenly appears where there was no door? Rumi has already arrived in this story with his call to stay awake so we can pass through the doorway where the two worlds meet. This liminal space beneath the lintel.

Here are a few personal openings that allow me to swim in the living waters, in the *Rio Abajo Rio*, the river beneath the river. 'We arrive there through deep meditation, dance, writing, painting, prayer making, singing, active imagination, or any activity which requires an intense altered consciousness. (We) arrive in this world-between-worlds through yearning and by seeking something she can see just out of the corner of an eye' (Clarissa Pinkola Estés).

The I Ching greetings and readings in response to a specific question. Sixty-four hexagrams – another doorway. I have mentioned the first of January creation of a collage, culling pictures from a wide range of magazines, removing the words and sticking them randomly on the sheet of cardboard. I number them and begin to write about each one. These collages know more about me than I know, so they lead me into otherworlds, wider loves. I also create collages with clients. A client

Route 77

looking for a career change, through her collage depicted the healing centre she was to buy in the Wilderness.

And rituals, yes, that places us in epiphany time:

Waiting with Arms Outstretched

the vase depicts Theseus
dressed in the robes
of King for a year, saying yes,
arms outstretched.

Pasiphae wife of the Minotaur
whom he slaughtered
in the maze, in the myth,
places an apple in his left hand.

Ariadne, daughter of Pasiphae,
who spun her line to the hero
so he could thread his way home,
into his right hand places an egg.

Theseus, king for four seasons only,
stands like Christ, like Adam, between
the apple of all endings
and the life pecking in the shell.

Dual citizenship in this and Otherworlds.

THE EMMAUS ROAD, THE INN, THE TRAVELLER AND A JOURNAL

> *Who is the third who walks always beside you?*
> *When I count, there are only you and I together*
> *But when I look ahead up the white road*
> *There is always another one walking beside you*
> *Gliding wrapt in a brown mantle, hooded.*
> (TS Eliot)

I love the *Emmaus Road* story. I love the Salley Vickers novel *The Other Side of You*. Literal and metaphoric travelling. Yes, I could write of time in Turkey. In old Istanbul, Cappadocia Street vendors, in Singapore, a Hong Kong retreat up a mountain, Europe. Australia. Nordic lands. Wine tasting on the estates high in hills of home.

Some places do feature on this map. The three week road trip in Ams's, Ice Queen Rav 4 – part work-play, part play-play. An oval lopsided loop from Pringle Bay to Parys to Cradle of Human Kind, Limpopo River, grey and greasy with fever trees (Kipling). Into Kruger to Ixopo BRC. Along the southern coast travelling west via son Adam at Zithulele and Coffee Bay. Addo to whisper to the Hefferlumps, (did not see one) Garden Route to son Dom... home again jiggity jig. Dodging most of 77 x 77 potholes. Celebrating friends en route.

Yet I'd rather follow another path in *Route 77*, travelling in a journal. With the help of Igno, I created *The Rough Writing Road*, a sixteen week self-directed Online Journaling Course. Our guiding metaphor? The rough road along the writing path. I prompt via stories, questions, quotations, poems, memories and suggestions. Drawn from many traditions and faiths. Helping you find your voice. As you walk you enter a great conversation with yourself and others.

Route 77

For a writer is a travel guide, the journal the bridge. Journaling offers an emotional and mythological map. In the mid-sixties, a psychologist, Ira Progoff, developed an Intensive Journal Process: *At a Journal Workshop*. Progoff takes the image of many underground wells all connected to a deep subterranean stream as a metaphor. An appropriate metaphor for the deep waters that lie beneath the dry earth.

One of the *Rough Writing Road* entries – this bare bone story that crossed my path, imagined made flesh:

The Way of Grief

she scribbled bits of Europe
in folio, in the ring-binder
her parents had given her.
daily she wove her spider thread
round pencil sketches
and ticket stubs stamped
with train dates and opera stalls.
she shaped impressions of a gallery,
a climb up a hill to reaches of snow,
market women and temple ruins.
the widow's pension
with an enamel water jug
and a turret above a canal
and her week of waitering
at Carlo's Cafe
filled four pages.
scripting her way south
she recorded a procession
of the Last Supper Christ
through candle streets.

Loves Within, Loves Without

<blockquote>

she was hardly home
when out of the African blue
blood cells sang her requiem.

matching dates and places
and pension addresses,
her parents embraced
the journey through the underworld.
they sat in the out-of-season
opera house, rode the metro
to her disembarking
and spoke to the widow
and Carlo of the water-side cafe.
taking her hours as guide
they shod their feet in journal leaves.
and walked the pages of her days.

</blockquote>

How do we walk our pages? I once took a group to Robben Island, once an island prison off the coast of Cape Town. (A great-grand father died there, a patient when the island served as an asylum.) Nelson Mandela, one of the prisoners. Though physically confined, his mind roamed the world. Back at the Waterfront on the mainland, my task was to facilitate a wordshop on the theme, 'How do we imprison ourselves, given that we are free to move?' What keeps us in prisons of our own making? Are we like Macbeth, 'cabined, cribbed, confined, bound in to saucy doubts and fears?'

Here's a Rumi tale:

The Caged Bird

The merchant has captured the bird and taken it from the forest to the city. One day the merchant informs the bird, "I'm going back

Route 77

to the forest. Is there anything you desire?" "Yes," says the bird, "Give me my freedom." "I will not do that. Is there anything else you wish for?" "Then tell the other birds what has happened to me." "Yes I will."

The merchant arrives at the forest and calls all the birds who assemble on boughs nearby. He tells them, "Your fellow bird is in a cage in the city."

As soon as the forest birds hear this news, as one they fall off the boughs, senseless to the ground. In some trepidation, the merchant returns to the city and tells the caged bird what he has seen. As soon as the bird hears this story, it falls off the perch to the bottom of the cage and lies there senseless. The merchant opens the cage, picks up the bird in his hands and puts it on a shelf, prior to burying it.

The bird fluffs and flaps its feathers and flies into the air, calling out, "Tell my fellow birds, I thank them for the message they have sent to me, via you, my jailer."

The beacons in such a travelling? Stories yes… Cairns and lighthouses arrive along the way:

Lighthouse Keeper

a wise man raised
it upon the rocks.
it rises, a monastic
tower, built to stall
the Viking tide.
the head, like Janus,
shines inwards onto

Loves Within, Loves Without

      rooftops at land edge
      and beams seawards,
      through a hundred suns,
      flashing it mirror message.
      It mingles in the colours of
      late sun then joins the stars.
      and when fog slither-loops
      a silver scarf around its head,
      the giant frog croaks his throat
      and puffs his chest to amplify
     across the rocks to troubled hulks.
    so may this pharology, this study of
   lighthouses, named after Pharos Lighthouse,
  Alexandria, one of the seven vanished wonders
of the ancient world, lead me to the keeper who
    stands legs astride, farsighted, ears attuned,
 sounding the deep, in the sea of unknowing -
the mare incognotum, a professional of the edge.

The Road to Enlightenment

the story might be that we won't
arrive at Nirvana City, ever
unlike Christian in Pilgrim's Progress.
for it's always the road, the road,
valley, forest, mountain.
the city lights dazzling
their mirage far in the distance.

the shadow falls ahead of us
as the sun swoops to light our backs.
we arrive at twilight at the seaside inn

Route 77

> where attachment catches us
> by the coat tails and sleeves.
> the eyes of the waitress hold us
> as she serves the roast pork platter
> and pours low cut, the blood jug of wine.
>
> the night cool on our skins
> we sit and sip in the courtyard
> under a moon enchanter
> rippling in the dark water.
> we'll never plumb its depths
> nor descend like the whale
> for we seek surface, fearing the bends.
>
> tonight we'll dream of a bird
> escaping a cage to flit into
> a larger cage then one larger than that,
> hopefully with thinner mesh. ad infinitum.
>
> certain of uncertainty we leave at first bird,
> find our staff which the innkeeper hid
> in some understair broom cupboard.
> dragging dream-infused a dawn shadow,
> we learn, light of step, to love
> the lore of the endless road.

Here's to that road. To pilgrimages. To the mystery traveller who walks beside us.

27 JULY

Yes, I love birthdays, mine and others. A way to end this poememoir — here's one of the invitations (2019) from the birthday boy, aged five, who stood at the Dalham Road gate, and asked the arriving guests, "What have you brought me?"

Invited you are (insert name) 12.03ish

Once upon a 1494 – or was it 1944? – winter's day there was a madhatter baby born 27 July in Kimberley wearing a Kaminski XY Dorian, a Panama fedora…shower resistant. His ancestors were the Dorians of ancient Greece. Their name mythologically derives from Dorus, son of Helen. He chanted in Dorian mode: the Ancient Greek harmoniai, a medieval musical mode and a modern modal diatonic scale. He shower sang:

> Seventy-six trombones caught the morning sun,
> With a hundred and ten cornets right behind.

But they told him 'You 75er. You're one trombone short.'
Gifts? Bring them not. Rather donate to Helderberg Hospice. Bring a poem, a story, a song, wear a HAT (not the Afrikaans dictionary), your good self for a circle sharing.
love Poet Doriate
Here are a few birthday snippets from yesteryears:

How to become a witness
(from friend Gert, 2014 for Dorian @70)

One may start by meeting another
in a taxi to East London
or on a hill in Ixopo

or in a story of the turtle who searched for the stork
or you could start by meeting in a shop
of writing works

The one may be the philosopher who is ready for his writing teacher
the other the writer who is ready for his question asker

Where-ever you meet, let the souls do the touching
let the frowns do the sharing

let the smiles do the wondering
let the hands do the noting
let the hearts do the thinking

And only then may you do the writing of being witness
the silent writing, the haiku writing, the story writing

Let the writing take you anywhere –
from Derrida and his tears about how difficult it is to bear witness
to Joseph Campbell the witness of a hero's journey

Let your story sharing take you to the mysteries
It is in their writing that witness-broers
let their stories converse:
only then we know: when I'm with you
i story more i write more
i think more i know more
i dream more i am more

more in witnessing you
more in witnessing me.

And a 2010 birthday letter from Father Dorian with four children's responses.

Dear children x 4

Here is an easy way to wish your father a happy birthday. All you have to do is select the options and return this email.

Father... You have reached the palindromic sixty-six. This is dyslexic/remarkable/so what?/

You are the best/worst/father we have so far had.

Father we are so glad/not interested in your being the men's 1000 metres champion swimmer at your local gym in the group: folically challenged, left-handed male, Kimberley born poets aged sixty-six years and no days /

Please unsubscribe me forthwith / only send such letters one a year

And the responses:

Adam

Dear Father

You have reached the palindromic sixty-six... this is not so remarkable as every eleven years you must pass through a palindromic age, so of all the birthdays in your life. If we look a little further into the future... you will see that seventy-seven is palindromic and a multiple of seven. Now that will be remarkable for you. (Prophetic. Here I am)

You are the best father that I have had so far. I will continue sampling and let you know if you have won the competition shortly. The child's decision is final and no correspondence will be entered into. Prizes cannot be exchanged for pensions.

Please retain this sense of humour as you leave your current palindromic age and head off to the next one.

With love

Adam (for your reference, child four)

Route 77

Dominic
Dearest Poem-egran-ate Dad,
At the hour of your birth,
sixty-six sun cycles later,
do you rise in this son's
inner eye and limbic heart.

The family. We were a strange little band of characters trudging through life-sharing diseases and toothpaste, hiding shampoo, borrowing money, locking each other out of our rooms, inflicting pain and kissing to heal it in the same instant, loving, laughing, defending, and trying to figure out the common thread that bound us all together. ~Erma Bombeck

I hope you were a happy birthday. Your form letter great fun. I trust that you received many happy returns from your children. You know, I routinely ask after myself. I find I never get a straight answer. Always just a wisecrack. What do I make of this? My psych textbook says my deal with the voices to only express themselves after 8pm in the evenings is an early sign of Schizophrenia. I'm not convinced though. I reckon cognitive slippage of word associations is a better measure of my being a poet that anything else. What do you think?

Who knows, perhaps the laughter shall keep me sane.

Love Dom out of context

Martine
Hello dearest dad
Loved the Birthday email and Ad's reply – funny.
P.S If I'd only ever done one thing right in my life, it would have been choosing you as my dad.

I love you. Me thinks that if my brothers get any sharper they might cut themselves!

Marts (Dad's Queensland Treasure)

Damian

Dear Gramps, happy birthday to our three-in-one father, father-in-law and grandpa. Out of all our folically challenged and poetic sixty-six year old fathers, we confess that you are by the far the best. Father, we are not interested in you being the champion 1000m swimmer if you're not going to put it to good use… like swimming over here to Texas for a visit. It's not THAT much further.

Please do not unsubscribe us from not not receiving letters not not not more than only once a year.

Love Damian for the Haarhoffs

So here am I a wealthy man. Glad and grateful. Apart from Endwords, here endeth the Poememoir.

ENDWORDS

WEALTH CYCLES

Annual income twenty pounds, annual expenditure nineteen six, result happiness. Annual income twenty pounds, annual expenditure twenty pound ought and six, result misery. (Charles Dickens)

What of the entrepreneurial shekels? It is possible to read money as we do the seasons? The Israeli Nobel Prize winner, S Y Agnon, tells a story of a rich merchant, at the peak of his fortune. His ships laden with merchandise are close to the harbour. On the way to market he loses a wallet under a bush. On his return he finds it with all his money intact. He breaks into irrepressible grief. At that point his fortunes decline, his life falls apart and he is left destitute. A storm wrecks his ships. On his way to spend shabbat with a friend, he stops at a bath house. In an altercation with a beggar, his clothing is ripped. Now he cannot even spend the sabbath with a friend. At that moment he begins to laugh wildly.

Reverse the rich man's reactions and there is no story. So here's to such cycles. I've included these seven wealth quotations to mark my travels from scarcity to abundance:

You are like a rich man entering heaven on the ear of a raindrop
(Seamus Heaney)

I keep the telephone of my mind open to peace, harmony, health, love and abundance. Then whenever doubt, anxiety, or fear try to call, they get a busy signal. Soon they'll forget my number (Edith Armstrong)

Not everything that can be counted counts, and not everything that counts can be counted (Albert Einstein)

You can't depend on your eyes when your imagination is out of focus (Mark Twain)

Wealth consists not in having great possessions, but in having few wants (Epictetus)

Work. Keep digging your well…Submit to a daily practice. Your loyalty to that is a ring on the door. Keep knocking, and the joy inside will eventually open a window and look out to see who's there (Rumi)

Three quarts of rice in my bag. A bundle of twigs by the fireplace. Listening to the night rain on my roof, I stretch out both legs towards the fire. (Ryokan)

I've also created a synonym wealth Alphabet – a double for each letter – one concrete, one abstract:

aviary abundance ballast balance chest charity diamonds discipline emeralds energy forest feasting grapevine generosity harvest hope incense increase jewels joy kaleidoscope kairos ladder largesse mountain magic new-moon numinosity opus opportunity pomegranate philanthropy quantum, quality rootedness radical sun service treasure tide umiak upsurge vestments venture well-point wellness xoanon xenogamy yggdrasil youthful zodiac zephyr

These are the mantras of enough.

FARE FORWARD TRAVELLER

Is the Trickster rather than the Magician my archetype? Yet I once played a magician in a play at the Windhoek Theatre. Some months later we were due to take the play to the children's ward in the hospital, appearing in our costumes. I had been away on sabbatical for some three months. On the appointed day, I went to the hospital in my costume and wandered around. People gave me strange looks. I asked, "Where is the children's ward? "A nurse responded., "Oh, that has moved to the new hospital." "And what is this place here?" "This," she responded with a cautious look, "is the mental hospital."

Like poet Stanley Kunitz, "I have made a tribe of my affections and my tribe is scattered." This story is about being spoken through, not from but through me.

So here's to the ancestors, blood and belonging ones. I began and end with poems for them:

Arriving at the Night Fire

in Motetema, Limpopo Province,
I feed the teachers
morning to late light,
a feast of stories.

as the sun sifts the room
one ladles a question
onto my plate.
it lies there like the pap*
we ate at lunch.

who did you inherit story-telling from?

a big meal question.
he watches me chew. first response
inside. I say, no one. it started here.
but this Lazarus has raised a ghost.
I take his question to my gut
to search for one who hands down gifts,
who multiplies fish and bread.

I answer his gaze. when I tell,
the story comes from somewhere else,
through me. you see this?
he slowly nods and smiles.

a match strikes a woodpile.
Europe and Africa,
blood and belonging,
reconcile in the telling.
it is the ancestors who story through me.
a night fire ignites my belly.

Tour Guide

through the bus windows
I see them huddle heads,
pointing at me, jabbering
these ancients.
Sixty-two of them
five generations.
me, at the bottom
of their vortex,

they have come to sight see
me. he has your eyes.

they clamber down the steps
what will he show us?
I hold the placard high
'Ancestors Tour
Welcome to Doriland.'
where will we go?
there are no suitcases to lug.
they travel light
as a swan feather.
we hug, shake hands,
double kiss like a helix.
I name tag them.

we head for the movie house
to watch three score plus years.
my father and mother point out
the river picnic. there we are.
they sigh, shake they heads,
pass comments, groan, applaud
No, no, the other road
you've fallen into that hole before
just like he did.
my grandmother nudges grandfather
who nods away a snore
stuck in his teeth.
he has your walk,
the way you settle your shoulders-
one double great to another.

they are curious about
what happens next –

the great shaker of story
for the movie affects them
as the archetype's play out.
me pushing against patterns
bright as blood cells.
bold as DNA strands.

after the movie
we spill out into the streets
and they walk through my life,
window shop, finger fabrics
I cook a meal, I eat alone
while they watch.
he still gulps like you
with no famine to drive him –
triple great to spouse.
I show them my study,
the family file of cuttings,
the collage I created to hold
the energy for the year.
they interrogate
the five Ws of me.
the geography and markets
the loves and laughter.

on their way back to the bus stop
the women insist on cruising
through the dark part of the town
where streets lights are stoned.
a brandy bottle rolls down the alley.
grandfather gropes then remembers
he no longer needs a shot.

> as they board the bus
> for ancestor land
> they have other askings in their eyes.
> will he break the cage that holds us?
> swing open the door wide?
> as they wave, their hands
> like swan necks,
> form question marks.
> will his spiral shrink inwards
> or spin out like a sparkle
> a swan wing wheel to become the milky way?

A final story: A man approaches a teacher, who is sitting meditating. He asks, "How can you sit there when there is so much pain, suffering and grief in the world?"

The teacher picks up a drinking glass and holds it in the air. "You see this glass? Look how it catches the light." Then she fills the glass with water and runs her finger around the rim. "Listen, now, how the glass makes music."

She puts the glass on a shelf behind her. "But I could easily knock this glass off with my elbow, or the wind could take it, and it would be shattered into a thousand pieces. So I presume that the glass is already broken, and I enjoy every moment of it." This echoes Rilke:

> Be ahead of all parting,
> as if it had already happened,
> like winter, which even now is passing.
> For beneath the winter is a winter so endless
> that to survive it at all is a triumph of the heart.

taken at a McGregor poetry festival

Here's to the fire in the glass and to Quince in *A Midsummer Night's Dream:*

> If we offend, it is with our good will.
> That you should think, we come not to offend,
> But with good will. To show our simple skill,
> That is the true beginning of our end.

SOME OF DORIAN'S PUBLICATIONS

Bordering (1991) Johannesburg: Justified Press.

Aquifers and Dust (1994) Johannesburg: Justified Press.

Tortoise Voices (2002) Mercer.

Drawing Water (2007) Leopard Press.

Poemegranates (2012) Leopard Press.

ZenPenYen (2022) Leopard Press.

The Writer's Voice: A Workbook for Writers in Africa (1998) Johannesburg: Zebra Press.

Mirror, Lens and Window, A Workbook on Journaling for Namibian Teachers in Training (2015) Basel Afrika.

The Wild South West: Frontier Myths and Metaphors in Literature set in Namibia (1991) Johannesburg: Wits University Press.

The Halo and The Noose; The Power of story-telling and story-listening in Business Life, co author, G Williams (2009, 2016) Cape Town: Graysonian Press.

Desert December (1991) Cape Town, Songololo.

Guano Girl (1994) Johannesburg, Justified Press.

Alice in Welwitschialand (Environmental Play) Performed 1992-94 National Theatre Namibia and Grahamstown Festival. (unpublished)

Tones and Textures: Photo-poetry from Namibia (text Dorian Haarhoff, photographs Amy Schoeman), (1996) Cape Town, Clifton Publications.

2 CDs: Tortoise Stories, Stories from Africa and the Great Elsewhere Vol 1 and 2, 2009 (My own and other stories)

Poetry CD, *Stone on the Stomach,* 2009

Sketch: Andrew Horne –Pringle Poet the fastest wordslinger in the Overberg

Ingram Content Group UK Ltd.
Milton Keynes UK
UKHW050705120623
423287UK00005B/14

9 780648 652458